Richard Yates Up Close

Richard Yates Up Close
The Writer and His Works

Martin Naparsteck

McFarland & Company, Inc., Publishers
Jefferson, North Carolina, and London

LIBRARY OF CONGRESS CATALOGUING-IN-PUBLICATION DATA

Naparsteck, M. J. (Martin John), 1944–
    Richard Yates up close : the writer and his works / Martin Naparsteck.
        p.   cm.
    Includes bibliographical references and index.

    ISBN 978-0-7864-6059-5
softcover : acid free paper ∞

    1. Yates, Richard, 1926–1992 — Criticism and interpretation. I. Title.
PS3575.A83Z75 2012
813'.54—dc23   2011047644

BRITISH LIBRARY CATALOGUING DATA ARE AVAILABLE

© 2012 Martin Naparsteck. All rights reserved

No part of this book may be reproduced or transmitted in any form or by any means, electronic or mechanical, including photocopying or recording, or by any information storage and retrieval system, without permission in writing from the publisher.

Front cover image: Richard Yates (photograph by Thomas Victor)

Manufactured in the United States of America

McFarland & Company, Inc., Publishers
  Box 611, Jefferson, North Carolina 28640
    www.mcfarlandpub.com

For
Taft
America
Molly-Maguire

Acknowledgments

Thank you to Professor Steve Street of Buffalo State College, to Professor Doug Brooks of Monroe Community College in Rochester, New York, and to the late Scott Chisholm of Utah State University for providing me with engaging conversations about the writings of Richard Yates. For the same reason, thank you to Andrea Barrett and Tim O'Brien. Thank you to Nancy Kress for similar conversations and for providing me with the physical space I needed to write this book. Thank you to Charles Niles, archivist at the Howard Gotlieb Archival Research Center at Boston University, for his always cheerful assistance in helping me navigate my way through 15 boxes of materials in the Richard Yates collection. And, primarily, thank you to Richard Yates for a short but edifying and kindhearted friendship.

Table of Contents

Acknowledgments vii
Preface 1
Introduction: Appreciating Richard Yates 5

1. The Autobiographical Nature of Yates's Fiction 15
    ORDER OF OCCURRENCE 24
    RICHARD YATES: A NONFICTION BIOGRAPHY 25
2. The Inevitability of Unhappiness: *Revolutionary Road* 30
    YATES AND HOLLYWOOD 39
3. The Lies of Richard Yates: *Eleven Kinds of Loneliness* 51
4. War Interrupted: *A Special Providence* 62
    RETHINKING A NEAR CLASSIC 74
5. The Depths of Transition: *Disturbing the Peace* 80
    AT THE CROSSROADS WITH DICK YATES 86
6. The Possibilities of Redemption: *The Easter Parade* 95
    YATES AND HOMOSEXUALITY 103
7. Static and Memory: *A Good School* 106
    THE PERFECT GAME 112
8. Cruelty and Optimism: *Liars in Love* 116
9. The Artist Ages: *Young Hearts Crying* 128
    THE CRITIC 134
10. Hope for the Youngest: *Cold Spring Harbor* 138
    UNCERTAIN TIMES 144
11. The Collected Stories 152
    THE UNCOLLECTED STORIES 159

Table of Contents

12. Rethinking Richard Yates	163
Appendix 1: Lie Down in Darkness	167
Appendix 2: Alternative Yates	169
Appendix 3: "The World on Fire"	173
Chapter Notes	175
Bibliography	185
Index	191

Preface

The structure of a book doesn't just happen. Or if it does just happen, the structure is flawed. Richard Yates was careful to assure that his novels, and his short stories, began at some point and arrived at another and that the journey between the two points was convincing. This book seeks to accomplish the same sense of direction within its covers. In deciding on a structure an author always has choices. What came first could have come second or fourteenth or last. What comes last could have come earlier or could have been omitted. Structure, Yates felt, was largely a matter of deciding what to include and what to exclude and what order everything should come in. These are the decisions made for this book.

First is this preface, which explains the book's structure. By knowing what's coming, a reader can more easily follow the arguments being made.

Next is an introduction that is intended to explain why the book was even written, why the novels and stories of Richard Yates are worth reading, and how a reader might most appreciate those novels and stories.

Third is a discussion of the autobiographical nature of Yates's fiction. Many writers draw from their own lives to write fiction, but few have drawn so heavily from the reservoir of personal experience. Every novel and nearly every short story is filled with details that have a corresponding factual basis in the author's life. This is so prevalent and so often repeated in the novels and stories that a reader could choose to read them in the order they occurred in Yates's life. For that reason, a section titled "Order of Occurrence" is included. A reader should remember, however, that Yates and most writers who write fiction based on their own lives make a distinction between autobiographical and autobiography. Writers may start with facts from their own lives, but they select them, reshape them, omit some, emphasize some points, deemphasize others, and in other ways make real-life facts into fictional facts. That is, "autobiographical" is not synonymous with "autobiography." If for example, someone were to read Yates's work in the sequence provided in "Order of Occurrence," a story here, a short story there, but to interrupt that reading with a reading of corresponding chapters in Blake Bailey's excellent 2003 biography of Yates, *A Tragic Honesty*, the differences would become clear. Some things in the biography are not in the fiction; some things in the fiction are not in the biography. Yet they are easily recognizable as being drawn from the same sources.

To help remind the reader of the distinction between Yates's life and his fiction, a nonfiction biography is included next. More accurately, it is an outline of his life, with particular focus on some points that will arise during the discussion of his writing, such as his alcoholism, his dislike of the Kennedys, his bipolarity, and his experiences in the Second World War.

That is followed by a sequential and detailed discussion of each of the seven novels and two collections of short stories that were published during Yates's lifetime. A tenth book, containing most of the short stories he wrote, concludes the discussion. Another book, the screenplay he wrote based on William Styron's first novel, *Lie Down in Darkness*, which was never produced, is discussed in an appendix because it is in important ways not really the work of Richard Yates but rather his adaption of a novel by his friend Styron.

The discussion of each novel is immediately followed by a discussion of some issue related, directly or indirectly, to the novel. These are:

Revolutionary Road— the movie based on the novel and Yates's intense dislike of Hollywood, both the place and the metaphor.

A Special Providence— why Yates was more disappointed in this book than any other he wrote and a comparison with novels of the Second World War written by some of his fellow veterans.

Disturbing the Peace—Yates and the role that alcohol played in his life and writing.

The Easter Parade—Yates's dislike for homosexuals and his fear that he might be perceived as one.

A Good School—a discussion of other novels based on attending private schools, especially John Knowles's *A Separate Peace*, and how Yates consciously sought to not write another version of the same story.

Preface

Young Hearts Crying—how Yates, and some of his friends, came to develop an intense dislike for Anatole Broyard, an influential book critic for *The New York Times* and onetime friend of Yates who wrote an exceedingly harsh review of the novel.

Cold Spring Harbor—a discussion of the book Yates never completed, *Uncertain Times*, and why he was uncertain he even wanted to write it.

The three books of short stories are treated somewhat differently. Rather than an extended discussion of an issue related to the books as a whole, a discussion of each story is followed by either an anecdote or commentary designed to help put the story in perspective. For example, following a discussion of "Jody Rolled the Bones," the publication of which helped establish Yates's career, is his comment that he wished he had never written the story. (This, by the way, is one of many points throughout this book that have never been reported in any other work about Yates or his writing.) Following the discussion of the individual entries in *The Collected Stories of Richard Yates* is a discussion of 15 stories written by Yates and not included in the volume.

The main section of the book closes with a reiteration of the key points made in the book and a bit of speculation about Yates's future in the American literary canon.

There are also three appendices: one discusses Yates's screenplay based on William Styron's first novel, *Lie Down in Darkness*; another lists alternate titles for stories and books that Yates considered and a few tidbits, such as alternate character names; and the third is about a treatment, that is, a synopsis for a movie, "The World on Fire," that he tried to interest Hollywood in but which no one bought.

A final point about the structure of this book: the overall discussion of Yates's writings is broken into three distinct but overlapping periods of his life. His first three books (*Revolutionary Road*, *Eleven Kinds of Loneliness*, and *A Special Providence*) all reflect a worldview that is both pessimistic and caring: according to this view, human beings are essentially lonely because they are dishonest about who they are. Pretensions lead to loneliness and loneliness leads to unhappiness. His fourth book (*Disturbing the Peace*) goes beyond that, reflecting a view of the world in which salvation, happiness, doing good, anything positive, is impossible. It is unredeemable pessimism in the extreme. But every book after that reflects some sense that redemption is possible, that some slice of happiness is within the reach of human beings, that life is, after all, not that bad. These last five books (*The Easter Parade, A Good School, Liars in Love, Young Hearts Crying,* and *Cold Spring Harbor*) are in no way optimistic. They are, more tellingly, just not nearly as pessimistic as their predecessors.

So many people who have read one or two books by Yates have been so depressed by the experience that they don't read more of his work. They might consider the overall pattern, the progression from caring pessimism to unremitting despair to the possibility of redemption, as a useful bit of advice.

Introduction: Appreciating Richard Yates

This is a work of literary criticism. And it is a memoir. That is an unusual but not an unprecedented combination. An underlying premise of this approach is that my friendship with Richard Yates in the mid-1980s, which mostly consisted of extended conversations about his writing, about writers he had read and others he knew personally, about writing and literature in general, and about any subject either of us brought up (baseball, a restaurant where George Washington once dined, the relative merits of Boston versus New York, about a dozen or two dozen other things), increased my understanding of his novels and short stories.

I, too, am a writer of novels and short stories, and I typically listened to what Dick Yates had to say as a student listens to an admired teacher. Of all the writing instructors I studied with, from elementary and high school in Pennsylvania's anthracite fields to college to graduate school, none helped me understand how fiction works and doesn't work better than Dick Yates.

Thus, a discussion of what I learned about writing (and by implication about Yates's writing) seems an appropriate place to start.

Robert Prentice, the protagonist in Richard Yates's second novel, *A Special Providence*, dislikes a Sergeant Loomis: "...he was such a God Damn actor: everything he said came out with the ponderous fraudulence of something in the movies; it was as if he had learned how to be a platoon sergeant by watching every Hollywood war picture ever made" (p. 262). Fifteen years later, in 1984, Yates published *Young Hearts Crying*, in which a character tells his ex-wife, "We spent our whole lives yearning. Isn't that the God damndest thing?" (p. 126). Seven novels and 27 short stories, Yates's output while he was alive, are united by those two sentiments: pretentiousness and yearning. Add loneliness and you have the three great and interlocking themes of Yates's total output.

Those were his themes. He also had a guiding principle for his style: honesty in the use of words. In his short story "Builders," the narrator, speaking in 1961 about something that happened in 1948, says that at the time he was wearing "a much-handled brown fedora" but adds: "'Battered' is the way I would have described it then, and I'm grateful that I know a little more now about honesty in the use of words. It was a handled hat, handled by endless nervous pinchings and shapings and reshapings; it wasn't battered at all" (*Eleven Kinds of Loneliness*, pp. 191–192). The cliché "battered hat," makes the speaker or writer look interesting (because it would become battered, for example, when in a bar fight, an event most people want to avoid, but most of us realize that people who are in bar fights lead more interesting lives than those who aren't). The replacement words, in particular "much-handled," make the narrator (and writer) look unappealing (uneasiness is hardly an attractive personality feature). Typical of Yates's style, honesty results from indirect confession.

Yates, the writer, sought honesty by fictionalizing the minutiae of the life of Yates, the man. Anyone who has read all of his published novels and short stories and then reads Blake Bailey's highly detailed biography of Yates, *A Tragic Honesty*, is likely to conclude that few, if any, fiction writers have been so autobiographical.

Yates's admirers are nearly unanimous in believing his first novel, *Revolutionary Road*, is his masterpiece, and many call it an American classic, better, some say, than *Moby-Dick* (which Yates thought was overrated[1]) or *The Great Gatsby* (which Yates admired as much as anything he ever read), and his short stories better than those of John Updike and John Cheever (two writers to whom he is often compared because so many of the characters of all three live in middle-class, suburban America[2]). Some critics would place him on a list of the ten or dozen best American writers in the decades following the Second World War. Among his biggest admirers are other writers who are often placed on similar lists, including William Styron, Tennessee Williams, and Kurt Vonnegut.[3] Reviews of his books in the daily and Sunday *New York Times*, *Time*, *Newsweek*, and most other publications were almost always very positive. But only one of his books had sales in excess of 10,000 copies. (*The Easter*

Introduction

Parade sold 120,000 copies when it was published in 1976, primarily because it was a Book-of-the-Month Club selection).

Yates's depiction of Loomis learning how to be a sergeant by watching movies, clearly a remark intended to be negative, is ironically mirrored by Yates saying he learned to be a writer by watching movies. He wrote in a 1981 article for *The New York Times* that as a child he read little but watched a lot of movies. Movies, he told me once, taught him how to shape stories, the difference between effective and ineffective dialogue, and how words are not interchangeable, that when a writer changes a word he moves closer or further away from being honest. Every character in his writing who watches movies a lot is, in fact, made less honest by the experience. In *Cold Spring Harbor* (1986) Rachel meets Evan, a liar and cheat and who once slammed a brick into another man's head. He's clearly someone she should stay away from. That's what her parents tell her. That's even what Evan's father tells her. But poor Rachel learned about romance from movies, an art form that often depicts a young man who is misunderstood by older people. Based on the evidence supplied by movies, she falls in love with him, and they eventually get married, after which he publicly insults her, hits her, and deserts her and their baby. Poor Rachel believed what movies told her, and she suffered for it. Yates told me Rachel was modeled on his older sister, Ruth, and Evan on Ruth's husband, Fred, who like the novel's character "looked just like Laurence Olivier." Stars of the screen seduce their audiences as much as they seduce other characters. Movies seduce us into believing damaging lies.

Yates was himself seduced by Hollywood, an experience that resulted in a lifetime of bitterness. In 1965 he went to Hollywood to write movie scripts and in the late eighties he returned to write for television, and each time he felt unappreciated, unloved, and used. Screenplays and television plots (treatments) he wrote were unproduced, and the one movie that carried his name as screenwriter and that was produced (*The Bridge at Remagen*) was so unlike the script he wrote that he refused to tell anyone about it. In the years I knew him we discussed movies and his first trip to Hollywood at least a dozen times, and he never once mentioned the film to me.

But, although he often spoke of his Hollywood efforts as disappointments, he did have some success there. A script he based on *Lie*

Introduction

Down in Darkness, William Styron's first novel, was never produced, but it was published in 1985, and the movie rights to three of his novels were sold, although none of them were produced while he was alive. Fifteen years after his death, his first novel, *Revolutionary Road*, was made into a film with two big stars, Leonardo DiCaprio and Kate Winslet. He was bitter about his novels not being made into movies while he lived, but nothing is as telling about his attitude toward Hollywood as what happened with *Hannah and Her Sisters*, a 1986 Woody Allen movie, in which Lee, a character played by Barbara Hershey, says to Elliot (played by Michael Caine), "Oh, you know, I, I love that book you lent me. *The Easter Parade*? You were right. It had very special meaning for me." There is no more conversation about the novel in the film.[4] The name of the author of the novel is not mentioned, but Yates told me, one night while we were in a bar in Boston, that he received 50 letters and phone calls because of that mention, which exceeded the combined total for all his other books. He also said, emphatically, that he resented that kind of influence coming from an art form he looked down upon. And few things are clearer in my memory of Dick Yates than his reaction to the time I asked him about the time he spent in Hollywood working on the Styron script. He was drunk at the time. He stabbed his finger into the tabletop between us with each spoken word, each with overriding bitterness: "I don't want to talk about that fucking time in fucking Hollywood writing for the fucking movies."

Years later we had a separate conversation about whether watching bad movies or reading bad books could help someone learn to write. The reasoning was that maybe if you could analyze what made a story bad you could therefore not do that in your own writing. Yes, he said, bad movies and television — and he thought almost all movies and almost all television was bad (I never once heard him praise a movie or TV show) — that could be useful. But not for books. You want to learn to write, he said, read good books and only good books.

Most of Yates's novels and stories are set in and around New York City, where he lived most of his life. Born in 1926 Yonkers, just north of the New York, the city and its suburbs was his intellectual and physical home for more than two-thirds of his life. (He lived in Boston for 11 years and more briefly in Iowa, California, Alabama, and elsewhere, often in temporary college teaching positions). But while he was a New York writer, one of his great regrets was he did not become, while he was alive, a *New Yorker* writer. The magazine, which he greatly admired, refused to publish any of his work until 2001, eight years after he died. When "The Canal," which is clearly inferior to at least a dozen stories he sent there while he lived (in fact, the magazine rejected the same story a half century earlier), was published posthumously, his oldest daughter, Sharon, picked up the box holding his ashes and said, "Way to go, Dad" (*A Tragic Honesty*, p. 611). His parents were divorced, and divorce appears repeatedly in his novels and stories. He saw his mother as pretentious, and nearly every mother in his writing who is a major character is pretentious. (One example: several of the mothers he created join the Episcopalian church because they view it as the church of aristocrats). His mother enrolled him in a private but not very good Connecticut school, which became the basis for *A Good School*, a 1978 novel that is a particular favorite among Yates's most ardent fans. In the closing days of World War Two, he served in the U.S. Army in Europe, and that experience was transformed into two-thirds of *A Special Providence*, a much-under appreciated 1969 novel.[5] The protagonist of that novel, Robert Prentice, pauses while searching a house for German soldiers to admire himself in a mirror. I mentioned that scene once to Yates and wondered if it was based on something he had done. He reminded me that he had previously suggested I make a distinction between "autobiographical" and "autobiography." The point was this: while he drew on his experiences to write fiction because there was nothing else he could write about with honesty, he needed to change it, mold it, to fit the requirements of the story.

The Atlantic Monthly accepted "Jody Rolled the Bones" for publication in 1953. It was Yates's first publication, and coming in a large-circulation, prestigious magazine, it provided more than his first success; following years of having stories rejected, it made him noticed in the literary community. I assumed he would remember the story with fondness, but three decades later he told me he regretted "Jody" had ever been published. The problem, he said, was that the protagonist, an army drill sergeant during World War II, was a stereotype. Yates in those 30-plus years had transformed from an unknown writer struggling for even a little bit of success to a writer nearly unknown to the large reading public but widely admired by fellow writers and critics, and while he had come to accept, even if unwillingly, his lack of financial success, he was determined to protect his reputation in the literary world. In 1961, with the publication of *Revolutionary Road*, which for some critics instantly achieved the status of a major American novel, he assumed a reputation that is, perhaps, best summed up in something Rust Hills, long a fiction editor at *Esquire* magazine, said about him in the 1980s: Yates was "one of America's least known great writers."[6] Yates knew he possessed that reputation, and while it was never a substitute for financial or popular success, he valued it greatly.

It offered compensations. Director John Frankenheimer employed him to write the screenplay for *Lie Down in Darkness*. Attorney General Robert Kennedy hired him as a speechwriter. Many women were willing to have sex with him. Eight colleges hired him to teach fiction writing, although he did not have a college degree. The Jerry Seinfeld television show did an episode based, loosely, on him.

And it cost him much. Every one of the rewards was matched by some significant failure in his life. The script he wrote for Frankenheimer was never produced. When the attorney general's brother was killed in Dallas and all high-ranking federal officials were expected to offer their resignations, Yates's was accepted. He was married twice and divorced twice, and many of his other relations with women were short-lived or unsatisfying to Yates. All but one of his college teaching positions were part-time or temporary and offered no chance of building an academic career, and the one that did offer some hope of a longtime career, Iowa, ended when he was denied tenure. As for the *Seinfeld* episode, he thought it distorted who he was and said he disliked it.

The one big reward his reputation provided, and he was very aware of this, was the ability to keep publishing his work even though he did not make money for his publishers.

Movies tell damaging lies. Distinguish between "autobiographical" and "autobiography." Yates was aware he was teaching me these lessons. Another one was that the ideal ending to a story is simultaneously inevitable and a surprise.

Sometimes he would mention a short story or novel that he thought was a good teacher. "The Eighty Yard Run" and "The Girls in Their Summer Dresses," both by Irwin Shaw, he believed could be helpful in teaching how stories work if read carefully. Reading carefully, he indicated, often meant reading some stories as he did: over and over until

Introduction

you understood how they worked. Stories should have an easily discernible three-part structure, he believed. He thought his best short story was "The Best of Everything." In part 1 we see a young woman, Grace, the day prior to her wedding to Ralph; you can do better, her roommate tells her. In part 2 Ralph is aware his attraction to Grace is based mostly on the fact that she is large breasted. In part 3, Ralph goes to Grace's apartment, where she asks him if he wants wine, and he asks for a beer. They're both virgins (the story is set in the early 1950s) and she's trying to seduce him. She's unsuccessful. This is not the classic structure Aristotle called for; it's Yates's intuitive sense of the three-part structure found in the stories, of all those he had read, that he liked most.

When I told him that Grace and Ralph struck me as two decent people who just shouldn't be married to each other, he asked me if I had read "The Eighty Yard Run." When we talked about Aristotle and three-part structures he asked me if I had read "The Girls in Their Summer Dresses."

* * *

The lessons were taught in the Crossroads, a bar in Boston's Back Bay, his favorite hangout for the decade he lived in the city. He lived for a few years in each of three different apartments in the neighborhood, which is within walking distance of both Boston University and the Massachusetts Institute of Technology. One of the apartments was upstairs from the bar. The comments he made on literature and writing were made in the Crossroads bar, in the apartment upstairs from there, in an apartment on Beacon Street a block and a half east of the bar (I was never in the third apartment), and in handwritten notes on the manuscript of a novel I'd written. Some were made in the half-dozen or so telephone conversations we had over a three- or four-year period. Most of the time, especially when we were in the Crossroads, he was drunk. He was drunk during most of the telephone conversations. Once he denounced a young dentist ("fucking kid," he said) who told Yates he would have to stop drinking before he would do the repair work Yates needed on his teeth. He was an alcoholic. The price of drinking too much was two divorces, losing his job writing speeches for Robert Kennedy, some teaching jobs, a few friendships.

He wrote about drinking. Nearly every adult male protagonist in his writing drinks too much. I learned things from Yates. Things about honesty in the use of words, and the value of structuring a story in three parts, and how reading and rereading and rereading good literature can help you write better. But more than anything else what I learned from Dick Yates is something I didn't want to learn: if your fiction is cemented in autobiographical details and you want to write good fiction, you give yourself an advantage by living a damaged life. Isn't that the God damndest thing?

* * *

Once, in the Crossroads bar, I mentioned to Yates the frequency with which *Time* magazine gave positive reviews to his novels; every novel he has published was favorably reviewed by the magazine. He went to the restroom and two men sitting nearby asked me who I was talking to; being mentioned in *Time*, they said, meant he was *somebody*. "Richard Yates," I said, "the writer." They said, "Who's Richard Yates?"

The books Yates wrote were praised by Tennessee Williams, William Styron, Mordecai Richler, Ann Beattie, Robert Stone, Alfred Kazin, John Ciardi, Dorothy Parker, Kurt Vonnegut, Granville Hicks, Tobias Wolff. But he was unknown in his lifetime to the larger reading public, a failure that depressed him. I've taught in ten colleges, and I've asked dozens of members of English departments who their favorite living authors were. Only one mentioned Yates. Almost all the others when I said, "How about Richard Yates?" asked who Yates was. That he is little known is a point no one is likely to dispute. That he is a great writer is the reason this book came to be written.

Yates was a great writer for the same mix of reasons all great writers are great: he dealt with universal themes (in his case, honesty and loneliness), and he dealt with them in a manner that is interesting, convincing, and, often, disturbing, disturbing, that is, to the reader who, if he or she is a thoughtful reader, is likely to read a work precisely because of the possibility it will disturb a deeply believed lie. Those who read only to have what they already believe confirmed lose out on the enriching experience reading can and should be; those who read only to acquire new information have too limited a view of the capabilities of literature. For the first group, Judith Krantz (some of whose books, by the way, were edited by one of Yates's daughters) is more appropriate; for the sec-

Introduction

ond group, James Michener wrote works that are as much encyclopedias as they are stories. But for those who read because they think of literature as a liberating art, Yates almost always pleases. He pleases not in the sense of entertaining but in the larger, more useful sense that at the end of the novel or the short story the reader is likely to understand himself and his fellow man better.

Thoughtful readers should want to read Yates.

Those who have not previously read Yates should approach his writing with a sense of caution. He has clearly mastered his art, but he is not artful. Perhaps more than any other widely respected American writer of the second half of the twentieth century, he places an emphasis on plot; his style, while impressive to those who stop to study it (its lack of clutter, its grace and simplicity, its carefully chosen words, its quickly convincing dialogue), is likely to pass almost unnoticed by the many readers who will be drawn into the sequence of events and interactions among characters. Characters and what characters do to each other are at the heart of all of Yates's stories and novels. Technique — at least the type of technique that might dazzle, the technique of William Gass or William Burroughs or even Norman Mailer — is clearly secondary. Unfamiliar readers must also beware of the continuing ability of a Yates story to depress. This undoubtedly is one of the major reasons Yates's work remains un-bought by much of the public. In a culture where stories seem to exist primarily to help readers and viewers escape from unsatisfactory lives, Yates's stories drive them deeper and deeper into their lives.

Yet among readers who read not just one work by Yates but several and perhaps all of his writings, one of the most frequent comments to be heard is that the writer has added something positive to their lives. He has, some readers say — and I am including here dozens of my own students and friends to whom I introduced the work of the writer — depressed them momentarily, enriched them permanently.

* * *

One certain reason Yates has not developed more of a following is the unfamiliarity with his work on the part of academics. And when they do read him, they don't know what to do with his novels and stories. Unlike, say, Burroughs or Gass or Mailer, Yates needs no explanation. He is — to use a favored academic word — accessible. A cynic might suggest academics do not teach Yates because doing so would expose them as useless; who, after all, needs a teacher to guide him or her through writing that is so clear? But that, I believe, is an undeserved charge. Academics don't teach Yates for pretty much the same reason the public doesn't buy him: they don't know him or his work. Like the two men in the Crossroads bar in Boston, they are likely to be impressed once they learn a little about him. Let them read a short story — say, "The Best of Everything" — and they will probably want to read a novel.

* * *

Yates, while he was alive, was the subject of only a half-dozen articles in literary magazines and one-third of a book of literary criticism; no article about his work appeared in his lifetime in an academic journal; the shortage of critical references, thus, is explainable: they barely exist.[7]

I believe a book-length study of Yates's full body of work can accomplish at least four useful purposes: it can place his work in a lifelong pattern that reveals stages of developments, and the relationship between the author's life and the author's work becomes clearer; it can pinpoint recurring themes, such as denouncement of movies, that provide insights into both the writer's view of his craft and his attitudes toward life; it can — to use a phrase Yates himself used in his short story "Builders" — let the light shine in, the philosophy, what precisely it is the writer was trying to say; and it can celebrate its subject. This last item is one often avoided in contemporary criticism, particularly in academic criticism, but it is not inappropriate for its subject.

In addressing this last item, I will make no pretense at objectivity, the bane of so much contemporary academic commentary. I will say, for example, that the first and last thirds of *A Special Providence* are as fine a novel as any produced by an American about the Second World War and that *Disturbing the Peace*, with its unrelieved attack on the varying treatments for alcoholism, fails as fully as the life it mirrors.

And in being willing to forgo any claims to objectivity, I will also make a larger point, that Yates's work is a case study that helps demonstrate that literary greatness — despite the claims of elitists — is not beyond the grasp of ordinary readers. That is a goal Dick Yates would aim for.

1

The Autobiographical Nature of Yates's Fiction

Yates's fiction drew its details heavily from his own life, but never does it slip into a mere retelling of that life. He used autobiographical sources without being autobiographical. The sources can be found in the repetition of details: Yates was born in 1926, making him 17 in 1943, the same age in that year as William Grove in *A Good School*; and he was 29 in 1955, the same age in that year as Frank Wheeler in *Revolutionary Road*; and 36 in 1962, the age Emily Grimes was that year in *The Easter Parade*. He uses the advantage of knowing what it was like to be a particular age in a particular year. Even the jobs are similar: Chester Pratt, a secondary character in *Disturbing the Peace*, is for a while a speechwriter for Attorney General Robert Kennedy, as Yates was in 1963; many of his characters, including Frank Wheeler and Emily Grimes, write public relations materials, and many have an older sister — Emily has Sarah, Phil in *Cold Spring Harbor* has Rachel — Yates knew with accuracy and sensitivity based on carefully recalled memory what it was like to write public relations materials and to have an older sister. But Frank Wheeler is not Yates, nor is Robert Prentice in *A Special Providence*, nor John Wilder in *Disturbing the Peace*, nor Michael Davenport in *Young Hearts Crying*. Yates shaped the lives and personalities of these characters to meet the needs of his stories; his fictional characters have a completeness in their lives, a sense of inevitable progression, that is either not present in real lives or at least not discernible. Because of the wealth of autobiographical sources, a reader will be excused from sometimes assuming Yates is writing a continuous fictional autobiography, but the same reader will increase his or her own chances of understanding the author and appreciating his art by recognizing that what is written has been shaped and ordered and polished and crafted — has, in short, been translated into a work of art — the way only lives in fiction can be.

The key autobiographical facts are these: Yates was born February 3, 1926, in Yonkers, New York; his parents divorced when he was three, and he and his older sister lived with their mother in New York City and a series of the city's suburbs. He was sent to a now-closed private school in central Connecticut, the Avon Old Farms School; after finishing there he entered the Second World War, arriving in Europe as an army infantryman during the closing days of the fighting, after the Battle of the Bulge, the last major German offensive. After the war he held a series of writing jobs, including one as a financial rewrite man for United Press and another writing PR for Remington Rand. During this time he wrote a great deal of fiction that was not published, but in 1953 one of his short stories — "Jody Rolled the Bones" — was published in *The Atlantic Monthly* as an "*Atlantic* First," that is, as the first story by a new writer to appear in a major magazine. In 1961 the publication of his first novel, *Revolutionary Road*, established him as a major literary figure; it received uniformly excellent reviews. In 1962 he was hired by film director John Frankenheimer to write a script based on William Styron's first novel, *Lie Down in Darkness*, but it was never produced, largely because stars Natalie Wood and Henry Fonda pulled out of the project. He worked on another script, about Iwo Jima, that also was not produced. *The Bridge at Remagen*, directed by John Guillermin and starring George Segal and Ben Gazzara, was produced in 1969, with Yates writing the screenplay. In 1963, partly on the strength of a recommendation by Styron, Yates was hired to write speeches for Robert Kennedy, then the attorney general of the U.S.; when President John Kennedy was assassinated in November of that year, Yates, like many other appointees in the administration, resigned. After that Yates, who never attended college, taught at the New School, Columbia, the Iowa Writers' Workshop, Wichita State University, Boston University, the University of Southern California, and the University of Alabama at Tuscaloosa. Except for these teaching posts, he lived largely in New York City and its suburbs and, for about a decade beginning in the late 1970s, in Boston's Back Bay. He married twice and was the father of three daughters, two from his first marriage, one from his second.

There is a consistency to the treatment of his fictional world that helps define Yates's view of the world itself. John Wilder in *Disturbing the Peace* is placed for a while in a psychiatric ward of Bellevue and realizes

1. The Autobiographical Nature of Yates's Fiction

it is the worst experience of his life. John Givings in *Revolutionary Road* is a long-term psychiatric patient whose doctor is shown to be insensitive to his problems; in *Cold Spring Harbor* both Charles Shepard and Curtis Drake are determined to keep psychiatrists away from their mentally ill wives. Few of society's institutions are portrayed favorably in Yates's fiction, but none of them are as unfavorably depicted as is the profession of psychiatry. Frank Wheeler uses his knowledge of psychiatry as a weapon in his disagreements with his wife, April, convincing her at one point she needs psychiatric help; his intellectualized discussion of psychiatry contribute to her demoralization. Dr. Brink in *Disturbing the Peace* helps poor John Wilder go over the mental brink. Every psychiatrist in Yates's writing seems little more than a quack, and they are portrayed with such consistency and so convincingly that it is easy to agree with the toast offered by Michael Davenport, whose wife Lucy has repeatedly turned to and repeatedly been failed by psychiatrists, near the close of *Young Hearts Crying*: "Fuck psychiatry."[1]

If those who are supposed to help, such as psychiatrists, cannot, who do those in need turn to for help? Over and over in Yates there is simply no one to turn to. Attempts to find happiness are typically aborted, and the very act of abortion is one of the most often repeated metaphors in Yates's fiction. Never is his discussion of abortion framed in a political context; much of it was written long before the 1973 Roe v. Wade U.S. Supreme Court decision legalizing abortion. It is openly discussed — argued about — by Frank and April Wheeler, but never is it clear what Yates himself thinks: the abortion and discussion of abortion in *Revolutionary Road* are there for the effect they have on the characters, not because the author is trying to convince readers to accept a pro-life or pro-choice or some other position. Messages are carefully avoided in all Yates's writings. His characters may have messages (Frank Wheeler says abortion is wrong, April tells him his arguments are "just words"[2]), but Yates lets nothing get in the way of his stories, least of all messages. Emily Grimes will have two abortions in *The Easter Parade*, and she will try to write an article about it, but the article itself is aborted because she cannot figure out how to say what she means. The reader may get the impression she is writing the article not so much out of a philosophic conviction as out of an attempt to rationalize what she has done. The article is aborted because her rationalization is never fully developed.

Over and over the abortions in Yates's stories and the use of the word "abortion" represent a failure of the character to give birth to something. Frank Wheeler cannot fully convince April she should not have an abortion; Emily Grimes cannot give birth to, cannot write, her article. Even when Michael Davenport offers to help his daughter Laura in *Young Hearts Crying* by paying for her to have an abortion, she turns out not to be pregnant: the abortion itself has been aborted.

A medically related problem that comes up even more frequently than abortion is alcoholism. Nearly every major character — John Wilder, Emily and Sarah Grimes, Michael Davenport — has a severe drinking problem. Even many secondary ones do: Grace Shepard in *Cold Spring Harbor* claims to be housebound because of an unspecified illness that in fact turns out to be alcoholism. These characters have typically turned to alcohol because they have nowhere else to turn. Their loneliness contributes to their drinking, and inevitably their drinking contributes to their loneliness.

Little wonder then that so many of the marriages in these novels and short stories fall apart. Alcoholism is not the only cause of marital strife. Often it is not even the major cause, and in a few cases it is not present at all, but it continually puts pressure on marriages that they are typically too weak to withstand. Alcoholism is clearly a contributing factor to the breakup of both of Michael Davenport's marriages in *Young Hearts Crying*, provides an excuse for Sarah Grimes's husband to beat her in *The Easter Parade*, and is the direct cause of John Wilder's at times weird behavior in *Disturbing the Peace*, which in fact is *about* alcohol-induced nervous breakdowns. But the marriages in Yates do not really need alcohol to tear them apart. What is more significant is that just as the characters who turned to psychiatrists found no real solace, neither were they comforted by their drinking. All their efforts to seek solace are aborted.

The marriage of the Wheelers falls apart because of their basic dissatisfaction with their lives. They have established a typical American suburban life: two children, a comfortable home, a decent job for Frank. It is that life — or, more precisely, life in general — that assures their unhappiness. Emily Grimes will live a "liberated" life and her sister, Sarah, an almost stereotypically married life, and despite the clear contrasts they will share one overwhelming characteristic, the one revealed

1. The Autobiographical Nature of Yates's Fiction

in the opening line of their novel, *The Easter Parade*: "Neither of the Grimes sisters would have a happy life."[3]

No one in any Yates novel or short story is truly happy. Unhappiness, resulting largely from the inevitable loneliness of human existence, is the one recurring, even stifling, theme of Yates's writing. It is because of loneliness that these characters seek help from psychiatrists, seek companionship in marriage, seek acceptance as artists or actors or poets, seek something, and life keeps failing them. Some will at least briefly turn to religion, but they do not find solace there, at least partly because they sought out religion for the wrong reason. Gloria Drake in *Cold Spring Harbor* wants her daughter, Rachel, married in an Episcopal church not because of any religious convictions but because she sees that church as aristocratic. Even in their selection of churches Yates's characters are pretentious; they yearn to be someone other than who they are. That desire to be someone else, and the inevitability they will not realize their pretensions, assures their unhappiness.

This view of the world is never explicitly stated by Yates (although now and then a character says something similar), but it becomes clear because of the way he has structured his stories. The taxi driver in "Builders" has a useful bit of architectural advice about how to build stories: among other things, start with a solid foundation and make certain to include large windows to let in light, to let in philosophy, to let in truth. The truth Yates tells is a clear explaining of the essential human condition, and the clarity of what he has to say comes not only from the clarity of his style but also from the unusual clarity and orderliness of his structure. Typically he has a clear beginning and middle and end, but he ties them together so well that often (although not always) it is virtually impossible to tell where one stops and the other begins, just as Flaubert said the sections of a story should blend together. And it is that structure that provides an inevitability to the plots, which is what Aristotle (in *Poetics*) and Flaubert and Hemingway wanted to achieve. When "The Best of Everything" closes with a clear sense that Ralph and Grace will go through with their wedding despite their obvious incompatibilities, there is no doubt as to why: their personalities, their choices in life up to the story's end, have made the wedding inevitable.

The combination of the inevitability of the plot and repeated details contributes to a feeling in reading Yates that his individual short stories and novels each form a small or large shining piece that combines with the rest to present a mosaic, a patterned view of the world. The philosophy that Bernie the taxi driver wants to shine through in "Builders" shines all the more clearly when one story is built upon another, when the full structure of Yates's collected works adds wings and new levels and enlarged rooms to the solid foundation. A secondary character — Bucky Ward in *A Good School*—sums up the light that again and again illuminates the interiors of these stories: "To come so close to all you've ever wanted in life and then never quite — never quite attain it — I suppose that's the nature of the human condition."[4]

That light is brightened by other characters' observations of their own lives. Michael Davenport laments that "we spent our whole lives yearning. Isn't that the God damndest thing?"[5] That is what makes so many people so lonely. They all want to be somebody other than who they are, and they are doomed to fall short of their goals. Emily Grimes wants to be accepted as an intellectual, as if that will in some way make her happy. She in fact does become an intellectual, but that not only does not assure her happiness but inevitably blocks it. When she reads poems written by her lover Jack Flanders she cannot enjoy them because she explicates them, something being an intellectual has conditioned her to doing. Frank Wheeler's intellectual ruminations about penis envy drive him further away from April and help make her self-inflicted abortion inevitable. Artists, likewise, contribute to their own unhappiness and that of people around them. Lucy Davenport dooms herself to getting hurt when she insists her friend, the successful painter Tom Nelson, give her an honest opinion about her paintings. When he calls them "nice," she knows she has no real talent as an artist. She has set herself up with artistic pretensions. And the artist Paul Maitland will hurt his would-be friend Michael Davenport by dismissing Nelson, Davenport's real friend, as a mere "illustrator." Artists and intellectuals in Yates are almost always pretentious, and their pretensions contribute to their own loneliness and hurt those around them.

All this might lend an air of inevitable depression to Yates's writing, and in fact that is often the case with his earliest works. No one is going to come away from completing *Revolutionary Road* or "The Best of Everything" with elation. Yet the later works represent a subtle but significant refinement of Yates's worldview. It is as if warmth has been added to the

1. The Autobiographical Nature of Yates's Fiction

brightness of the light illuminating the interiors of the building he is constructing. *Young Hearts Crying* ends with Michael Davenport accepting the fact he does not know if his second wife will ever join him in Boston; *The Easter Parade* closes with Emily Grimes having turned to and been accepted by her nephew, an Episcopal priest; "Oh, Joseph, I'm So Tired" comes to its conclusion with the reader willing to forgive, because he understands the loneliness and frustrations that caused it, the insensitive anti–Semitic remark Helen makes. The hint of redemption — although never actual redemption — present in the stories and novels following *Disturbing the Peace* is at times so subtle it might go unnoticed except for its frequent repetition. Any readers of the full body of Yates's work will notice it and will probably be grateful for it, for it offers hope for the future of their own lives that they have seen reflected in the writing.

There may be a tendency by some readers to want to reject the truths Yates reveals because they make the reader uncomfortable. A minor scene in one of his stories provides a key to understanding this difficulty: the narrator in "Builders" says that when he was younger he wore a "much handled brown fedora" but that then he would have called it "a battered hat" because that was before he knew about "honesty in the use of words."[6] The hat, the narrator says, is "much-handled" because of his own nervousness and is not at all "battered," a word that suggests it was hit by or against something. Thus, the narrator's honesty in the use of words has revealed something about him that is not flattering. Over and over in Yates, details are presented that reflect poorly upon key characters, upon characters so well drawn readers see themselves in them. They are drawn so well not because Yates inundated his stories with details (Joyce Carol Oates once complained about the lack of details in his novels) but because of his ability to select those details that are most revealing. There is a sense of incompleteness that ironically contributes to the accuracy with which readers can see the characters. No one ever in their own lives observes people in totality, so Yates never pictures them that way. Sometimes the name of a character is not given, such as the lead actor in the play that opens *Revolutionary Road*, reflecting a reader's limited knowledge of the real world; readers often do not know the names of people around them. Memories are even more incomplete; the sketchiness of *A Good School*, a story recalled by the narrator of the foreword and afterword — William Grove — is justified by the minor incident Grove relates at the close: once he was riding in his car and heard on the radio a brief bit of a recording that reminded him of his father singing "Danny Boy," but most of the song was lost in static. That is how things are remembered, and that is how Yates presents them. He does not clutter his stories with details. Every detail he gives tells something significant about the characters' personalities or their lot in life. It is a dangerous way for most writers to write because of the possibility the details will be poorly chosen, that details needed to explain a character's motivation will be missing, that details selected will not really be revealing. One of Yates's two great accomplishments as a stylist is his almost-never-failing ability to include only significant details and to leave a reader with the impression he has not omitted any that are.

His other great accomplishment as a stylist is his ability to say complicated things simply. Almost never will a reader need to turn to a dictionary to find the meaning of a Yates word, and never will he have to read a sentence or paragraph a second time to decipher its meaning. The clarity of the style is one of its hallmarks (the other being the "honesty in the use of words"). At times the style is downright colloquial. Yates does in his narratives often resort to the idiomatic tones of the American middle-class; that is, he as well as his characters sound as if they are middle class Americans because they use the same groups of words and have the same tonal quality in their voices. But his phrases never have the shallowness or inaccuracy of emotion that is typical of clichés. The idiomatic tones, in fact, are a strength because they ease the reader into the story; Yates makes the reader comfortable with his voice because it is the way the reader talks and writes and it is what the reader listens to and understands. Many of his characters use clichés, but even that tends not so much to reveal their shallowness (a technique often used by other writers) but rather allows their inner feelings to come through without their knowing it. When Helen in "Oh, Joseph, I'm So Tired" says, "*None of my best friends are Jews,*"[7] her hurt and loneliness and frustrations are revealed, even though she will probably never realize just how revealing her remark is.

That is typical of what makes plot so important in Yates. It is virtually impossible to discuss Yates's novels without repeating what the plot is. The plot and dialogue and details and everything else combine

1. The Autobiographical Nature of Yates's Fiction

to make up the characterizations, and it is the clarity of the characterizations, what makes these men and women, boys and girls, unhappy, that reveals the truths, the light that Bernie Silver wants to shine in through the large windows.

Thus, it is not surprising that Yates learned about stories as a child by watching movies. That was a fairly typical experience for someone growing up in the thirties and forties, but not necessarily for someone who turned to a literary career. He did not begin a significant amount of reading until he was 17. And what he learned from movies is that they get life wrong: a secondary character, Aaron, in *Cold Spring Harbor* complains that "the movies don't even pretend to show the truth about the army and the war, any more than they ever show the truth about love."[8] Over and over movies in Yates's novels and short stories are depicted as portraying a fraudulent view of life, and over and over that can contribute to the unhappiness of the characters. Rachel in *Cold Spring Harbor* marries Evan at least partly because movies taught her lies about love and thus made it easier for her to overlook Evan's obvious faults. In *A Special Providence* Robert Prentice will find himself in a fight with a bigger man at least partly because a sergeant has learned how to be a sergeant by watching movies. That sergeant has a sentimentalized method of solving problems between soldiers: have them go off someplace alone and fight it out. Prentice does and is beaten up. False sentimentality, so typical of movies — and of many novels and certainly of television — is what Yates most wanted to avoid in his writing.

And he did. There are sentimental scenes in Yates's work — the attempted suicide by the chemistry teacher in *A Good School* will make almost any reader feel sorry for him — but the sentiments are always saved from the melodramatic. There are sentimental moments in Yates because there are sentimental moments in life. But his insistence on honesty in the use of words, on the inevitability of the plots of his stories, and on the illuminating quality of the light shining in contributes to a sense of fidelity with life, veracity of experience. And the fidelity and veracity can make a reader uncomfortable. Few readers appreciate the revelation that their basic state is one of loneliness and unhappiness.

Readers see themselves in his characters and are uncomfortable with what they see. Yates never makes it easy for a reader to lie to himself about who he is. He never performs the services a writer of escapist fiction performs. He does not allow the reader to escape, even temporarily, from the dishonesty and loneliness and pretentiousness of his life.

But that is exactly what draws readers to Yates. He enriches them not with entertainment but by helping them to understand themselves. He reminds them their loneliness and dishonesty and pretentiousness — their dissatisfactions — are not unique but, rather, are universal and, as is made clear by the full body of his work, that is clearly redeeming. The reader is offered a possibility of salvation from his own loneliness and dishonesty and pretentiousness by Yates's ability to clearly reveal them. He has, in a sense, fulfilled the biblical directive: the reader shall know the truth and the truth shall set him free.

Order of Occurrence

Bill Grove, the main character in *A Good School*, also plays an important role in "Oh, Joseph, I'm So Tired," which takes place years before the novel opens, and in "Regards at Home," which takes place years after it closes. Those connections reflect a connection among all of Yates's work. A reader could examine the interplay of themes and character development that results from reading the stories and novels in the order in which they occur.

Of course, by reading them in the order in which they were written a reader can trace the writer's development. But by reading them in the order of occurrence the result, at least in the case of Yates, can be almost the same as reading a continuous and very long story. Some of the characters, even when they have different names, will seem to be almost the same person. That can be misleading, because each is intended to be and each is likely to strike all but the least generous of readers as actually being a separate character. The most notable possible exception is the similarity between Robert Prentice and Bill Grove.

Nevertheless, reading the works in the order of occurrence may appeal to some readers. The list that follows is a suggested reading order for those who want to try the experiment. Keep in mind that in not all cases is the year of occurrence of the story clear, although almost always a reasonable guess can be made. *The Easter Parade*, because of its 40-plus-year time span, does not fit comfortably into the list, so it is

1. The Autobiographical Nature of Yates's Fiction

excluded. Some stories, such as "A Natural Girl," fit in only if accepted as digressions, because their key characters have no notable counterparts anywhere else. Other stories, such as "Lament for a Tenor," are also excluded because they are not included in published books and are therefore not easily accessible to most readers.

Reading the stories in the order of occurrence, of course, emphasizes the autobiographical nature of Yates's fiction.[9]

The list:

"Fun with a Stranger"
"Doctor Jack-o'-lantern"
"Oh, Joseph, I'm So Tired"
"Trying Out for the Race"
A Special Providence, part 2
Cold Spring Harbor
A Good School
"Jody Rolled the Bones"
A Special Providence, prologue, parts 1 and 3, epilogue
"A Compassionate Leave"
"The Best of Everything"
Young Hearts Crying, part 1
"No Pain Whatsoever"
"Out with the Old"
"Builders"
"Regards at Home"
"The B.A.R. Man"
Young Hearts Crying, part 2
"A Really Good Jazz Piano"
"A Glutton for Punishment"
"A Wrestler with Sharks"
"Liars in Love"
Revolutionary Road
"Saying Goodbye to Sally"
Disturbing the Peace
"A Natural Girl"
Young Hearts Crying, part 3

Richard Yates: A Nonfiction Biography

So much of Richard Yates's writing is based on his own life, a reader determined to understand his fiction will benefit from a short nonfiction biography of the man that focuses on points that recur in his fiction.

He was born on February 3, 1926, in Yonkers, a suburb just to the north of New York City. His parents, Vincent and Ruth (Maurer) Yates, divorced when he was three years old, and he and his lone sibling, an older sister named Ruth, grew up living with their mother in and around New York City. In 1941, at age 15, Yates was enrolled by his mother in Avon Old Farms School, a private school in Avon, Connecticut, a suburb of Hartford. He graduated in 1944 and shortly thereafter entered the U.S. Army. He took basic training at Camp Pickett in Virginia, was trained as an infantry rifleman, and on January 8, 1945, was sent to Europe as part of the 75th Division (sometimes called the Diaper Division because so many of its members were so young; Yates was still 18). He participated in a battle in Belgium (and was awarded the Combat Infantry Badge, given to all soldiers who see action), got pneumonia, spent time in a military hospital, and later became part of the military occupation force in Germany. At some point he got tuberculosis, which permanently damaged his lungs, and that combined with an adult lifetime of heavy smoking (several packs of cigarettes a day) and drinking (he became an alcoholic) would result in thousands of coughing fits, several hospitalizations, and eventually his death. He was demobilized on January 15, 1946, two years after he entered the army, but spent five months in tent camps in France before he was sent back to the states.

He then worked for United Press in New York rewriting financial news. In 1948 he married Sheila Bryant and the next year he went to work writing publicity materials for Remington Rand. In April of 1951 he and Shelia moved to Paris and lived on a disability pension he received from the Veterans Administration. Ever since he had left the service he wrote fiction, mostly short stories, but was unsuccessful in getting anything published until 1953, when his story "Jody Rolled the Bones" was accepted by *The Atlantic Monthly*. For the next six years, while continuing to write stories and work on his first novel, he wrote freelance PR articles for Remington Rand. To supplement that income and the little bit he was now earning for his fiction, he taught creative writing courses at the New School for Social Research and Columbia University, both in New York. For much of his adult life he taught part-time or in temporary full-time positions in colleges around the country, an occupation that he told me drew energies away from his writing.

In 1961 his first novel, *Revolutionary Road*, was published and his life changed. It was a critical success, receiving nearly unanimous favorable reviews, and was nominated for the National Book Award (it lost to Walker Percy's *The Moviegoer*). The book did not sell well, but Yates was now established as an important writer.

His success resulted in receiving a Guggenheim Fellowship in 1962 and being hired by film director John Frankenheimer and, later, United Artists to write screenplays, none of which were ever produced. (He wrote a screenplay for *The Bridge at Remagen*, a movie that was actually

1. The Autobiographical Nature of Yates's Fiction

produced, but the final version was so different from the script that Yates wrote that he refused to acknowledge it was his, even though he received screen credit for it.) His experiences in Hollywood left him embittered toward the movie industry for the rest of his life.

He picked up odd jobs now and then, including, in 1962, editing a collection of prize stories by young writers.[10]

For 11 months in 1963 he wrote speeches for U.S. attorney general Robert Kennedy. Although he felt his efforts made Bobby Kennedy a better public speaker who drew louder and more enthusiastic applause than he previously had, this experience also left Yates embittered. He resented the Kennedys for being born rich and for not earning what life had given them.

His literary reputation brought him, also in 1963, a grant from the National Institute of Arts and Letters and an offer to teach at the Iowa Writers' Workshop at the University of Iowa, perhaps the most prestigious writing program in the country. He taught there from 1964 to 1971 in the only tenure-track position he ever held in a college. The job ended when he didn't get tenure, still one more experience that left him embittered.

While teaching at Iowa he also found time to write screenplays for Columbia Pictures; again, none were produced. In 1965 he was admitted to the Neuropsychiatric Institute at UCLA for mental problems that would plague him the rest of his life. He was diagnosed as bipolar, a condition that was either caused or worsened by his alcoholism. He would be institutionalized several more times (including in New York's Bellevue Hospital), would be under the care of many psychiatrists, and would take several medications for his condition. He came to hate the profession of psychiatry.

Still, his reputation as an important writer brought rewards. In 1966 he received a grant from the National Endowment for the Arts and in 1967 he received another from the Rockefeller Foundation.

His marriage to Sheila Bryant ended in divorce in 1959 (they had two daughters, Sharon and Monica). In 1968 he married Martha Speer. They had one daughter, Gina. (Yates once told me he was particularly proud of the fact that his three daughters got along well even though Gina was 15 years younger than Monica and had a different mother than Sharon and Monica.) Despite his mental, drinking, and financial problems, Yates worked hard at being a good father. He and Martha divorced in 1975.

The drinking and mental disorder interfered with his writing. His first novel, *Revolutionary Road,* considered by most of his fans to be his masterpiece, was published in 1961 and a collection of short stories, *Eleven Kinds of Loneliness,* in 1962. But his third book, a World War Two novel called *A Special Providence,* was not published until 1969. Then another six years passed before his fourth book, *Disturbing the Peace,* was published. *Disturbing the Peace,* about an alcoholic with a mental disorder, was, Yates believed, his one bad book. Most critics agree with him. But writing it seemed to release him, and he entered into an extended period of productive work. In 1976, *The Easter Parade* appeared. In 1978, *A Good School. Liars in Love,* a collection of stories, was published in 1981. *Young Hearts Crying* was published in 1984. In 1985 another book, his screenplay for William Styron's first novel, *Lie Down in Darkness,* was published, although it had been written in the early 1960s. In 1986, *Cold Spring Harbor* appeared. From the late seventies to the mid-eighties, he kept himself on a steady schedule, writing each morning and afternoon, seven days a week. But his drinking continued at night. Every night.

Yet he was also able to do some teaching, including stints at Wichita State University in Kansas, Boston University, Emerson College (in Boston), the University of Southern California, and the University of Alabama. And he continued to be honored for his writing, including a grant from the National Institute of Arts and Letters in 1975, the Rosenthal Foundation award in 1976 for *The Easter Parade,* a National Magazine Award for the short story "Oh, Joseph, I'm So Tired" in 1978, and a $25,000 grant from the National Endowment for the Arts in 1984.

He died in a Veterans Administration hospital in Birmingham, Alabama, on November 7, 1992, where he had been admitted for treatment of various of his ailments.

At the time of his death he was working on another novel, which he called *Uncertain Times* and which was partly based on his time as a speechwriter for Bobby Kennedy. It has not been published and it may be too incomplete to be publishable. In 2001 *The Collected Stories of Richard Yates* was published, containing all 11 stories in his first collection, all seven in his second, and nine more not previously collected in book form.

1. The Autobiographical Nature of Yates's Fiction

* * *

There are, of course, many things that occurred in Richard Yates's life that did not make it into his fiction. Among these is the fact that he and John Cheever, a writer with whom he is often compared because they both wrote about middle-class America (although their middle classes seem distinct — Cheever's is often wealthier), lived at separate times in a house on the same estate in Scarborough-on-Hudson, north of New York City. The estate had been owned by Frank A. Vanderlip, who was Assistant Secretary of Treasury under President William McKinley and who negotiated a $200 million loan from National City Bank to pay for the Spanish-American War. Vanderlip later became (no surprise to cynics) president of National City Bank. His estate included several homes, and he and later his children rented out some of them. Although the house Yates lived in (originally built as a machine shop and later converted to a cottage) was modest, the fact that it was on an estate that included a five-story mansion appealed to Yates's mother, Dookie.[11]

One detail about life at Scarborough-on-Hudson that may have been a model for Yates was the presence of an amateur acting company that members of the surrounding community participated in.[12]

2

The Inevitability of Unhappiness: *Revolutionary Road*

Revolutionary Road is a novel that is easy to misread. Because abortion plays such a central role in the plot and because the two main characters spend so much time arguing about it, an assumption that the novel is *about* abortion can easily be made. That would be a particularly tempting assumption a half century after the book was first published; but the novel appeared more than a decade before the U.S. Supreme Court's Roe v. Wade decision legalizing abortion and it is not set in the social/political context that dominated the discussion of the issue in the decades following that decision.

The novel, Yates's first, is about, rather, failed dreams and the inevitability of unhappiness. It opens with the lead characters facing great expectations; the Laurel Players, a newly formed community theater in western Connecticut in the early spring of 1955, present their first production, *The Petrified Forest*, a work notable because its seriousness shows the ambitions of the inexperienced company and because of the opportunity it provides for the leading lady, April Wheeler, to deliver the rhetorical line, "Wouldn't you like to be loved by me?" (p. 9).[1] April Wheeler is attractive, sophisticated, and usually charming; she is exactly the type of woman most men would love to be loved by. But the play and the lives of April and her husband, Frank, are tragedies. The actor playing the leading male role spills a glass of water onstage, and April, the lone really talented performer in the production, fluffs the delivery of some of her lines. In the climactic scene, offstage gunfire is too loud and the actors cannot be heard. "When the curtain fell at least it was an act of mercy" (p. 10).

The lives of April and Frank Wheeler, and those of their friends, Shep and Milly Campbell, are just as pretentious. They are all actors

2. The Inevitability of Unhappiness

playing at a game called marriage, a game they happen to be not very good at. Their lives in many ways parallel the performances of the Laurel Players. By the end of the novel April realizes that her life with Frank has been earnest and pretentious, like the Laurel Players. A good part of that pretentiousness results from the sense Frank and Shep have of themselves as intellectuals. Frank will not call the Campbells "friends" (p. 135) precisely because he thinks of them as less intellectual than him and April. And Shep, who once rebelled against his mother by attending a Midwestern technical school rather than an Ivy League college, has a decade later come to feel he has denied himself his birthright and tries to adjust by listening to classical music and reading literary journals. His frustration is so great that he calls his wife, Milly, an "ignorant cunt" (p. 140) and punches the wall. He is embarrassed by his four sons, aged four to eight, because they act middle class (just as in *A Good School* Robert Driscoll is embarrassed by his son, who he thinks is not masculine). Shep is even embarrassed by the titles of books he has when Frank looks at them (but typical of Yates the reader is not told the titles, reflecting how people really see the world, with many details missing; similarly, the name of the director of the play is never given). Milly feels uneasy when the Wheelers visit because she thinks they are stuck up, that they feel intellectually superior to her and Shep. But Shep really suffers from that fault far more than Frank or April, for he sees in April the epitome of the sophisticated, intellectual woman, one with the appealing traits Milly clearly lacks. At one point Shep whispers, to hear how it will sound, "I love you, April" (p. 146).

April's unhappiness leads her to having sex, just once, with Shep, but when he then tells her he loves her she is clearly annoyed, because she recognizes the essential phoniness of the remark. She knows he loves her not because of who she is but because she conveniently fits his image of the perfect woman. Her ability to make such a recognition makes her the most heroic figure in the novel. Just prior to the climactic scene, she will think that if a person wants to do something "honest" or "true" (p. 311) he or she has to do it alone. It is a sentiment that could come right out of the mouth of a character in Hemingway (who happens to be one of the writers Yates most admired[2]). Her ability, at least at the end of the novel, to avoid anything essentially phony leads her to catch an impulse to sign a final note to Frank "I love you" and instead write just "April" (p. 310).

Shep, who finds April so attractive, never becomes capable of that kind of honesty. At the end of the novel, while April is dying on an operating table in a hospital, he tells Frank he is going for coffee, because he is not willing to admit he really needs to go to the men's room.

But no one in the novel is more basically dishonest than Frank, who in many ways *is* an intellectual, well educated (Columbia), widely read, with carefully thought out opinions on complex issues; but his intelligence is typically Procrustean, allowing him to adjust his facts and his logic to fit his purpose. Nowhere is this more evident than when he tries to convince April not to have the abortion she wants by claiming to have once read about a woman who wanted "to open herself" (p. 231) to let a penis hang down, suggesting the desire to abort a pregnancy is a form of penis envy. He adds that *if* girls have penis envy, they normally get over it by emulating their mothers, something April could not do because her mother gave her to an aunt to be raised. Frank's simplistic interpretations of Freud incisively reflect American liberal-intellectual conversation in the 1950s at its most pretentious.

John Givings, a secondary character with certified mental problems — he is institutionalized — is a more accurate observer of the psychological condition of the other characters than is the overly intellectualized Frank Wheeler. Givings is taken by his parents to visit the Wheelers because they hope such a visit will provide a stabilizing influence on their son. John tells the Wheelers that their home on Revolutionary Road, in the Connecticut suburbs of New York City, "looks like a place where people live" (p. 184). This Wheeler family of an attractive wife, an intellectual husband, a son and daughter, in a pleasant community, is seemingly an American ideal. John Givings, better than anyone else in the novel, understands why the Wheelers have decided to move to Paris, where their plans call for Frank to think and walk while April works. John's understanding of their motivations leads Frank to tell April, "I guess that means we're as crazy as he is" (p. 192). Frank clearly means April is the one who is crazy, but he is not without some hang-ups of his own. Throughout much of the novel he spends time making a stone walk in front of his house because he thinks of it as man's work; the walk remains unfinished at the end of the novel. And when the roommate of the woman he is having an affair with tells him the affair is bad for her friend, Frank tells her she is "meddling" and that she is a "pain in the ass" (p. 269), because that is how a man is expected, he thinks, to react to such an accusation. The essential cruelty of his remarks is revealed when he then does break off the affair. His *manliness* has caused him to commit his one overt act of cruelty in the novel. He comes close to another when he tells April about the affair, which he blames on April's talk of having an abortion, talk he says that might have in some way threatened his masculinity. It is more Freudian hogwash and is kept from being cruel in its effect only because April does not care.

John Givings gets away with far more cruelty precisely because his mental illness is certified. When he hears that the Wheelers have changed their plans for going to Paris he rejects Frank's explanation that it is a result of their inability to pay for both the move and another child and accuses Frank of getting "cold feet" (p. 286). John's mental illness allows him to be rudely honest where others feel social restraints forbid such conduct. Recognizing that Frank and April are not getting along well, John points to April's enlarged abdomen and says, "I'm glad I'm not gonna be that kid" (p. 288).

Frank later tries to dismiss John's rudeness by saying it results from his insanity, which he then defines as "the inability to love" (p. 290), causing April to laugh and say he is calling her insane because she does not love him. She then becomes hysterical, and Frank thinks that if this were a movie he would slap her, but he doesn't, indicating, as happens often in Yates, that movies present a false view of life. He says she does love him, and they argue about that. Arguing, in fact, is their major form of communication. She often sleeps on the couch while he is in the bed and at one point does not talk to him for two days. He becomes very aware of how much he dislikes his life and once even looks forward to a visit from the Campbells primarily because it means April will have to talk to them.

During that visit Frank notes that the next day will be his thirtieth birthday and tells a story about spending his twentieth birthday under fire during World War II. It is a story he has told before, and April looks at him with a "pitying boredom" (p. 68) that makes him feel middle aged. Theirs is clearly a marriage that has lost its capacity for warmth.

But there are touches of at least pretended warmth. April and the children, Jennifer and Michael, hold a surprise birthday party for Frank, and when he and April first decide to go to Paris they have "a love affair" because they look forward to being "new and better people" (p. 126). Having a dream, something to look forward to, has eased the tension between them. The Wheelers even congratulate themselves on having not turned into typical suburbanites like the Campbells, and Frank compares the emotions he has for their planned trip to Paris to those he had the first time "on the line" in war — "I just felt this terrific sense of life" (p. 130) — and April says she felt that way the first time they made love. The reader can easily doubt April's sincerity on this point, and a clue to understanding any of Yates's characters is figuring out if they are being honest when they explain their emotions.

Despite what for a time seems to be marital bliss, Frank realizes his marriage has become "unsentimental" (p. 224), and that allows him to justify an affair with a secretary who works in his office, Maureen Grube. That affair, however, is never a major cause of problems between Frank and April. When he leaves for work on the last day that April is alive, Frank asks her, "You don't really hate me, or anything?" and she answers, "No, of course, I don't" (p. 299). She knew about the affair at that point but had come to realize that she neither hated nor loved Frank. Their fights were not so much with each other as with what had become of their lives.

Frank often complains about living in the suburbs and frequently refuses to recognize that he is middle class and a suburbanite. He sees that as drab, uninteresting. He dislikes even the idea of having a stable childhood and is clearly jealous of April's more "dramatic" (p. 38) upbringing. Her father killed himself, her mother died an alcoholic, and she was raised largely by her aunt Claire; one time April's mother came to visit with her boyfriend but stayed only two days, and when April's father came and stayed only an hour the best he could do for a present was a trinket from a whiskey bottle. Hardly a childhood a child would want to have, but Frank, as an adult, envies it; the envy is, of course, a result of an anti–middle-class bias, a revolt against a stereotypical American life. The very setting, a pleasant Connecticut suburb of New York City, could provide the backdrop for any of hundreds of stories about how something goes wrong in an idyllic life, about how a tragedy — a murder, a kidnapping, a hurricane — disrupts the happiness of a typical American family; it is, instead, a story about what is wrong with the idyllic life itself.

2. The Inevitability of Unhappiness

When the book was first published, it contained a note on the front cover from critic Alfred Kazin calling it "a powerful commentary on the way we live now. It locates the new American tragedy squarely on the field of marriage." Yates, however, has said he did not agree with that statement[3] and adds that not only does he like those characters but also if they did not live in suburbia they would probably have to live in the slums of a city. He once sarcastically sang a few lines from a song called "Little Boxes" that referred to suburban homes as being made of "ticky tacky" and that was popular in the late 1960s and which attacked the sterility and sameness that some social critics say then dominated American suburbia.[4]

Yates's rejection of this interpretation of the novel is consistent with his insistence that a story should be about its characters and should not be dominated by a message. Still, he does not reject the notion that a story may also be about an issue of concern to more people than those who appear as characters in it. Yates typically presents characters who reflect views on all sides of an issue, as with Helen Givings, who in sharp contrast to the Wheelers and Shep Campbell has grown to love her home, after many moves, and who sees love as "positive" (p. 154). More important, however, than that contrast is the interrelationship of the Wheelers and Givingses. Helen hoped the Wheelers would help her son John find a sense of stability, but when they tell her they plan to move to Paris she realizes her hopes are useless. Her plan to help her son is based on her sense of community, while the Wheelers can plan to move away precisely because they lack that sense of community.

The plans to move to Paris, in fact, represent an attempt to escape from the middle-class, suburban life the Wheelers blame for their unhappiness. After all, Frank does not plan to write or paint or do anything particularly creative there but rather to think and walk; he'll be "finding himself" (p. 109). When his first reaction to April's announcement of the plan is that it is unrealistic, she delivers a long speech about how their current lives are unrealistic. She specifically adds that everyone, not just writers and artists and those with definite talents, has a right to "lives of their own" (p. 115). The point, of course, is that typical American suburban life denies people lives of their own.

April has little trouble at first convincing Frank of the appeal of walking and thinking in Paris, but then the appeal of his current life provides attractions of its own. He starts to get ahead in his job — at least he gets praise and a vague promise of a better position. He is drawn to both lives, as alien as they are. He looks forward to telling the Campbells of their plans precisely because telling someone will make the plans seem more real and in effect cement the decision. At the same time, he is too embarrassed to let Mrs. Givings know their plans call for him to not work in Paris. Nearly no one approves of their plans. The Campbells privately agree the plan is "immature" (p. 149); Helen Givings tells her husband it is "unsavory" and that she thought the Wheelers were more "settled" (p. 163). Even the Wheelers' daughter, Jennifer, cries because she is upset about the move. Frank suggests the move is "inconsiderate" (p. 180) to the children, a remark that causes April to snap at him and accuse him of changing his mind. The plan is clearly far more April's than it is Frank's.

When the Wheelers do change their mind about going because of April's pregnancy, however, not everyone is happy. Shep Campbell in particular had hoped to get over his infatuation with April by picturing her moving away and coming back ten years later less pretty.

Frank had not been fully honest with everyone about the Paris plans and wanted to keep opportunities for advancement open in his job with Knox Business Machines. He told Bart Pollack, who had strongly hinted at a promotion for Frank, that he was leaving the company but did not mention Paris, leaving Pollack with the impression he had another job. What had impressed Pollack about Frank was a simple sales letter Frank wrote. That at first seemed like an incidental detail, but it eventually opened up new opportunities on the job for Frank and thus provided him with an important alternative to moving to Paris. This is typical of Yates's plotting: simple details serve multi-purposes, adding unity to deceptively complicated plots. When Frank tells April that Pollack wants him to write a whole series of similar sales letters, something that will increase his importance to the company, he is disappointed — even angry — that April does not share his pride in his office success. Nowhere are the differences in expectations from life clearer than when Frank and April react so dissimilarly to this success. He refuses to think of the opportunity Pollack offers as a compromise, telling himself it is an acceptable "plan in its own right" (p. 208). By the time the book ends, after April's death, Frank is working, not for Knox, but for Bart Pollack Asso-

2. The Inevitability of Unhappiness

ciates, which does PR work for Knox. Milly Campbell sees Frank at that point as "courageous" (p. 329), but Shep, who more closely shared April's outlook, thinks Frank is lifeless and that Frank, unlike April, would never have had the nerve to kill himself.

The climactic scene in which April performs a self-inflicted abortion that results in her death has, as much as anything else in Yates's writing, opportunities for varying interpretations. Clearly April was aware she might die and the abortion might be seen as essentially suicidal. But she tidied up after herself, as if she did not want anyone to think she was not neat, and called for an ambulance. Rather than suicidal, she might have been accepting the possibility of death as better than the possibility of continuing a life like the one she lived. Coming close to death might have been a way of convincing Frank to not back out of the planned trip to Paris. Yates does not so much fail to dictate the precise motive as he accurately reflects the uncertainties — brought on by anguish — swimming in April's mind.

She had once previously considered an abortion, when she was pregnant with Jennifer, seven years before they planned for her to be, but Frank talked April out of it. His principal objection was not moral but rather that she had made a key decision without consulting him. When she is pregnant for the third time and she suggests an abortion, Frank conducts a "courtship" (p. 216) to convince her not to have one. This time he does think it is morally wrong. She responds by saying "moral" and "conventional" are the same thing and that his arguments are "just words" (p. 223). Their arguments over the issue of abortion reflect in many ways the arguments over the issue that have continued for several decades. Their arguments have the same tone of rationalization that has long dominated both sides of the issue. Not that that proves either side wrong, but rather that it reflects, as is typical of so many of Yates's characters, a basic dishonesty. Logic in the mind of a Yates character is a weapon for winning an argument, not for reaching a conclusion.

The real problem between the Wheelers defies their logical analysis; it is essentially a matter of emotional incompatibility. A remark made by Mrs. Givings offers a metaphoric explanation of what neither April nor Frank could articulate. Mrs. Givings had given the Wheelers as a gift some sedum plants, and she finds them in the basement after April dies. She asks her husband rhetorically, wouldn't he think someone would take care of a "living, growing thing?" (p. 337). Of course, just as the Wheelers did not properly care for the plants, so, too, did April's parents and Frank not properly care for April (whose name suggests the growing season that both opens and closes the book).

Mrs. Givings may be willing to blame both Frank and April for not caring for the plants, but others are quite willing to blame themselves for April's death. Frank feels responsible for not letting her abort the pregnancy a month earlier when it would have been much safer. Shep wonders if his one sexual encounter with April is in any way responsible. There are more than enough guilt feelings to go around.

The key abortion scene occurs, in effect, offstage. The details are provided by secondhand observers, not directly by Yates. Milly and Helen Givings and Shep and Frank each fill in some of the details as they talk to others. This shift in point of view at a key moment in the story is common in Yates and it has at least two notable effects: it wipes away the tendency of melodramatic writing that accompanies such scenes in other writers; after all, avoiding melodrama in a scene involving the deaths of both a beautiful woman and an unborn baby may be impossible; and it broadens the impact of the climax, emphasizing how April's death has affected the lives of those who were part of her life.

Having key action take place offstage was typical of many ancient Greek plays, and that is not the only similarity this novel has with them. John Givings, to some extent, serves the same role as a Greek chorus, although he never becomes a mere dramatic device but is, rather, a fully developed character; Yates avoids turning John Givings into the stereotypical insane-observer-who-is-the-only-really-sane-person-in-the-story by endowing him with some opinions that are clearly wrong (such as his assumption that Frank might help him find a lawyer to get him out of the mental hospital). The most notable similarity, however, may be the least visible. Like the ancient Greek plays, the novel has a clearly defined beginning introducing characters, conflicts, and settings; middle, where all these elements interact; and ending, where the conflict is resolved; it is essentially the same structural formula followed by Sophocles, Aeschylus, and Aristophanes and advocated by Aristotle in *Poetics*.[5]

Revolutionary Road is thus a classical story set in contemporary America. Just as the best of the ancient Greek plays were about universal emotions, so, too, is the first of Yates's novels about something everyone

2. The Inevitability of Unhappiness

can feel, a sense of not being satisfied with life. That is where the revolution is. In their unhappiness, Frank and April Wheeler revolt against their lives. They traveled down, as much as they lived on, a revolutionary road, and at the end of it they found not freedom but defeat and tragedy.

* * *

A common complaint among readers of Yates's novels and short stories is that they see themselves in his characters and they do not like what they see. Neither Frank Wheeler nor Robert Prentice, nor anyone else in either of Yates's first two novels (or in his first collection of short stories, *Eleven Kinds of Loneliness*), is likely to be willingly adopted as a role model by anyone. Still, they are far from evil and can even be amiable. Their lack of appeal lies in their unalterable glide toward unhappiness; they are each complete, yet each is devoid of even a remote possibility of redemption from their loneliness. For the reader seeking emotional escapism, Frank Wheeler and Robert Prentice and so many other of these characters are worse than depressed: they are depressing. For readers seeking some sense of the truth of their own lives, some sense of what the world is really like, they are discomforting.

Yates and Hollywood

When I interviewed Richard Yates in a bar in Boston's Back Bay, the Crossroads, in 1984 and I asked him about writing film scripts in Hollywood, he avoided answering the question. I asked again; he avoided again. But with the third or fourth time I asked, after he had downed eight or nine double shots of Jim Beam with water and two bottles of beer — Rolling Rock — he lost his patience, which he never did before the whiskey and beer and which he almost always did after, he leaned toward me, jabbed a finger into the table between us with each word, and said with modulated but unmistakable anger, "I don't want to talk about that fucking time in fucking Hollywood writing for the fucking movies."

Yates hated Hollywood. And he longed for it. It was not a love/hate relationship. It was far too complicated for a cliché. When his first and best novel, *Revolutionary Road*, was made into a movie — what promised, at least briefly, to be a big movie — in 2008, 16 years after Yates died, there was at least a potential that he would achieve one of the things he hoped Hollywood would give him: a wider readership. The movie starred Kate Winslet and Leonardo DiCaprio, the first film they appeared in together since their 1997 megahit, *Titanic*. And it was directed by Sam Mendes, Winslet's husband, who received an Academy Award in 1999 for directing *American Beauty*. *Revolutionary Road* was released to a few theaters in big cities on December 26, 2008, so it would be eligible for that year's Academy Awards, and had its worldwide release three weeks later.

To understand Yates's likely reaction to the film, it will be helpful to provide more details about his attitudes toward Hollywood.

He did eventually talk to me about his time in Hollywood. The next day when he wasn't quite so drunk and years later when I made subsequent visits to Boston. Here's one of the stories he related: William Styron was asked by director John Frankenheimer to write a screenplay for his first novel, *Lie Down in Darkness*, but Styron, who was married to a rich woman, didn't need the money and wasn't attracted to Hollywood's alleged glamour and turned down the offer. Styron, however, had read *Revolutionary Road*, which he very much admired, knew Yates needed money, and suggested to Frankenheimer that he ask Yates to write the script. The offer was made, Yates accepted, and he ended up in Hollywood in 1962. Yates told me that Frankenheimer intended to have Henry Fonda play the role of the father in the novel and that the daughter would be played by Natalie Wood, who had indicated a strong willingness to accept the role, although at the time she was getting a lot of offers for other movies. Eventually, she turned down Frankenheimer's offer, and the director then suggested another young and attractive actress. Jane Fonda. Anyone familiar with the plot of *Lie Down in Darkness* will immediately recognize the problem. In a key scene the daughter and father share a very passionate kiss. When Henry Fonda learned of Frankenheimer's suggestion, he was infuriated and said he wouldn't have anything to do with the movie or the director. Yates, while telling me all this, resorted to a cliché, something he seldom did in speaking or writing: "Hollywood," he said, "is a small town." No famous actors would work on the film after word got out about Frankenheimer's aborted plan. Frankenheimer was crazy. The money people, the ones needed to fund the project, lost interest. *Lie Down in Darkness*, because of its strong hints of incest, always promised to be a difficult project, and now it

2. The Inevitability of Unhappiness

seemed like an impossible one. Yates told me the story with a small, sad smile and a soft shrug of his shoulders. And with a belly full of booze. Was it accurate? No one else has related this story. Liquor can be liberating and encourage people to reveal secrets they would otherwise keep to themselves. It can also distort the truth. But when he told me the story I'm certain Yates believed that Frankenheimer's suggestion that Jane Fonda passionately kiss her father in front of millions of moviegoers destroyed whatever hope he had of building a career as a screenwriter.

There was another afterword to the story. Natalie Wood, he said, was just as pretty in person as on the screen, and he found her death by drowning, in 1981, very sad. Once she spotted him at a party and told him how sorry she was that she had pulled out of the film, that if she hadn't done that, he no doubt would have been a successful screenwriter.

Since then, other directors have expressed an interest in making *Lie Down in Darkness* into a film, but so far, none have.

Yates mentioned that he worked on a script about Iwo Jima while in Hollywood and said it never reached production stage. I talked to him about writing for Hollywood a half-dozen or more times and not once did he mention *The Bridge at Remagen*, a 1969 movie directed by John Guillermin that starred Ben Gazzara and George Segal. And which gave Yates, in very large lettering (as large as lead actors normally get and about twice the size of what is normally given to screenwriters), credit for the screenplay. He didn't want anyone to know about his role in the movie. Decades later a videotape of the movie was released, and that retained Yates's name as the sole screenwriter. But in 2000, when the movie came out on a DVD, Yates shared screen credit with William Roberts. Although it came nine years after his death, Yates would have been pleased with the decision to downplay the role he had in writing the script. Blake Bailey, Yates's biographer, said Yates didn't list the film on his résumé. Too many changes were made between the script Yates wrote and the film that was produced for Yates to consider it his own work, but more important than that is the fact it is a bad film, populated by stereotypes acting in clichéd situations. From Yates's viewpoint, *The Bridge at Remagen* was just another typical Hollywood movie.

Perhaps the clearest expression of Yates's emotional reaction to Hollywood comes in *A Special Providence*, his second novel, when Robert Prentice is in a fight with another soldier because a sergeant learned how to be a sergeant by watching movies. The sergeant thinks if two soldiers can't get along, they should settle their differences with fists. So he tells Prentice and the other soldier to go off by themselves and have the fight, and when they do Prentice is beaten up. Prentice, like Yates, was an 18-year-old private in France near the end of World War Two, and he realizes what he doesn't like about the sergeant: "...he was such a God Damn actor: everything he said came out with the ponderous fraudulence of something in the movies; it was as if he had learned how to be a platoon sergeant by watching every Hollywood war picture ever made" (*A Special Providence*, p. 262).

Yet it is unsurprising that Yates learned about stories by watching movies as a youngster. That was a common experience for anyone growing up in the thirties and forties. In one of the few nonfiction articles Yates wrote, he said he didn't read much as a child, but he often went to movie theaters. Movies taught him, he told me, how stories are shaped, how dialogue works and doesn't work, how changing a word here or there can move you closer to the truth. Or can create a lie.

He also learned from movies that they get life wrong: a secondary character, Aaron, in *Cold Spring Harbor*, Yates's final book, complains that "the movies don't even pretend to show the truth about the army and the war, any more than they ever show the truth about love" (p. 136). Again and again movies in Yates's seven novels and more than two dozen published short stories are depicted as portraying fraudulent views of life, and over and over that contributes to the unhappiness of the characters. Rachel in *Cold Spring Harbor* gets married at least partly because movies taught her lies about love and thus made it easier for her to overlook her boyfriend's obvious faults.

Yates captures poor Rachel's attitudes toward Hollywood:

> The movies were wonderful because they took you out of yourself, and at the same time they gave you a sense of being whole. Things of the world might serve to remind you at every turn that your life was snarled and perilously incomplete, that terror would never be far from possession of your heart, but those perceptions would nearly always vanish, if only for a little while, in the cool and nicely scented darkness of any movie house, anywhere [*Cold Spring Harbor*, p. 88].

In *Cold Spring Harbor*, Rachel meets a far from admirable young man, Evan, who lies and cheats and once bashed in another young man's

2. The Inevitability of Unhappiness

head. Her parents warn her to stay away from Evan, and even his father warns her he's no good. But Rachel has learned from movies that such young men are really good people at heart, so she has an affair with him and marries him, and he insults her in public places, beats her, and abandons her and their new born baby. Movies taught poor Rachel a damaging lesson.

Helping make the connection more complete, Yates said several times that Rachel was based on his only, and older, sister, Ruth, and that her husband, Fred, like Evan, "looked just like Laurence Olivier." Movie stars seduce their fans. Movies, more generally, seduce us into believing lies.

In *Disturbing the Peace*, Yates's third novel, the character John Wilder recalls with admiration what some people would think was the rude behavior of soldiers at a base movie theater:

> Funny thing; in civilian movie-houses people'd sit still for any kind of trash — you'd never hear anybody laugh out loud in a love scene or anything like that — but in the army there was nothing magic about the big silver screen any more, and we all got to be very vocal, brutal, movie critics. We could spot a fake plot or a fake "message" a mile away; we'd stomp and laugh and yell obscenities at anything cheap or trite or hoked-up or sentimental, and I remember thinking Jesus, these guys are like me; we've all been raised on movies, and we're just now beginning to figure out what frauds most of them are [pp. 97–98].

Yates's own experiences with the film industry are captured in his short story "Saying Goodbye to Sally": Jack Fields is a 36-year-old novelist who goes to Hollywood to write a film script and has an affair with Sally Baldwin, an attractive secretary of about the same age. He fancies himself a 1960s version of F. Scott Fitzgerald having an affair with Sheilah Graham, but near the end of this long story (60 pages, making it by far the longest of any of Yates's published stories) Sally calls him a "Counterfeit F. Scott Fitzgerald who comes stumbling out to movieland" (*Liars in Love*, pp. 270–271).

Dozens of other references to movies appear in Yates's stories and novels, every one of them negative.

Hollywood purchased options to three of Yates's novels: *Revolutionary Road*, *Disturbing the Peace*, and *The Easter Parade*. Yates, as much as he looked down on Hollywood, hoped one of them would be made into a movie so he would get both money and a larger readership. But none of them made it to the screen before he died in 1992.

Although one sort of did.

In *Hannah and Her Sisters*, a film written and directed by Woody Allen, the Barbara Hershey and Michael Caine characters hold a brief conversation about Yates's 1976 novel, *The Easter Parade*, and although his name is not mentioned, Yates told me he received about 50 fan letters and phone calls as a result and that that was more than he received for all his other books combined, and he resented that Hollywood influence.

Yates had several other connections to Hollywood.

Monica, his second-oldest daughter was the model for the Elaine Benes character on the *Seinfeld* TV comedy series (she dated one of the producers), which once did an episode about Elaine's father, clearly based on Yates, coming to dinner. After viewing the episode, according to Bailey, Yates complained that much of the minutiae was wrong: Benes wears a hat, and Yates didn't; Benes is a veteran of the Korean War, Yates of World War Two; and Elaine tells stories in the present tense, something Monica didn't do. Again, Hollywood got it wrong.[6]

Yates was hired in the late 1980s by an ex-student, David Milch, producer of TV's *Hill Street Blues*, to work on treatments (story-like ideas that might be developed into scripts). Yates didn't even like Milch, whom he had taught at the University of Iowa. Working for Milch made Yates miserable. None of his treatments ever made it to the screen.

In *Lonesome Jim*, a 2005 movie, the protagonist, Jim, played by Casey Affleck, tells his girlfriend, Anika, played by Liz Tyler, that Richard Yates is one of his favorite authors and that all of his books are out of print. The screenwriter, James C. Strouse, was a fan of Yates, and the plot is clearly autobiographical. The lead character, Jim, at age 27, has left New York, where he barely made a living as a dog walker and failed to establish a career as a novelist. He returns to his home in Indiana, where his mother is arrested and charged with sending illegal drugs through Federal Express. The overwhelming tone of sadness that dominates the low-budget movie (it was made for about a half-million dollars) is reminiscent of Yates's writing.

(At least a few people mistakenly think there is one more Yates connection to the movies; several web sites say that in the 2004 movie *Million Dollar Baby* [which won the Academy Award for Best Picture] the character Frankie Dunn, played by Clint Eastwood, is reading a Richard Yates book. But they are wrong. The scene they refer to occurs just before the

2. The Inevitability of Unhappiness

halfway point of the movie, and the Hilary Swank character, Maggie Fitzgerald, asks the Eastwood character, "Whatcha readin'?" Frankie turns to Scraps [Eddie "Scrap-Iron" Dupris], played by Morgan Freeman, and asks, "What the hell she say?" and Scraps says, "Wants to know what you're reading." At this point, some listeners evidently think that Frankie answers, "Yates." But the script, written by Paul Haggis, clearly says: "Yeats." And Scrap replies by saying, "Talk a little Yeats to her, show her what a treat that is." Throughout the movie, Frankie is trying to teach himself Gaelic, so a reference to the great Irish writer William Butler Yeats is consistent with his character.)[7]

Yates's first novel, *Revolutionary Road*, opens with an amateur production of a play in a community theater in Connecticut. One actor forgets a key line, offstage gunfire is much too loud, and the only talented actor on the stage, April Wheeler, performs as badly as everyone else. "When the curtain fell at last," Yates writes, "it was an act of mercy" (*Revolutionary Road*, p. 10).

As much as Yates wanted the money and increased book sales a movie production of one of his books would have brought, perhaps the fact that none of his books were made into a film until after he died might also have been an act of mercy. He so disliked movies and the way Hollywood treated him, he no doubt would have disliked the movie *Revolutionary Road* because it left so much out that he had put into the novel and in the process distorted what his novel was about; seeing one of his books translated to the big screen would have caused pain.

In *Young Hearts Crying*, Yates's next-to-last novel, a character tells his ex-wife, just as Yates once said to *his* ex-wife, "We spent our whole lives yearning. Isn't that the God damndest thing?" (p. 126). A decade and a half after his death, Dick Yates went back to the movies. Isn't that the God damndest thing?

* * *

The money and the increase in sales of his books that came from the movie version of *Revolutionary Road* would no doubt have pleased Yates. The movie itself would have displeased him. Maybe even angered him. It's not a bad movie, but it omits so much of the novel, so much that gave the novel emotional and intellectual depth, that he might even have felt betrayed.

The problem with the movie was summarized a year and a half after it was released in an article that wasn't even about the movie, doesn't mention its title, and omits Yates's name. It appeared in the May 24, 2010, issue of *Time* magazine, in an article about superstrong beer (beer with 32 to 40 percent alcohol by volume [most beer is in the 4 to 8 percent range]). Sean Gregory, in summing up his reaction to drinking a bottle of the strong beer, concludes his article with this: "...instead of watching an NBA playoff game, I took in a depressing movie in which Leonardo DiCaprio and Kate Winslet play a married couple who keep screaming at each other. I must have been hammered."[8] The idea that you have to be drunk to want to watch the movie is harsh, but the sentiment that the movie is depressing is consistent with how critics and the public reacted to it. The novel is also depressing, but the novel offers insight into human nature that is totally absent from the film.

Part of the problem, no doubt, is that movies can't handle all the material that goes into novels. Many writers have noted that. For example, science-fiction writer Nancy Kress has opined that in terms of quantity of material, a movie is about the same length as a novella.[9] However, a larger part is that moviemakers, particularly directors and screenwriters, conceive of stories differently than do novelists or short story writers. An examination of some key differences between *Revolutionary Road* the movie and *Revolutionary Road* the novel reveals differing perceptions about storytelling.

The movie opens with April and Frank meeting at a party in New York City, while the novel opened with the Laurel Players, the amateur acting group to which April belongs, rehearsing for the performance of their play, *The Petrified Forest*. The movie, thus, sets up the relationship and in doing so deemphasizes the specialness the Wheelers see in themselves. The novel, by opening with preparation for the play, emphasizes April attempting to make herself special. Having acted in college and being the only actor in the Laurel Players with any acting talent, she has reason to feel superior to the others in the play. The movie, in fact, omits nearly everything about the play. We are not even told its title. We don't hear a single line delivered by anyone. We see only the falling of the final curtain and hear members of the audience both applaud politely and comment about how bad the performance was. For the novel, the play is the thing.

2. The Inevitability of Unhappiness

The idea of acting is itself metaphoric. We all act at being someone other than who we are, the metaphor says, and we're not very good at it. The metaphor takes on larger and ominous meaning as the novel progresses and April and Frank act at being superior to their neighbors and friends. But the title of the play is another metaphor. They live in a world, suburban America in the 1950s, or, more generally, middle-class America anytime, that petrifies them, that keeps them from growing and realizing their full capabilities. When April, as Gabrielle in the play, asks the leading man, "Wouldn't you like to be loved by me?" (*Revolutionary Road*, p. 9), we understand this accurately reflects April's attitude about herself. The line is omitted from the movie, and we are left with an April absent her self-confidence. In the movie we know April is attractive because we see that Kate Winslet is attractive. We don't know that April knows how good looking she is.

Another, less obvious but significant, change is the house in which much of the action is set. Sam Mendes, the director, decided to do all shooting on location and in sequence. The purpose of in-sequence shooting is so actors can get a sense of the development of their characters as the story unfolds. That's the way most stage plays are performed, but it's unusual for film because of the added costs. If, for example, there's an on-location scene in Paris and the next one is in New York and that's followed by another in Paris, it's obviously cheaper to film the two Paris scenes back-to-back, rather than fly cast members back and forth across the Atlantic. Mendes is well known for using the stage approach as a way of improving an actor's performance. The purpose of on-location shooting, of course, is to increase the sense of realism for both the audience and actors. The house used for shooting in Connecticut is significantly larger than the one Yates used in the novel. While Yates does not describe the house in detail, he makes it clear that it is modest. The house in the movie is larger and would clearly belong to a family that is financially better off than the Wheelers. Mendes was aware of that, but he said a house like the one in the novel would have been too small to shoot in.[10] Kristi Zea, the film's production designer, also said a house that the Wheelers could have afforded was too small to film in. Leonardo DiCaprio explained that when the audience sees a scene with just him and Kate Winslet in it they should remember that there are also cameramen, sound people, the director, and others present. Plus their equipment. In a house the size of the one in the novel, there wouldn't have been room for all of them. The change is understandable, but the result is to make the Wheelers seem wealthier than they really are. Neither the novel nor the movie mentions Frank's salary or the cost of the house, but financial considerations cannot be dismissed in evaluating the story line. Frank, for example, is concerned that they cannot afford a move to Paris. April's suggestion that she could make enough for them to live on by working as a secretary has no hint of a downgrading in their lifestyle. But it's unlikely that on a secretary's salary they could live anywhere as nicely as they do in the movie. In the novel, it makes more sense.

(Yates and I once joked about *The Waltons*, the 1970s TV series [it ran from 1972 to 1981] in which a family that supposedly lived in poverty in rural Virginia during the Great Depression resided in a house the size of a mansion, owned their own mountain, and sat down to a feast for every meal. A character in Yates's *Young Hearts Crying*, Ben Duane, is clearly based on an actor in *The Waltons*.)

Omissions significantly alter the character of Shep Campbell. In the novel, he is fully developed and has the third most important role in the story. In the movie, he is merely a prop, someone for April to have sex with once, which helps complicate and therefore develop her character but adds nothing to who he is and why he does what he does. In the novel, Yates gives Campbell a thorough background: He was raised by a wealthy, divorced mother, and he rebelled against what she considered "cultured" by becoming "a tough son-of-a-bitch" (p. 138). He refused after World War Two to go to Princeton or some other prestigious college and instead attended an unnamed technical college in the Midwest and became an engineer. He married Milly, got a job at a hydraulic plant in Phoenix, and then realized he didn't like his life. He came to believe he had denied himself his birthright, and he longed for what he saw as the sophistication of the East, listened to classical music, and read literary journals. That explains his attraction to April, whom he views as the epitome of sophistication. In frustration, at one point, he calls Milly an "ignorant cunt" (p. 140). He imagines April, as Gabrielle, saying to him, "Wouldn't you like to be loved by me?" (p. 151). Since the movie omitted the line when it was spoken in the play, it couldn't bring it in later when it helps shape the character of Shep Campbell.

2. The Inevitability of Unhappiness

And, just as telling, in the novel Shep is embarrassed when Frank looks at the books in his home. Shep thinks the titles are not sophisticated enough (Yates doesn't tell us any of the titles). Thus, Shep is jealous of Frank not just because of his wife but also because of his presumed intellectualism. Frank's intellectualism and Shep's jealously of it are omitted from the film.

Also omitted from the film are references in the novel to Frank building a walk on his property. He sees his effort as manly work. It helps make the novel's Frank a complete character, one who has a physical side. The film's Frank lacks any physicality other than engaging in sex with April and Maureen.

The biggest omission, however, is Frank's sense of intellectuality. He sees himself as an intellectual, and he uses his intellect in a futile attempt to manipulate April. He is so in love with the idea of himself as an intellectual that he sees his attempts to talk April out of having an abortion as "very like a courtship" (p. 216). His failure to convince April, in fact, makes him aware that he is not nearly as intellectual as he has pictured himself. Among other problems, he comes to realize that they should not have had their discussion in the living room because it contained "shelves on shelves of unread or half-read or read-and-forgotten books that had always been supposed to make such a difference and never had" (p. 221). Just as bad, the room contains "the loathsome, gloating maw of the television set" (p. 221), which in the mid–1960s was seen, even more so than today, as proof that the owner's intellectuality was limited. There is little in the movie to indicate that Frank sees himself as an intellectual and, more important, nothing that indicates he comes to a disquieting realization that he's less intellectual than he once thought he was.

Other changes each have their own minor bits of importance. In the novel, Frank tells Shep about the abortion and overtly blames himself for April's death, an attitude that, if it is present in the movie, can only be surmised. Shep, in the novel, wonders if he is in any way responsible for April's death; the movie has no indication of Shep's self-imposed sense of guilt.

The changes make the film a shallow story, one filled with shouting and anger and accusation but absent the intellectual pretensions and self-doubts that add complexity and depth to the characters. The film is about a social sterility that many people associate with the Eisenhower fifties, while the novel is about universal pretensions that transcend any historical period. Watching the film, a viewer can be left with the feeling that the times, the mid-fifties, made the Wheelers who they were. The dominating feeling when reading the novel is that we all pretend to be someone other than who we are and that lie makes unhappiness inevitable. It is beyond a decade; it is part of human nature.

3

The Lies of Richard Yates:
Eleven Kinds of Loneliness

Every Richard Yates character is a liar.

Eighteen of Yates's short stories have been collected in two volumes: *Eleven Kinds of Loneliness*, published in 1962 and containing stories written mostly in the 1950s, and *Liars in Love*, a 1981 collection with stories written in the late seventies and early eighties. Despite the two decades between the two volumes, they are remarkably consistent in quality and tone, the most notable difference being a sense of unrelieved sadness dominating the first collection and an occasional glimmer of hope, or at least of the possibility of hope, in the second; it is essentially the same pattern followed in the transition from his early to his later novels.

* * *

The stories can be grouped for convenience. Two, for example, "Doctor Jack-o'-lantern" and "Fun with a Stranger," are about grade school children. But that distorts their impact; each stands as a thoroughly complete work in no way dependent on another. Even those stories that contain characters found elsewhere in Yates's writing, such as the mother and son in "Oh, Joseph, I'm So Tired," who appear in *A Good School*, can be read, understood, and appreciated without knowledge of any other work.

And that is the best way to proceed with a discussion of the stories, as individual entities.

* * *

In "Doctor Jack-o'-lantern" Vincent Sabella, a new pupil in Miss Price's fourth-grade class, becomes the teacher's pet, largely because she pities him, and the other kids understand better than their teacher that he is a liar and a not very likable boy. By the end of the story Vincent will betray Miss Price's hopes by drawing a picture of her naked and writing dirty words underneath it. A key to Vincent's problems is his consistent lying in a vain attempt to gain respect; he is not even very good at telling simple lies. He claims, for example, to have seen a recently released movie, *Dr. Jekyll and Mr. Hyde*, but calls it instead *Doctor Jack-o'-lantern*. Vincent turns out to be a Mr. Hyde and the chemical he drinks to transform into Dr. Jekyll is Miss Price's well-meaning but misdirected kindness. As in so many of Yates's stories, the central character contributes to his own unhappiness by his inability to be honest.

One key to fully appreciating Yates's intent in this story is understanding that Miss Price's attempt at kindness fails largely because she doesn't confront Vincent's dishonesty early enough. When he lies about seeing *Dr. Jekyll and Mr. Hyde*, calling it *Doctor Jack-o'-lantern*, she tells the class, "It's a *perfectly natural mistake*" (p. 12).[1] Only later, when Vincent tells a story about his father being shot by a cop, does Miss Price tell him, out of the hearing of other students, he should have "told us something about your real life instead" (p. 13). Where did Vincent learn to lie? The answer is made clear when Vincent, worried that two boys who saw him draw the picture of Miss Price will squeal on him, threatens them, imitating Edward G. Robinson: "I don't like squealers, unnastand?" (p. 15). Movies teach us to lie, and those who should teach us better don't teach us effectively enough not to lie.

* * *

"The Best of Everything" may be Yates's single most widely read work because it has been reprinted so often in anthologies. It is a classically structured work with a clear beginning, middle, and end. In the first part the focus is on Grace the day before her marriage to Ralph; she is clearly brighter than Ralph and has different interests. The second part focuses on Ralph, who seems to be marrying Grace mostly because she is "stacked" (p. 31); there is little in personality, interests, or intellect to draw them together. In the third part Grace and Ralph are together in her apartment and for the first time they have the privacy to make love, but he is not sophisticated enough to notice her subtle advances. She offers him sherry and he turns it down saying he is already full of beer, emphasizing an almost-class difference between them. The story ends with a clear sense they will go through with the wedding the next day

3. The Lies of Richard Yates

although it is evident they face an unhappy life together because neither is honest enough to admit understandable doubts about the impending marriage. It is a story that can make many readers uncomfortable because it seems to be such an accurate portrayal of so many marriages they will be familiar with.

I tried to discuss this story with Yates several times, and every time I did he responded only with a polite smile and, usually, a nod or two. Never with a comment. Almost every other piece of his writing I talked to him about, he would agree or disagree with something I said, but with "The Best of Everything" he reminded me or an athlete who had just turned in a stellar performance, maybe thrown four touchdown passes or hit three home runs, and who wanted to seem appropriately modest but still proud of the accomplishment. Yates knew "The Best of Everything" was among the best pieces of writing he had ever done.

* * *

"Jody Rolled the Bones" was Yates's first major publication, appearing in *The Atlantic Monthly* in 1953, and provided future fans with a good introduction to his style and themes. Yet there is much in it that will seldom appear again in another Yates story, particularly the use of a stock character, one seen in movies and television shows and other pieces of writing by other writers, in this case a Sgt. Reece, a highly competent drill instructor who is disliked by army trainees because he is so tough on them. Reece lets the men know with certainty their lot in life by leading them in "a singsong chant" about a soldier being away from his girl while his best friend, Jody, rolls the bones (dice) of life, winning the girl: "Every time you stand retreat, Jody gets a piece of meat" (p. 48). Under the mean and nasty Reece the men learn to like what he calls "soldiering" (p. 49) and will clearly become good soldiers; when he is replaced by a new drill instructor, Rudy, who is far more likable and liked, the men grow slack and stop caring about soldiering. The obvious stereotyping, however, is redeemed by careful crafting: the tightness of the plotting, the clarity of the style, the subtlety of characterizations. It is the work of a master craftsman.

I was only mildly surprised when Yates told me he wished he had never written the story. I knew Sgt. Reece was close to a stereotype and thus inconsistent with every other character Yates had created. I reminded him that as an "*Atlantic* First" the story was a major push for his career. He agreed but added that he thought it inferior to all the other stories in *Eleven Kinds of Loneliness*.

A stereotype is, by its very nature, a lie, a way of seeing people that is based more on convenience or ease of analysis than it is on careful observation or rigid intellectual honesty. Yates's characters are always, in one way or another, liars, but the author designed his style to avoid being like them.

* * *

"No Pain Whatsoever" is one of several stories by Yates about men who have tuberculosis (another is "Out with the Old"). For four years Myra Wilson has taken the bus every Sunday to visit her husband, Harry, in a Veterans Administration hospital on Long Island, east of New York City. One Sunday friends insist on driving her out and Jack, her boyfriend, goes along for the ride. Like many Yates characters, Myra tries to justify her actions by seeing the world not as it is but in a way that excuses what she does; she thinks, "Wasn't it almost like being a widow?" (p. 62). While Jack waits elsewhere, Myra visits her husband, who is "rake-knitting," something he learned from occupational therapy, showing how the hospital is making him useless. Myra has brought Harry magazines, and he reads an article in one while she is there, almost as if he is avoiding spending time with her. He says he feels "no pain whatsoever ... as long as I stay ... more or less in a normal position" (p. 68); that is, the reader will understand, Harry will feel no pain from his unfaithful wife if he does not notice her unfaithfulness. A reader may wish to speculate about whether Harry's dishonesty, not noticing his wife's infidelity, adds to his unhappiness, which would be a reversal of the normal Yates approach. But this is more Myra's story, and her dishonesty, her cheating on her husband, clearly has great potential for hurting someone else, Harry; that view makes the tone of this story consistent with the larger body of Yates's work.

A minor incident in the story offered an opportunity for me to once question Yates on a point that that seemed unclear to me in his writing. In the story, Red Cross entertainers enter the ward to sing Christmas songs, but before they can begin, a nurse announces that visiting hours are over. In much of Yates's writing, hospitals are not very pleasant places,

3. The Lies of Richard Yates

and I asked him if he thought hospitals were often uncaring. The scene in the story seemed to suggest, after all, that a hospital employee, the nurse, was preventing families from spending time together around Christmas. Veterans Administration hospitals, he said emphatically, had been very helpful to him. He was very appreciative for what they had done for him. I asked, with deliberate vagueness, about other hospitals (I wanted to avoid mentioning psychiatric hospitals, like Bellevue, where his experiences were decidedly unpleasant). He said he was talking about VA hospitals only. His final, unfinished and unpublished novel, *Uncertain Times*, is dedicated to the "men and women of the United States Veterans' Administration, past and present, in gratitude for their courtesy and kindness no less than for their excellent medical care" (*A Tragic Honesty*, p. 602).

* * *

In "A Glutton for Punishment," Walter Henderson as a nine-year-old excelled at pretending he was shot and falling over dead. Nearly 25 years later he is fired from his office job and he decides not to tell his wife, convinced he will have a new job in a few weeks. But when he gets home his nervousness gives him away, and his wife insists he tell her what is wrong. He does so by touching his heart while falling into a chair and saying "they got me" (p. 93), just like a kid pretending to be killed. That is, he avoids lying to his wife about being fired by lying to himself about life being a game to play at.

Several minor details in "A Glutton for Punishment" are reminiscent of other Yates stories. For example, Henderson works in a cubicle, as does Frank Wheeler in *Revolutionary Road* and Bill Grove in "Regards at Home." The office cubicle is a symbol for Yates, as it is for so many others in American culture, of the uniformity and blandness of the American work space, a technique to depersonalize the worker for the greater benefit of the corporation. And when Henderson's wife (her name is not given) insists he tell her what is wrong, Yates frames the response in terms of movies: "...the movie camera started rolling again. It came in for a close-up of his own tense face, then switched over to observe her movements..." (p. 92). Henderson, like Rachel in *Cold Spring Harbor* and a dozen other Yatesian characters, has learned how to act in real life by imitating movies, by responding to the demands of the camera rather than the needs of his wife.

Richard Yates Up Close

* * *

In "A Wrestler with Sharks" Leon Sobel quits a well-paying sheet metal job to join a much-lesser-paying biweekly tabloid, *The Labor Leader*. He says most people think the world has only two types of people, sharks and those eaten by sharks, but he is a wrestler with sharks, he is a man who will use his writing to bring social justice to the world. He has written nine books, none of them published, because, he says, they told the truth and people want to read the truth only from a name they know; that is why he joined the paper, to make a name for himself. This paper, however, almost never gives bylines and when Sobel threatens to quit unless he gets one and then does not get it he not only is forced to quit but also reveals himself as being more interested in the goal of making a name for himself than in promoting social justice. He has lied to himself about his own goals in life.

"A Wrestler with Sharks" almost won the first Aga Khan Prize for fiction awarded annually by the *Paris Review* literary magazine. It is one of the most prestigious short story prizes in the United States. George Plimpton, editor of the magazine, decided to offer a $1,000 prize for a short story as a way of attracting promising writers to a publication that at the time (the mid-1950s) was publishing mostly work by writers who seemed destined for oblivion. At the time, $1,000 was considered a very sizable sum for a short story. Plimpton recruited Saul Bellow, Brendan Gill (of *New Yorker* fame), and Hiram Haydn (at the time a well-known novelist) as the judges. The winners were Gina Berriault,[2] John Langdon, and Owen Dodson. Plimpton accepted the judges' decision, but he said, "Well, we have winners of the contest and judges have chosen all the wrong people.... They made the wrong choices." He published the winning stories but also published four of the losers, including a chapter from Jack Kerouac's *On the Road* and stories by Evan S. Connell and Nadine Gordimer, all three of whom built more substantial reputations than the three winners. (Gordimer won the Nobel Prize in Literature in 1991.) The fourth losing story he published was Yates's "A Wrestler with Sharks." Blair Fuller, a friend of Plimpton's since their days as students at Harvard, said, probably echoing Plimpton's view, that "Wrestler" was "a wonderful story." It appeared in the Summer 1956 issue of *Paris Review*.[3]

3. The Lies of Richard Yates

* * *

In "Fun with a Stranger" Miss Snell, about 60, is a strict and humorless third-grade teacher who often makes her pupils cry by scolding them. She is contrasted with Mrs. Cleary, the third-grade teacher across the hall, whose pupils always seem to be laughing. Miss Snell tells her pupils, "When we learn a new word it's like making a friend" and "you can't very well have fun with a stranger" (p. 117). When the two classes go together on a field trip to a train yard, Mrs. Cleary is friendly, while Miss Snell is so "pitiful" that the pupils wanted "to get her into the bus and back to school" (p. 120). The last day of class before Christmas break Mrs. Cleary's class has a bright party; Miss Snell waits until the end of the day and passes out wrapped presents: ten-cent two-color erasers. As the title suggests, Miss Snell will always be a stranger to her pupils and they will never be able to have fun with her.

"Fun with a Stranger" can be contrasted with "Jody Rolled the Bones," in which Sgt. Reece has many of the same traits as Miss Snell, but Reece does his job well (training new soldiers) and Snell's personality clearly excludes the warmth that would help her pupils develop socially. "Fun with a Stranger" is often dismissed as a small, even uninteresting story that is not bad but far from one of Yates's best. However, if considered as an antidote to "Jody Rolled the Bones," a story that provided Yates with his first publishing breakthrough but which he later regretted publishing, it can be seen as a corrective, Yates this time avoiding the stereotype and the clichéd analysis in favor of the realistically bland. "Fun with a Stranger" is a better story than "Jody Rolled the Bones" because it more honestly portrays a common personality type.

* * *

In "The B.A.R. Man" John Fallon, a 29-year-old insurance clerk, fights with his wife, unsuccessfully tries to pick up a girl at a bar, and is ditched by what he thought were newfound friends. Walking the streets of Manhattan he comes across a demonstration on behalf of a leftist college professor and in his frustrations attacks him. The story is about how a man's frustrations (in marriage, with friends, with life in general) lead to an act of political violence. It is more openly political than is typical of Yates. In it, the liberal Yates (he was once a speechwriter for Attorney

General Robert Kennedy) explains, without condoning or condemning, the motivations of a conservative resorting to violence.

The story is set in the mid-1950s, and Fallon is a veteran of the Second World War. Part of his frustration is caused by his sense that he wasn't a very good soldier. When he goes to lunch with some co-workers who brag about their time in the navy, he tells them he was a B.A.R. man. That is, he carried the Browning Automatic Rifle in his platoon. He does not seem to realize that he had a job that was often viewed as being given to a big, dumb solider who wasn't much good for anything else. He does not tell them that he fired it only twice and that neither time did he hit anything. The argument with his wife is over something so minor — he doesn't want her to wear padded bras — it seems to confirm that he is a typical B.A.R. man. Everything he does for the rest of the story, in fact, is consistent with that view, the big, dumb soldier. In a bar he dances with a girl named Marie and makes crude advances that repulse her. Fallon goes to buy a pitcher of beer, and when he returns he finds that Marie and her girlfriends have left. The accumulated combination of small humiliations — with his job, with his wife, with the girl in the bar — makes life very frustrating for John Fallon. Those frustrations make the deliberate irony of the story's opening sentence resonate at its end: "Until he got his name on the police blotter, and in the papers, nobody had ever thought much about John Fallon" (p. 129).

* * *

In "A Really Good Jazz Piano" two Americans, Ken Platt and Carson Wyler, admire Sid, a black American who plays a really good jazz piano, because, they think, he stays in France out of integrity rather than face, with his white girlfriend, prejudice in the U.S. But when they hear Sid curry favor with the owner of some Las Vegas nightclubs in the obvious hope of returning to the U.S. to make more money, Wyler turns against him. Sid, in fact, already told Ken and Carson he wanted to return to the states so he could make more money, and Sid's girlfriend, Jacqueline, is clearly annoyed when Ken says such a move would mean Sid is prostituting himself. When Sid openly brownnoses Murray Diamond, the owner of the Las Vegas nightclubs, asking him, for example, what songs he would like to hear, Carson derides him to Ken: "this big phony Uncle Remus routine" (p. 164). A few minutes later, Carson is deliberately rude

3. The Lies of Richard Yates

to Sid, momentarily pretending he doesn't know who he is, and Ken suppresses his dislike of Carson, because without him, he realizes, he would be a social outcast unable to attract the attention of women. That is, Ken prostitutes himself just as much as he accused Sid of doing.

This story can be contrasted with "The B.A.R. Man." Both portray standard, but not stereotypical, political types. In "The B.A.R. Man" a conservative turns to violence, and in "A Really Good Jazz Piano" a liberal (Wyler) is not all that liberal in the way he treats someone he ceases to admire. At one point Wyler even says of Sid's behavior, "This is damn near enough to make you lose faith in the Negro race" (p. 165), indicating he will support the rights of an idealized black, not one who has the same faults as whites.

* * *

"Out with the Old" is set largely in the TB ward of a Veterans Administration hospital on Long Island, just east of New York City (it's named for the first time in this story: Mulloy Veterans' Hospital). Tiny Kovacs, about 30, six feet, six inches tall and "broad as a bear" (p. 172), is a practical joker who is not well liked. For New Year's Eve he wants to dress up as a baby representing the new year, but at first no one wants to dress as the old man representing the old one, and Tiny's feelings are hurt. He feels dignity only when he goes home on a Christmas pass or when he wears his Christmas robe. Another patient, McIntyre, goes home for a Christmas Day visit and learns that his unmarried, 18-year-old daughter, Jean, is pregnant. And he argues with his wife and son, Joseph (we're never told the mother's name). McIntyre's wife snaps, "Willya please quit bothering everybody?" (p. 181). When Jean refuses to tell her mother the name of the father of her baby, Joseph says, "Maybe she don't *know* the guy's name" (p. 181) and McIntyre slaps his son hard. Back at the VA hospital, McIntyre tries for a week to write a letter of apology to his daughter and to offer to help her, but he can't get it right. This is similar to several other Yatesian characters — like Robert Prentice in *A Special Providence* and Bill Grove in *A Good School*—who write and rewrite letters and are often not satisfied with the final product (and not unlike Yates, who told me that by the mid–1980s he had himself on a schedule of writing eight hours a day and often produced only a few hundred words each day and who extolled the virtues of rewriting and rewriting and still found rewriting frustrating). McIntyre never finishes the letter.

On New Year's Eve Kovacs dresses as the New Year's baby and McIntyre as the old man representing the old year. The story ends with Tiny's arm around McIntyre's neck, two very different men brought together by their loneliness.

"Out with the Old" is one of five Veterans Administration hospital stories written by Yates. Three others — "No Pain Whatsoever," "A Clinical Romance," and "Thieves" — are also set in VA hospitals, and one, "A Convalescent Ego," is about a man who has just been released from one. As noted in the discussion of "No Pain Whatsoever," VA hospitals were the lone American institution Yates ever praised.

* * *

The narrator of "Builders" — Bob Prentice, who is the main character in *A Special Providence* — promises that although he is a writer this is not going to be another story about a writer. He is wrong but in the process provides some lessons on how to write a story. A young Prentice is hired by a taxi driver, Bernie Silver, to write at $5 apiece stories based on Silver's experiences in his cab. The experiences are either contrived or not interesting and the two men eventually give up the venture. What is of most interest here are two points about writing stories, one made by Silver, the other by Prentice. Silver tells Prentice that writing a story is like building a house and that it needs a solid foundation and windows to let in light (philosophy or truth). Although "Builders" closes with Prentice claiming he has not built this story well and that he does not know where the windows are, he is clearly wrong, and Silver's blueprint can be read as an outline for all of Yates's stories. Prentice, meanwhile, sets a standard that can be a credo on style. He recalls that long ago he wore "a much-handled brown fedora" and says that then he would have called it "a battered hat." Now, however, he has learned "about honesty in the use of words" (pp. 191–192). That honesty comes from careful and precise choosing of words that are often reworked and reworked. The hat was never battered (a word that suggests it was hit with or against something) but was rather handled and reshaped over and over by its nervous owner. The honesty in choosing "handled" rather than "battered" reveals something about the narrator that is not flattering, and

3. The Lies of Richard Yates

that is why such honesty is not often found in writers. The windows to let in the truth and the honesty in the use of words as the central element in style are what set Yates's short stories and novels apart from those that are merely good.

Yates told me "Builders" was a "blowout," meaning he wrote it quickly, perhaps in a single sitting. He was able to do that, he indicated, because it was so heavily autobiographical. He did, however, rework it before including it in *Eleven Kinds of Loneliness*.

* * *

Richard Yates once told Andre Dubus that "the arrangement [of the stories in a book-length collection] is important to the reading" and that he "arranged *Eleven Kinds of Loneliness* by moving from the simplest story to the more complex."[4] Yates may have had some standard for complexity in mind when he arranged the 11 stories in the collection, but neither reviewers when the book was first published nor later commentators, including this one, have noticed it.

* * *

Among the big fans of *Eleven Kinds of Loneliness* is the British pop/folk singer Tanita Tikaram, who in 2002 released an album with the same title. (I call her British, which is simply an attempt to avoid an awkward adjective: she was born in Germany to a Malaysian mother and Indian/Fijian father and raised in England.) She wrote all the songs for the album (12 songs, despite the title). Her liner notes thank a friend for "introducing me to Richard Yates and his excellent collection of short stories." None of the songs tie directly to any of Yates's stories, and the main element the songs and stories have in common is a general tone of sadness.

4

War Interrupted: *A Special Providence*

Richard Yates's stories serve a useful purpose where some others — many best sellers or most movies, for example — do not because his writing reflects a different sense of why someone should read or see a story. A person might read or see a story to admire its technique. What other reason can there to read most of the novels of, say, William Burroughs, who sometimes cut and pasted his manuscripts, cutting them arbitrarily lengthwise, shuffling the pieces, and pasting them together haphazardly in a deliberate attempt to destroy any semblance of plot? The idea is to emphasize words and to destroy plot (and in the process character development). It is deliberately similar to what some twentieth-century painters and sculptors did; the emphasis is on shape and texture and color and the relationship of each to the other. That is, much modern painting and sculpture is dominated by technique, not content. Sometimes this can be enticing (as when Walt Disney created *Fantasia*, in which the method of telling the story becomes more interesting than the story). Often it is confusing. Worse, often it is insulting, because artists have so often criticized audiences for not understanding them, even when there is no content to understand. Storytellers who emphasize technique, fairly or unfairly but certainly expectedly, seldom attract a mass audience.

Most people read or see stories for some other reason. One of these is adventure escapism. As with Robert Louis Stevenson's *Treasure Island*, a story that invites its audience to places and actions they are unlikely to encounter in a real life. It is harmless and rewarding, entertainment that enriches by providing a wider view of the world.

Too often, however, the escapism is purely emotional, like soap operas, presenting a view of the world the way a person wants it to be,

4. War Interrupted

not the way it is. Movies over and over show that when a man falls in love with a woman that woman will, eventually, fall in love with him. Love in the movies does not prepare the viewer for unrequited love, which, sadly, is one of the most common emotional experiences most people will encounter.

Yates, as much as any other post–World War II American storyteller, deals with a fourth purpose, truth-telling. And that is the major positive function stories perform for society. But Yates, whose work is as easy to read as that of any writer in recent American literature, never built a substantial following, precisely because his stories make the reader uncomfortable. Yates never provides emotional escapism, he is not interested in adventure escapism, and his technique is always a function of his content, never an end in itself.

The structure of his second novel, *A Special Providence* (published in 1969), provides a key to evaluating it. As in his 1984 novel, *Young Hearts Crying*, parts 1 and 3 make a continuous story, in this case about a young man going off to and being in war; part 2 sticks out, focusing not on the soldier but on his mother. A prologue and epilogue, however, support the inclusion of part 2 by emphasizing the relationship between mother and son; parts 1 and 3 make an excellent war story, as fine a war novel, in fact, as has come out of World War II, which is no small claim, considering that the war produced Norman Mailer's *The Naked and the Dead*, James Jones's *From Here to Eternity*, and Joseph Heller's *Catch-22*.

Mailer's work, however, is Procrustean, with its inserted dialogue between lieutenant and general discussing military life as a microcosm of civilian society, its too neatly delineated characterizations, and its contrived motifs, ranging from the soldier who dies in the opening scene because he tries to clean his excrement in the midst of combat to the general tossing his cigarette butt on the floor and ordering the lieutenant to pick it up as a way of demonstrating order in society. And Jones's style is more concerned with energy and flow than with preciseness or grace. Heller's work is more a political contrivance, a statement about war and insanity, than an accurate depiction of the complexities that drive and afflict men at war. Yates's overlooked World War II masterpiece suffers from none of these faults, although it has a major structural weakness: If parts 1 and 3 stood as a complete novel (or novella) it would depict the closest thing there is to a universal emotion among soldiers: a sense not of cowardice or bravery or camaraderie but of inadequacy. Nothing more unites all soldiers and nothing is less discussed by them.

The mother, Alice Prentice, seeks in many ways to shape her son; she is a sculptor and sometimes uses her son as her model. When he was not yet a teenager, she sculptured a "Portrait of the Artist's Son," and much later, when he is still in Europe after the war has ended, she tells a friend of her plans to do a second "Portrait" of her son: "I'll exhibit them side by side — the boy and the man — and together they'll be my sort of crowning achievement, the justification of my whole career" (p. 237).[1] The bit of obvious symbolism makes clear Yates's point, that the son has been molded by the mother. Yet the son, Bobby, will not come home from Europe and will go to college instead in England; the war will have made him into a man who can break out of his mother's mold.

When she made the first "portrait," Alice planned to enter it in the prestigious Whitney Annual show in New York, despite clear evidence that she was not a particularly good sculptor. But her desire to enter the sculpture shows that her pretensions are as much for her son as they are for herself, and it is that pretentiousness that causes many of Bobby's problems; it is the pretentiousness he rebels against.

Robert J. Prentice (who is also the main character in the short story "Builders" in the 1962 collection, *Eleven Kinds of Loneliness*) has been sent to a "good" private school (just like William Grove in Yates's 1978 novel, *A Good School*), not because that is in his best educational interests but because that fits Alice's image of herself and her son. (Prentice and Grove, by the way, have so much in common they may strike some readers as essentially the same character.) While he is a student at the private school his father dies and Prentice cannot recall having had any affection for him, which does differ from *A Good School,* in which Grove remembers his father with warmth. (It differs also from "Lament for a Tenor," a short story Yates published in *Cosmopolitan* in 1954, in which the protagonist, a boy at a private boarding school, consciously tries with great difficulty to remember his recently deceased father with affection.) Prentice does, however, admire his father's honesty; at the last meeting between the mother and son before the son goes off to war he becomes angry with her for lying about being known as a sculptor, and he does not want her to have illusions; he thinks of his father as someone who did not live by illusions. The mother is working at the time in a factory

4. War Interrupted

making mannequins, an indication of the nature of her talent as an artist. Her husband, George, when he was still alive, often sang "Danny Boy" (just like Bill Grove's father in *A Good School*), but George was realistic enough to know "I've got a good amateur voice, that's all" (p. 328).

But Alice does have some success as a sculptor. Her head of Bobby is accepted in the Whitney Annual, and a photograph of it is published in *The New York Times* (a photograph of a sculpture done by Yates's mother once appeared in the old *Herald Tribune*), and for several years she teaches sculpturing in an arts and crafts class in White Plains, a suburb of New York City (Bill Grove's mother in *A Good School* sculpts and is commissioned to do a head of President-elect Franklin D. Roosevelt in "Oh, Joseph, I'm So Tired" [included in *Liars in Love*]). But when Alice moves to the wealthy community of Riverside, renting a studio and home at Boxwood, an estate owned by the elderly and enormously wealthy Mrs. Vander Meer, the view of herself as a sort of artist-in-residence makes it too easy for her pretensions to dominate her emotions. She sees the wealthy Mrs. Vander Meer as "aristocratic," a quality she admires (as did Mrs. Grove — who remains otherwise unnamed — in "Oh, Joseph, I'm So Tired") and Mrs. Vander Meer comments on Alice's courage in being a woman artist, which she says must be very lonely. Alice's ex-husband, George, and friends advise her against making the move to Boxwood, seeing it as financially unwise. But she is "committed to it now with a desperate optimism" (p. 187) based far more on the non-existent opportunity to have a rich patron than real financial commonsense; the rent is too high and she will lose half of her students by moving from White Plains to Riverside.

Living at Boxwood makes her bolder. There she carves stone directly, instead of working only in clay, and sees herself "moving into a brave new freedom of expression" (p. 189). She finds great pleasure in teaching, often saying silly, meaningless things like "this shape doesn't fully relate to *this* shape — not in a really dynamic way" (p. 190). Many of Yates's artists — painters in *Young Hearts Crying*, poets in *The Easter Parade* (1976) — have a habit of speaking dribble when they talk of their art. The dribble is a form of jargon, and artists, like members of any profession, use it partly to convince others they possess special knowledge or a special way of thinking about things and partly to convince themselves they really are members of the profession. Alice talking about shapes not relating to each other is essentially the same as a lawyer talking legalese.

The special providence Alice sees as belonging to herself and Bobby is primarily artistic, and there are no notable intellectual pretensions on her part. She accepts the judgment of a school administrator, for example, that Bobby's IQ is "slightly above average" (p. 194 [Bill Grove in "Regards at Home," in the 1981 collection, *Liars in Love*, has an IQ of 109]).

But it does lead her to expect special treatment and allows her to feel resentment when she does not get it. When she needs money to pay her rent and the tuition at Bobby's school she wants to ask her friends, Maude and Jim Larkin, to lend it to her, but she does not have the courage to ask, so she dislikes them for not volunteering to give it to her. She has come to expect favors from the rich — Jim makes a lot of money writing radio scripts — as her due as an artist.

George, her ex-husband, pays the bills, even though that is in excess of their divorce agreement. She has come to trust that God "will provide for her" (p. 197), and when Jim Larkin, like George, advises her to move to a less expensive town and that makes it even harder for her to ask him for money "she hated him for it" (p. 197). Despite George's help, she and Bobby are forced to resort to hiding when bill collectors show up at the door. And her view of Mrs. Vander Meer as her personal patron-of-the-arts is shattered when the wealthy woman's son, apparently with his mother's approval, threatens to sue to collect past-due rent, and when Alice is not invited to a Christmas party at Boxmeer "this was a terrible blow" (p. 190). When Alice does receive official notice she is being sued by the Vander Meers, she rushes to the Larkins' home and accuses them of not helping her.

Alice's residency at Boxmeer, what she had seen as her great opportunity to live as a true artist should, thus turns into a financial and emotional disaster; her lone bright spot is when a teacher tells Bobby pictures he draws are imaginative, probably because of who his mother is.

To escape the bill collectors she moves to Texas to live with her sister, Eva, and Eva's husband, but when they do not get along Alice in a pique walks five miles in oppressive heat along an unpaved road to Austin, where she uses her last 25 cents to tip a bellhop. She then orders an expensive meal in the hotel restaurant and calls George in New York to ask for money. If God will not always provide for her, she is correct

4. War Interrupted

in assuming George will. He sends the money. This could have a deus ex machina effect if Yates were not careful to provide an explanation for George's coming to the rescue: one night George takes Alice to dinner and surprises her by asking her to marry him again; she agrees to think about it, but a week later, before she replies, he dies (probably of a heart attack).

When she storms out on Eva, Alice soon comes to realize how rude she had been to her sister but decides she can handle the matter sometime in the future by writing an apologetic letter, and she determines that also in the future, when things get really bad, she will say, "Remember the Caliche Road" (p. 234) — caliche being the chalk-like substance kicked up by jackhammers doing roadwork as Alice and Bobby walk to Austin — it is like "Remember the Alamo," another Texas rallying cry, and if that is not enough she will remember Bobby's advice about the heat: "Let's pretend it isn't happening" (p. 234). Bobby's willingness to pretend reflects her influence, but he can be excused: he is a 12-year-old; she is an adult.

Her over-willingness to pretend, to act as if she is someone other than who she is, leads her to abuse her friendships. She at one point imposes on a friend of friends to take photos of her sculptures to show to New York art dealers. And her pretentiousness leads her just as easily to blame others for her failures. When no art dealers are interested in handling her work, she decides to sell the antiques and art that a former lover, Sterling Nelson, left behind when he deserted her, but appraisers say they are worthless, that the paintings are fakes: "Sterling Nelson had come back over the years to deceive and desert her again" (p. 199).

Sterling Nelson was able to desert her because he did not *need* her, a point emphasized when she feels envy as Eva tells her that her husband, Owen Forbes, does *need* her. There are other men in Alice's life besides George and Sterling, but the one who might have been the most compatible died in a motorcycle accident before they could marry (just as George will die before they can remarry). His name was Willard Slade, and he was an unkempt, rude student, thought of as a genius by other students at the Cincinnati art school he and Alice attended when she was younger, and it was he who introduced her to sculpture; as a result she dropped painting to sculpt.

There is plenty of reason to feel sorry for Alice — her boyfriend's death, the poverty she sometimes lives in, her loneliness — but her pretentiousness makes her a character who is far from appealing. Nowhere in the novel does she become less sympathetic than when she is rude to her sister, Eva, who has allowed Alice and Bobby to move in with her and her husband, Owen. Alice thinks of Owen as "gross and ugly" (p. 215) because he accurately criticizes Bobby as being lazy, and she tells Eva, "I know you only married him because he was all you could get" (p. 219). When Eva reminds Alice that she is a "guest," Alice replies she is really a "prisoner" (p. 223). And when Alice does finally storm from the house, she tells Eva, "I hope I'll never see you again" (p. 224). Alice's rudeness and lack of gratitude are clearly the result of her own loneliness, but that explains and does not excuse it.

The loneliness is what Bobby inherits from his mother, and it is something he cannot avoid, but the pretentions that caused it for Alice are what he most seeks to avoid. Near the end of the novel he has a fight with a fellow soldier, Walker, who just before the fight begins says "this is it" (p. 317), a remark that angers Prentice because it sounds phony, like it is from a movie, and "he wanted to kill all the posturing fraudulence in the world" (p. 317). Walker easily handles Prentice in the fight, knocking him around, and then good-naturedly decides to quit, even apologizing for earlier having called Prentice "yellow." Prentice is disappointed the fight did not really prove he was not yellow, and he can picture another soldier — Quint — saying, "Do you think everything is going to work out the way it does in the movies?" (p. 320). Prentice does take pride in his cuts, bruises, and swellings, and he is glad when the "Hollywood heart" (p. 320) of a Sgt. Loomis — who is clearly a good soldier but nevertheless hated by members of his squad because "he was such a goddamn actor" (p. 262) who probably learned how to be a soldier by watching movies — is pleased that Walker has his arm around Prentice's shoulder. These are just several of the numerous references in this novel (and elsewhere by Yates) in which the false images of movies are contrasted with the reality of war and love and the rest of life. There are, in fact, 13 times that this novel refers to movies in a manner that depicts them as basically fraudulent.[2]

The mother's pretentiousness, which seems reinforced by the basic fraudulence of movies, is one of the two undercurrents that propel the story. The other is the son's fear of not doing his job as a soldier well.

4. War Interrupted

While still at Camp Pickett in Virginia he is known as "the fool of the platoon" (p. 32). Prentice is a general fuckup, but he takes pride in marching well, something no one else notices. In other writers this quiet pride might contribute to a character's dignity, but in Yates, who always strives to avoid false sentimentality, it lends a tone of the pathetic. When Prentice arrives in Europe — after the Battle of the Bulge, the last major German offensive — he manages to get left behind as his outfit marches out of one town to another, and he has to rush to catch up. The one soldier he has become friendly with, John Quint, the platoon's intellectual, bawls him out in front of the others: "I'm through being your God damn father" (p. 75); the remark brings Prentice close to tears. The quote by Quint comes near the end of the first chapter and is a typical chapter ending for Yates, providing a clear indication of where the story will go while recapping what has just happened: Prentice is a fuckup (a term that will be applied to him later by a sergeant), and that results at least partly from being raised by a mother who has pretensions of being special and not having had the presence of a father.

Before leaving for Europe Prentice frequently rewrote the letters he sent to a prep school buddy (William Grove in *A Good School* also rewrote letters before mailing them), and he is happy Quint talks to him about serious matters, like social issues and economics (just as Frank Wheeler in *Revolutionary Road* and Emily Grimes in *The Easter Parade* like being considered intellectuals and as Grove in *A Good School* wants to become). Prentice has a great need to have the approval of others.

When he picks up a girl in a Baltimore bar and goes to her home, he lights a cigarette so he will be debonair, but she doesn't notice. And when they make love, it is over too quickly for either of them to enjoy it. This pattern follows Prentice throughout the war: he does most things poorly, and the few things he does well are not noticed. He does not even have enough confidence to brag to Quint and others about his sexual conquest because he thinks they will ridicule him.

In Belgium Prentice gets sick with an unknown ailment (later discovered to be pneumonia) and his company commander, Captain Agate, tells him to go on sick call. Prentice is too sick to reply but shakes his head no. Others in his company tell him that if he is going to stay with them he should stop being a fuckup. Quint also becomes sick and suggests to Prentice that they go on sick call together, but by the time part 1 ends

Prentice will three times have passed up opportunities to tell Quint it was all right to go on sick call, a point that becomes crucial in the last third of the novel.

The fear of being a fuckup and the false bravado created in an attempt to overcome that fear is thus a basic and driving emotion in the story. That part of the novel is powerful in the same way Stephen Crane's *The Red Badge of Courage* is, in that it captures a basic and possibly universal emotion in a social setting — war — that strips away the complexities of society that normally obscure such elemental revelations.

When he does finally get into combat, Prentice charges forward, yelling "follow me" and "convinced that this was the bravest thing he had ever done in his life" (p. 275). Later he stops inside a house to admire his soldierly appearance in a mirror. When he learns that another soldier "had become a hero" (p. 283) by killing a German, Prentice is envious: "*I* could have done that.... If only I'd had the chance" (p. 283). Hearing his own and other stories of combat, Prentice comes to consider his own actions in battle "ludicrous" (p. 284). He thus comes close to accepting the view others have of him, that he is a general fuckup.

He feels unjustly treated when first a Sgt. Rand, then a Sgt. Finn, reprimand him for falling behind doing a night advance. He tells Finn not to "pick on" him, and Finn tells him, "I got no use for fuckups" (p. 289). That is a key phrase and captures Prentice's basic fear, that he will appear incompetent (in contrast to the Hemingway hero, who achieves grace largely by extraordinary competence, especially when displayed under pressure).

Later, when a Sgt. Bernstein asks Finn if he can have Prentice in his squad for a while and Finn agrees, Prentice is proud that Bernstein wants him but ashamed that Finn gives him up so easily. He fails to wake up in time to relieve a soldier on guard duty at 2 A.M., and a little later, when Prentice finally does go on guard duty, "he suffered little spasms of self-loathing" (p. 296).

Prentice, of course, is not the only person who does not do things right. Wars produce more than their share of incompetents, and while the soldiers are waiting for an American artillery barrage of a German-held hill before storming it they are hit by an "an American artillery shell, half an hour too early and 500 yards too short" (p. 300). More shells fall and a soldier named Krupka is killed, and a lieutenant named

4. War Interrupted

Coverly panics and runs away. Prentice, lying in a gutter and covering his face with his arm, is thankful that "at least we won't have to take the hill now" (p. 303).

On another night march, it is the private named Walker who screws up by getting lost in the dark, and Prentice is glad that now someone else is the target of the "fuckup" charges. A few days later both Prentice and Walker get a chance to redeem themselves by volunteering for a dangerous mission. Capt. Agate, who is drunk, sends a squad of about a dozen men under the command of a Sgt. Koversky on a combat mission, but Koversky has the men fire a few shots and return with him; he does not want to go on a mission for a drunk. Agate accepts Koversky's fraudulent report, and Prentice and Walker lose their chance to redeem themselves. Yates calls the faked mission "an abortion" (p. 300), echoing his use of this metaphor in *Revolutionary Road* and *The Easter Parade*.

Even in his sleep Prentice can be a fuckup. One night he sleeps in a barn on what he thinks is straw and next to another soldier, but in the morning he learns he has slept next to a pig on a straw-covered pile of pig manure.

Capt. Agate's drunkenness is paralleled by his treating himself to eggs and wine he has found, and there are small hints throughout the story of officers being better treated than enlisted men, but this is hardly a novel, such as Mailer's *The Naked and the Dead*, in which a rigid and oppressive military social structure is a dominant theme. Conversely, the officers in this story have at least as many noticeable faults as the enlisted men, providing one of several sharp contrasts with war as portrayed in World War II movies, which typically presented an approving picture of those charged with leading men into combat.

Prentice does not notice the general incompetence around him, focusing instead on his own. Before seeing their first combat, Quint tells Prentice they both probably have pneumonia and should go on sick call, but Prentice says no, that he would not feel right doing that before going into combat. Instead of focusing on the possibility that Quint might really be seeking a way out of combat or on his own small but legitimate act of bravery, Prentice focuses instead on the guilt he feels for sounding falsely heroic.

Prentice has a huge capacity for feeling guilt. When he is released after five weeks in a military hospital, where he was placed because he did have pneumonia, he learns Quint was killed by a land mine and feels guilty, reasoning that if he had not acted falsely brave and had agreed with Quint to go on sick call earlier, Quint would not have been around to step on the land mine. Prentice likes to "savor" (p. 253) his guilt. He thinks drinking too much wine might have made him too drunk to go back one final time and tell Quint he would go on sick call with him. Although many of Yates's characters drink heavily, this remorse for a particular act connected to drinking is rare in his writings.

When Prentice is about to enter combat for the first time, he senses a chance for "redemption" for Quint's death; he determines to seek that redemption in "whatever was left of the war" (p. 264). But when the Germans surrender, everyone seems happy except Prentice, who feels his chance to atone for Quint's death has been denied him. The hapless Walker volunteers for duty in the Pacific, but no one takes him seriously and he is laughed at, making Prentice glad he did not also make the mistake of volunteering. The company is assigned to guard some displaced Russians, and Prentice remarks that he is surprised that even more men did not volunteer for the Pacific war as a way of avoiding the "chickenshit" (p. 309); Walker overhears the remark, interprets it as an insult, and gets in a fight with Prentice. In the midst of the fight they are both restrained by other soldiers, and "Prentice was greatly relieved to be in bondage but he knew it was important to keep struggling for the sake of appearances" (p. 310). His pretensions here reflect both his mother's influence and a typical bit of movie-inspired acting.

Sgt. Loomis — the one who learned how to soldier by watching movies — tells them to go into a field alone in the morning to fight it out, as a way of ending their feud. Prentice reluctantly agrees. He has had very little experience fighting, some "formless and tearful playground pummelings" (p. 315) and three fights in his first year in prep school that he not only lost but did not even really try to win, entering them mostly with the hope of surviving. He is, however, determined to try to win this one, even though Walker outweighs him by 30 pounds. In a real sense, then, this particular war experience has made him more manly, and the fact he loses the fight becomes insignificant.

Prentice gets a letter from his mother about that time saying when she learned the Germans had surrendered "I just fell on my knees and cried and cried and offered all my thanks to God" (p. 321). He can hear

4. War Interrupted

her voice and it sounds just like Walker's when he tried to befriend Prentice after winning the fight: both of those voices had a "lying, sentimental message" (p. 321).

Alice Prentice can thank God precisely because she is convinced she has been graced with a special talent, that she has a special providence. She thinks of herself as being like Ruth in a Keats poem (p. 137), the poem referring to the biblical "Book of Ruth," thus bringing into the story, as the title suggests should be there, a definite, if vague, religious theme.[3] Yates is hardly a religious writer, but over and over his characters have a sense of religiosity that has a strong influence on their behavior (other examples being the short story "Oh, Joseph, I'm So Tired" and the novel *The Easter Parade*, which in many ways is about redemption). Like Ruth in the poem, Alice is sick for home, sick for Plainsville, Indiana, where she grew up and "when everybody knew she was the baby of the family" (p. 137). Bobby, the son, by the time the war is over, does not feel that homesickness, one clear clue to his having broken free of his mother's influence.

Alice's religiosity is closely tied to her pretentiousness. Although she was raised a Methodist, she joins the Episcopalian church, because she thinks Episcopalians aristocratic.[4] When she sees Bobby in the choir she has a great "sense of being exactly where she belonged" (p. 193), that is, among aristocrats. (The mother in "Oh, Joseph, I'm So Tired" proclaims that she "believes in the aristocracy.") Bobby joined the choir as a "crucifer," presenting an obvious possibility for symbolism: Bobby can be seen as being responsible for his mother's suffering, but the "crucifer" is simply the person at the head of the procession as the choir moves out of and into the vestry. It is Bobby's leadership role that fills Alice with pride.

Whatever special providence guided Alice, whatever faith she had in her ability as an artist, a sculptor, deserving of special treatment by the rest of society, she is unable to infuse it into Bobby, her major work, her crowning achievement. In a strong sense the story is in a long and honorable tradition of fables, including the Greek Pygmalion, who sculpted from ivory the perfect woman, and the Italian Geppetto, who carved from wood the wondrous Pinocchio, But Yates is not a writer of fables, and the realistic conception of his characters requires their fate be different. Alice, unlike Pygmalion or Geppetto, has not shaped a creation that will assure her happiness, and Bobby achieves an opportunity for happiness only by breaking free of his mother's mold, breaking free of the pretensions that resulted in an inevitable fear of being a fuckup. The real special providence is the inevitability of the child reshaping himself; that is what the heavens have ordained.

Rethinking a Near Classic

A Special Providence was ordained to own a place in literary obscurity. While some of Yates's stories, especially "The Best of Everything," are widely reprinted in anthologies and at least one of his novels, *Revolutionary Road*, is often called a classic or a masterpiece, his World War II novel is virtually ignored by critics (not surprising, of course, since the full body of Yates's work has never received the attention it deserves). Part of the blame, however, for the obscurity of *A Special Providence* must lie with Yates's decision to frame the war story within the smaller story of the son's relationship to the mother. Incompetence and fear of incompetence are universal enough traits to make the war story one of the major American World War II novels.

I once spoke to Yates about this, and he at first insisted that the story was really more about the mother/son relationship than about the war or soldiering, but the next day he brought up the subject and said he thought about it all night and "maybe" he made a mistake. Then he added, "Probably did." (Stewart O'Nan, writing in 1999, offered high praise for the war sections: "...much of the war writing [is] flinty and reminiscent of Hemingway's best work in *A Farewell to Arms*..."[5]).

* * *

The basic facts of Richard Yates's military service (as recorded by Blake Bailey on pages 75 to 88 of *A Tragic Honesty*) are these: He was inducted into the U.S. Army on June 17, 1944, at age 18. At six-foot-three and 160 pounds, he was skinny but had no difficulty passing his physical. He scored 109 on an army IQ entrance test, leaving him one point short of the 110 he needed to qualify for Office Candidate School. He took basic training at Camp Pickett, Virginia, and was assigned to the 289th Infantry Regiment of the 75th Division. With the rest of his

4. War Interrupted

unit, he was sent overseas on January 8, 1945. When he arrived in England, he and the rest of his regiment were immediately put on a troopship and sent to France and then put on a train and sent to Belgium. Yates volunteered to be a runner, delivering messages within the division, a job he performed despite coming down with pneumonia, which permanently damaged his lungs. He was put in a military hospital, located at an old Catholic girls' school, for five weeks. When he was released in March, he returned to his unit, which had since moved into Germany. By this time, the Germans were in retreat and unable to stop or even significantly slow the Allied advance. Yates would later say he fired at a lot of trees and that he was "shit-scared." He did receive the Combat Infantry Badge, a medal given to everyone who is in ground combat. Although other members of his units believed Yates performed well, or at least no worse than most other soldiers, he would often jokingly, and sometimes not so jokingly, deride his own efforts as a soldier. Bailey believes that attitude might have resulted from an incident when his unit was crossing the Dortmund-Ems Canal in Germany and Yates was assigned to carry a 50-pound spool of communication wire and, in the confusion common to combat, he became lost, as many soldiers did that day, and later a sergeant berated him. Bailey notes, however, that Yates later spoke of his wartime experiences with pride. When the war in Europe ended on May 8, 1945, Yates celebrated by getting drunk. He was then assigned to a Camp Pittsburgh, a temporary camp set up to process soldiers back to the states, where he was a clerk filling out forms. In December of 1945 he worked as a cub reporter for a newspaper in England, the *Halifax Courier and Guardian*, while still in the service. It was part of a military/civilian work program designed to ease soldiers back into civilian life. He was discharged from the army on June 9, 1946, at Fort Dix, New Jersey, with the rank of Private First Class. He was given the Good Conduct Medal, an indication he did not get into any serious trouble while in the military.

* * *

Dick Yates knew I was a Vietnam veteran before he met me. I had written to him asking for an interview and told him in that letter that I was a veteran and that I had published two novels and several stories and articles about the Vietnam War. The first time we met — in the Crossroads bar in Boston — he asked me about my time in Vietnam. The subject came up every time we met. As did his time in the army.

Much of the discussions about our military experiences was very general. He asked me if I enjoyed being in the military. I said it was not as bad as I expected, that after basic training, in fact, after the first two weeks of basic, when sergeants scream at you a lot to get you accustomed to no longer being a civilian, military life wasn't much different from most civilian jobs, especially if it's a civilian job you don't much like. Yeah, he said, same for him; you can get used to anything. Even my time in Vietnam wasn't too bad. Less routine there, in fact. Same for him, he said, about being in Europe at the end of the war. Of course, I said, being in the Signal Corps and being assigned to repair and maintain electronic equipment meant I didn't actually see much of the war. Yes, he said, he spent more time in the army not in the war than in it. Some sergeants and some lieutenants and at least one captain I knew were assholes, I said, but most of them were all right, probably make pretty good next-door neighbors, people who are easy enough to get along with. He nodded, said he could agree with that. "And you know," I said once, "being a veteran had some small perks. Meant you automatically were assigned a modicum of respect, didn't have to prove you deserved it." I added that I didn't think that was worth two years of my life, but, hell, it was something. He liked that. "You're right," he said. He smiled and repeated, "you're right."

We talked about John Wayne. We agreed that Wayne's later super-patriotism seemed hypocritical considering his unwillingness to join the military during the Second World War. Dick asked me about ballplayers: didn't many of them just play ball for army or navy or marine teams during the war? That was true of Joe DiMaggio and Bob Feller and a bunch of others who were already in the majors when the United States entered the war, I said. But Ted Williams I knew saw combat as a fighter pilot in Korea. Gil Hodges wasn't yet in the majors, and he saw action in the Pacific. Dick asked me if I played ball in the army. I played on a company softball team while at Fort Monmouth for six months before going to Vietnam, and sometimes that meant I got extra food, deserts especially, after a game. But that certainly didn't keep me out of Vietnam. He said he didn't remember ball teams in any of the units he was in and that it wouldn't have made a difference anyway, that he wasn't an athlete. Wished

4. War Interrupted

he was, he said. At least good enough not to embarrass himself on a ball field or basketball court.

"When you were in the war," I asked, "did you think then that you were taking part in something you could someday write about?" Yes, he said. He knew that Hemingway had written about his war experiences. But of course Stephen Crane had written a good book about war and he hadn't been in a war before he wrote the book. But, Yates added, he didn't think his experiences in the army were story material. That is, he thought that while he was in the army. I noted that Norman Mailer and Joseph Heller and Thomas Heggen established their reputations by writing about the war. I added, "And Kurt Vonnegut." Vonnegut, Yates said, was already successful when *Slaughterhouse Five* was published. "Yeah, but that's the one that got him a larger readership, his war novel." Yes, Yates knew that, and he was well aware that so many other writers in his age group established themselves by writing fiction that in some way came out of their World War Two experiences. He was aware of that, he said, while he was writing *A Special Providence*.

But he wanted to change the subject. Did I have problems writing about Vietnam? Was it too difficult to recall? He kept hearing that, that Vietnam veterans had more trouble writing about their experiences than veterans of other wars. I told him I had the same problems I had writing about anything, no more, no fewer. Things like, was I getting it right, was I taking too many words to explain this action, was I overly concerned with detail just because I knew the detail, did I select the right word or did I settle for the almost right word. The same problems. He said his son-in-law was a Vietnam veteran and had several times expressed an interest in writing about the war. "Fiction or nonfiction?" I asked. Dick wasn't certain. Said his son-in-law hadn't figured out yet what he wanted to write or if he really wanted to write. At least that is what Dick had concluded from talking to him.

Had I read *Born on the Fourth of July* by Ron Kovic? Yes, and I started to tell him something about a review of the book I had read that annoyed me, but he interrupted me to ask if I knew that the book had been so heavily rewritten by an editor at the publishing house that she should have shared the byline with Kovic. I didn't know that. What was I going to say? he asked. There was a review of the book on page 1 of *The New York Times Book Review* by C. D. B. Bryan, and in it Bryan said, by implication, that up to Kovic's book there had been so few good books about Vietnam by veterans of the war because people who were smart enough to write the good books were also smart enough to avoid the draft. Pissed me off, I said. Still pisses me off to think about it. Dick said, "Can't blame you. I would be pissed off if somebody said that about World War Two soldiers." We started to talk about something else, but a little later, maybe 10 minutes later, maybe 15 or 20, he said Bryan was a fop. The comment came out of context, and I realized he was giving me a gift, something negative to know about C. D. B. Bryan. Problem was, I wasn't certain what a fop is. "I'm not sure what a fop is, Dick." "Sort of like a dandy," he said, "somebody who cares too much about how he dresses and acts." I nodded. My way of thanking him for the information.

More than a year later, I asked him if his son-in-law had written anything based on his time in Vietnam. No, no, he said, and he didn't think he would. But who knew.

The one writer who wrote about Vietnam that he praised — the only writer, in fact, whom wrote about Vietnam who he praised — was Tim O'Brien. He had met O'Brien several times. Yates was living in Boston then and O'Brien was living in a small town about 25 miles north of the city, and sometimes they would be together at a party or a reading or something. Yates particularly liked the short story "The Things They Carried," which he read when it first appeared in *Esquire*. And he liked *Going After Cacciato*. He hadn't read many novels about the war, he said, and he probably would, someday. But wasn't O'Brien something?

And most of the time war literature entered our conversation, I asked about *A Special Providence*. Did he know that every time a new edition of one of O'Brien's books came out, say in trade paperback or mass market paperback, it was at least slightly different from any earlier version? He always changed a few words or shortened a scene or something. No, he didn't know that. "Ever think you might do that with *A Special Providence*?" "You mean, cut out the parts about the mother?" "Well, yes, that was what I was thinking about." "No, the book is written. It's done." He said he conceived the book with the mother parts in it and that's the book he wrote. Maybe someday he would write another World War Two book and it would be just about the war or just about the soldiers, but as of the moment he didn't have any plans for that, and

4. War Interrupted

as for *A Special Providence*, well, it was written, it was done, and good or bad or something else, it was what it is. I brought the subject up so often, at least a half-dozen times over about three years, that I thought he would become annoyed with me. He had certainly let me know that other subjects I brought up, especially his time in Hollywood, annoyed him. But never my suggestion that *A Special Providence* would have been a great book if it was just about Prentice and his time in the army, his soldiering, and if the mother was brought in, if at all, just in some short flashbacks. But he was always politely adamant. No, that's not the book he set out to write, and if he was going to write that book ... well, it's not the book he wrote. Maybe someday. But I understood "maybe someday" to mean "no, I'm not going to write another war book."

5

The Depths of Transition: *Disturbing the Peace*

Disturbing the Peace, except for a brief final chapter set in 1970, takes place in the early 1960s, during the years John F. Kennedy was president, and that background offers contrasts on how losers like the main character, John Wilder, react to winners, like JFK. This novel, like Yates's short story "The B.A.R. Man," explains a type of political personality, and there is a lot of talk by characters about blacks, bigotry, and other politically oriented subjects. One character, Chester Pratt, is even a speechwriter for Attorney General Robert Kennedy. But, despite the political overtones, the novel can just as easily be read as a psychological study of a man whose heavy drinking brings on a nervous breakdown.

Wilder realizes that he has a compulsion to let others know the worst about himself and that he confuses what is weak and ugly in him with what is "interesting" (p. 139).[1] He is probably the least sympathetic of any major character in a Yates novel, and Wilder has accurately identified the reason why. Much of the plot, in fact, revolves around his willingness to allow a movie to be made of the lowest point in his life, the few days he spends in a mental ward at Bellevue because of his excessive drinking.

The opportunity to make the movie arises when Wilder has an affair with 20-year-old Pamela Hendricks, whose friends at Marlowe, "the single most expensive college in America" (p. 120), use Wilder's personal problems as the subject of a low-budget film they produce on the college campus. By reaching into the depths of his life — the time spent in Bellevue — Wilder in a sense reaches new heights: having a movie made about himself. Much of the plot resembles a roller-coaster ride: over and over throughout the story Wilder will have ups and downs, dips and curves,

5. The Depths of Transition

just like an amusement park ride, just like, also, someone suffering from severe mental stress.

A major part of that stress comes from Wilder's strong sense of inferiority. At one point he yells at doctors, "I've been a turd under everybody's feet all my life and I've just figured out there's greatness in me" (p. 12). Even at a point when things are going well for him, he is defensive: "Hadn't he served a long enough apprenticeship among the losers of the world?" (p. 161). The low point on the roller coaster comes when he is committed to Bellevue and he realizes "nothing in his life had ever been as bad as this" (p. 38). While Yates's stories frequently depict depression, no character in any other of his writings sinks as deeply into the pits as does Wilder at Bellevue. The whole book, in fact, runs the full gamut of mental problems: delusions of grandeur, suicidal tendencies, imitation of Christ, a sense of inferiority.

That sense of inferiority stems largely from viewing others as being more successful than he is. Wilder is consistently, for example, confronted by men who are more attractive to women than he is. George Taylor, his boss at *American Scientist* magazine, where Wilder sells advertising space, brags about his sexual conquests, and that contributes to Wilder's continued drinking, the primary physical cause of his mental problems. Very near the end of the novel Wilder will tell an attendant in a geriatric center where he is temporarily staying that he wants to die and the attendant, Randolph, will say there is something far worse in store for him: "you're going to live" (p. 263).

Having to live in a world where he is constantly exposed to people like the Kennedys is a continuing source of Wilder's feelings of inadequacy. Although no member of the Kennedy family ever makes a direct appearance in the story, they hover like giant, blazing stars over everything that occurs. His first argument with his girlfriend, Pamela, comes when they discuss the Bay of Pigs fiasco: she is a JFK fan, he is not, and she says he is against Kennedy because the president is tall and has a reputation as a "cocksman ... he's everything you're not" (p. 121). When he briefly devotes more attention to his son, who is having his own stress-based problems because of his father's behavior, and his son starts to recover, Pamela leaves to go to Washington to live with, of all people, Chester Pratt, who has just been hired to be a speechwriter for Robert Kennedy. Wilder's best friend, Paul Borg, praises Robert Kennedy and

Wilder's wife, Janice, praises the whole Kennedy family. The people who are most important in Wilder's life, his best friend, his mistress, his wife, never let him forget how much they admire the Kennedys. Near the end of the novel Wilder will claim to have killed John Kennedy (as well as many blacks and his wife and son). Also near the end is a clear clue that Wilder's sense of competition with the Kennedys is not unfounded: Pamela has moved in for the second time with Pratt, who thinks of her as "his little Frontier girl" (p. 271); "New Frontier" is a term the Kennedy administration applied to itself. (At the same point Pamela will say to Pratt, "You're so nice and tall" [p. 273]; Wilder is short.) But one of the keys to understanding why Wilder has the problems he does comes when he understands too well the motives of Lee Harvey Oswald in assassinating John Kennedy:

> Kennedy had been too young, too rich, too handsome and too lucky; he had embodied elegance and wit and finesse. His murderer had spoken for weakness, for neurasthenic darkness, for struggle without hope and for self-defeating passions of ignorance, and John Wilder understood those forces too well. He almost felt he'd pulled the trigger himself [p. 196].

Except for the word "neurasthenic," this is a typical example of Yates's writing at its best. "Neurasthenic" is untypical because many readers will have to consult a dictionary to find out what it means (it refers to a feeling of inadequacy) and almost never does that happen when reading Yates; he is particularly adept at finding the simplest ways to accurately say complicated things. And that is what is so typical of the passage as a whole; it summarizes a complicated, deep-set emotion that clarifies a perhaps universal trait. And — also typical of Yates — it will allow many readers to see something inside themselves that they do not want to admit is there. Yates at his best can make readers uncomfortable, and that certainly helps explain why he has never attracted a wide, popular readership.

The word "neurasthenic" is not the lone stylistic oddity in this novel. A great deal of information is given to the reader in the form of dialogue by the characters; in no other Yates novel or short story does this happen with such frequency. There is some apparent playing with names: one psychiatrist, a Dr. Brink, takes Wilder to the brink of insanity with his quack treatment, and Wilder himself is clearly *wilder* than most men. And there is even an unusual structural device in having a scene

5. The Depths of Transition

in which the main character does not appear, when a doctor explains why Wilder will have to be moved to a new institution. Yates in all his other writings focuses on a single character (*The Easter Parade*) or divides his books into clear sections that form separate although interlocking stories (*A Special Providence* and *Young Hearts Crying*) or frequently jumps around a large number of characters (*A Good School* and *Cold Spring Harbor*). And there are coincidences in the plot that are nearly totally absent from any other Yates work; the ability of Wilder and Pamela to continue their plans to make a movie is helped when her father gives her $50,000 to go to Hollywood to pursue her movie career; it keeps the plot going, but it is something that *happens to* the main characters, not something they cause, and that is extremely unusual in Yates, as it is in most writers who have a serious critical reputation.

That type of coincidence, of course, is common in movies, and one thing that does appear in *Disturbing the Peace* that also appears frequently elsewhere in Yates's writing is a depiction of movies as essentially phony, partly for that reason. Wilder remembers going to movies while he was in the army and how soldiers would stomp their feet and laugh and call out obscenities if there was anything on the screen that struck them as "cheap or trite or hoked-up or sentimental" (pp. 97–98). His fellow soldiers, Wilder believed, were raised on movies but had become unforgiving critics of the art form.

Another notable institution consistently portrayed as fraudulent in Yates's writing plays a prime role in *Disturbing the Peace*, the whole profession of psychiatry. When Wilder is committed to Bellevue, nearly a week passes before doctors get around to interviewing him. A fellow patient, a Dr. Spivack, will accurately refer to the hospital as "a relic of the nineteenth century. This isn't a psychiatric ward ... it's a madhouse" (pp. 54–55). Spivack reflects a typical Yates view of the profession: many Yates characters will see psychiatrists or be in psychiatric institutions, and not a single one will benefit from the experience. Wilder is treated by being institutionalized, by being given drugs, by being talked to; nothing works. Part of the problem, of course, is Wilder's own inability to quit drinking. Psychiatrist Myron Brink tells him to stop drinking; psychiatrist Burton Rose gives him the same advice; he goes to Alcoholics Anonymous meetings. And through it all he continues to drink. At one point he convinces himself that he will be the first man to come back from being mad without the aid of psychiatry and that maybe that is the same as being a Messiah; a doctor is there to witness it, Wilder is convinced, to "authenticate the miracle" (p. 256).

Although religion plays important peripheral roles in other Yates novels, this is the only one in which it comes close to being a central theme. Over and over there are direct links between mental illness and religion. Patients in Bellevue say they will save someone, meaning save a cigarette butt for him, but there is an obvious religious implication that patients themselves are aware of. Wilder at one point accuses Pamela of having had an affair with "God," which is the nickname students at Marlowe College have given to philosophy professor Nathan Epstein. At another point Wilder deliberately poses like a crucifixion. His middle initial is *C*, meaning his full initials could stand for "Jesus Christ Wilder." And while at Marlowe he blames his problems on Epstein, that is, on "God."

Epstein, or "God," is actually kind to Wilder. He tells Wilder he is "the most admirable man in this [moviemaking] venture" (p. 142) because he can find "order in chaos" (p. 143).

That provides an example of the continued repetition in Yates's work of minor points; a highly similar phrase, "order out of chaos," is used in *Revolutionary Road* (on page 214) to describe what time imposes on life. It is essentially what the writer does with the mass of details that constitute the lives of his characters. The repetition is evident again when Wilder says, "I have never depended on the kindness of strangers" (p. 158), which reverses the famous line ("I have always depended on the kindness of strangers") in Tennessee Williams's *A Streetcar Named Desire*, a play that assumes an important role in *Young Hearts Crying*. The most important secondary theme in this novel has ties to another Yates novel in the role of the mother. Wilder's mother is a "vegetable" in a nursing home, like the mother of Emily and Sarah Grimes in *The Easter Parade*, and although she never makes a direct appearance in the story, Wilder is quite willing to blame her for his mental problems. His parents manufacture Marjorie Wilder's Fine Chocolate Candies and he had refused to go into business with them; when he sees a display of the candies in a supermarket, he knocks it over, calling it "an accident-on-purpose" (p. 231). Wilder's resentment at seeing the candy display is a typical Yates plot device to tie the protagonist's problems to his mother, just as Robert

5. The Depths of Transition

Prentice in *A Special Providence* and William Grove in *A Good School* have problems resulting from their mothers.

Wilder has other family problems as well, with his wife, Janice, and that may seem to be consistent with the fuller body of Yates's work: there are, after all, marital problems in every one of Yates's novels and in many of his short stories, but in most cases the reader will have no difficulty feeling sympathy for both the husband and wife. *Disturbing the Peace* is the lone Yates novel in which the reader is likely to feel sympathy for only one partner, the wife. Wilder cheats on his wife; he lies to her about attending A.A. meetings; he threatens to kill her and their son, and he is, in general, inconsiderate of her feelings and needs, even though at one point their relationship seems to improve and Janice thinks of them as having a second honeymoon and John thinks "this is probably where he belonged" (pp. 192–193). But he returns to his drinking and a point made earlier by Janice seems once again justified: he has stayed away from home for several weeks and calls his wife and son to blame the absence on his being in a hospital; Janice tells him, "Tommy and I have learned not to expect very much of you" (p. 162). Janice had from the beginning of the novel resigned herself to the lack of romance in her marriage, and Wilder is painted so clearly as an unsympathetic character that the wonder is why she would tolerate him at all.

That is a typical problem in *Disturbing the Peace*. It is the one novel that is likely to be least satisfying to Yates's admirers.[2] It has some unconvincing coincidences, unexplained details, and some heavy-handed attempts at symbolism. It marks a clear change in direction for Yates, a point when he stood at a crossroads and chose a different path. Everything prior to it has a sense of doom; everything after it at least a flicker of hope. It is as if by creating a character who reaches the pits Yates was able to go on and create characters who, while perpetually unhappy, have at least a possibility of redemption. *Disturbing the Peace*, in a sense, disturbed the writer's existing patterns and marked the emergence of new ones.

Disturbing the Peace does not achieve anywhere near the same degree of truth-telling as Yates's more successful works, and perhaps it falls further short than any other novel he has written. An uneasy but tempting analogy with Hemingway is possible: it as if Hemingway in such "middle" works as *Across the River and into the Trees* moved beyond grace (under pressure) into gracelessness, enabling him to write *The Old Man and the Sea*, certainly — with its emphasis on enduring despite hardship — the most Christian of his novels. Yates in *Disturbing the Peace*, by descending into a purgatory, purged his novels of their inevitability. The works that follow deal as much with loneliness and dishonesty as those that precede, but they each hint at, regardless of how vaguely, a way out. They each suggest that whatever is worst in life need not be inevitable.

At the Crossroads with Dick Yates

Although I consider *Disturbing the Peace* Yates's only bad novel, in one important way it more thoroughly reflects the Dick Yates I knew in the mid–1980s than anything else he wrote. It's about drinking, and the time I spent with him involved a great deal of drinking. In fact, drinking was involved even in the phone call I received from him that led to our friendship.

I had written to his publisher asking them to forward my request for an interview, and one day weeks later, late at night, he called, but when I answered the phone I couldn't understand what he was saying. At first I didn't know it was him. He slurred his words the way a drunk slurs words, and with some annoyance I asked the caller to repeat what he had said. He did, with some care that clearly required effort, and I understood that the man calling me was Richard Yates. He said he was willing to be interviewed and asked when I wanted to come "up here." I didn't know where he lived, so I asked where "up here" was. "Up here, up here, Boston, up here." We would be friends for several years, and during all that time he never developed an ability, once he was drunk, to hide any annoyance he felt.

* * *

The first time we met was at the Crossroads, a bar in Boston's Back Bay, where he ate and drank, I later learned, nearly every day for the 11 years he lived in the city. For a while he lived on Beacon Street, a block or so away from the bar, and for a while he lived on Commonwealth Avenue, just to the north of Beacon, and for a while he lived in an apartment above the Crossroads.

5. The Depths of Transition

The first time we met, I was about two hours late. I had never been to Boston before, and I missed the exit off the Massachusetts Turnpike I should have taken and ended up downtown and had a hard time finding my way out. And when I got to Back Bay, I couldn't find a parking spot. When I arrived at about 9 P.M. for our 7 P.M. appointment, I had no difficulty recognizing him. He was tall and thin and looked very much like the picture on the dust jacket of his then-latest novel, *Young Hearts Crying*, the one taken by Jill Krementz, wife of his friend Kurt Vonnegut. Even the fact that he was sitting alone at a booth in a small side room seemed appropriate; all of the autobiographical characters in his highly autobiographical fiction seemed so lonely.

There was a bottle of Rolling Rock on the table, next to a glass filled with something else. I later learned it was water mixed with whiskey. A few dozen times over the years I saw a waitress bring him a glass almost filled to the top with water, probably about eight ounces, and a shot glass filled with Jim Beam. The waitress would put the two glasses in front of Yates and after a few minutes he would pick up the whiskey glass, pour it into the water, and almost always use his finger to stir it. Only two or three times did I see him use the stir stick the waitress usually provided.

I asked him about the Rolling Rock and he told me one of his daughters recently visited and brought a six-pack of the beer as a gift. He said he didn't have much preference for which beer he drank. It was just a chaser. The real drink was the whiskey.

It was clear to me that when I arrived he had been drinking for some time. It was visible in his face and, even separated by several feet, I could smell it on him. But he wasn't drunk, at least not in the sense that he lost command of his basic politeness and caring personality. He told me that he had already eaten but that I should feel free to order some food. I declined, and mostly we chatted and agreed to delay the start of the actual interview until the next day. He had two or three more Jim Beams and waters while we talked but stayed with the same bottle of Rolling Rock. I had two beers, which was then and remains today pretty much my limit.

The next day, a Saturday, we met in the afternoon, talked about a dozen things, and then he had something to do. He didn't say what. He had coffee that afternoon, and our session lasted only about an hour.

But we met that night, again in the Crossroads, at seven, and the waitress asked him if he wanted something; he may have said "the usual," but I'm not certain. She brought him a Rolling Rock in a bottle, and a glass of water and a shot glass with whiskey. There was no glass for the beer. I ordered a beer and I was given a glass with the bottle. I mentioned Hollywood and he politely brushed me off. He indicated we could talk about that later. I knew he had not enjoyed his time in Hollywood, so I didn't push the point.

Sometime long after nine, maybe after ten, after Yates had completed one Rolling Rock and was halfway through a second, or maybe it was the third, after seven or eight or nine Jim Beans with water, I mentioned Hollywood again. I was not done with my second beer. He didn't answer, and we talked about something else for a few minutes, and I asked again about Hollywood, and he leaned over the table between us, jabbed his forefinger into the table on each word, and said in a voice dominated by a hiss, "I don't want to talk about that fucking time in fucking Hollywood writing for the fucking movies."

A pattern developed. In four trips to Boston in two years, meeting with Dick Yates at least three times per trip, I saw him drink and drink and drink, always whiskey and water with beer as a chaser, and the more he drank the more easily he lost his patience and the more he said "fucking," pretty much his only curse word. Before the drinking began each day, and indeed, before his third or fourth or fifth whiskey and water, he was polite, usually thoughtful, often helpful.

* * *

The Crossroads is about a 15-minute walk from Fenway Park. He never went there. About a 10-minute walk from the eastern edge of Boston University, where he sometimes taught. The Crossroads was the center of his life in Boston. Except, of course, when he was in his apartment, writing. There was little food in his apartment; I was in two of them, the two on Beacon, and in each one saw him open the refrigerator, which had long been uncleaned. Some beer, some bread, something left over. Less than a third of the space inside the refrigerator was occupied. He did his eating in the Crossroads. Several times I was with him he ordered the fisherman's platter, which consisted of fried clams, fried onion rings, a piece of, I think, fried whitefish, a few other things, all

5. The Depths of Transition

fried. At his suggestion, I ordered the same, and, although I try to eat healthy, enjoyed the meal. There was a lot of it and all of it was flavorful. Several times when he went to the men's room or when I was waiting for him to arrive, I chatted with waitresses about him. They knew he was a writer of some renown but had not read his books. They liked him. Even if he drank too much, he was polite and didn't make crude jokes. Usually, they said, he was in the bar alone, but sometimes other men joined him. The waitresses had the impression those other men were writers.

The Crossroads then had one room with a long bar and another one that was smaller and walled off. He almost always sat in the same booth, where he had a view of the door. If I arrived earlier than him for a meeting, I always sat with my back to the door. I was back in the Crossroads in 2010, and the wall is gone and the booth he sat in no longer exists. There is, however, a reminder of Richard Yates in the bar: a framed article from the *Boston Globe* about Yates and the bar he hung out in.

On my second trip to Boston, my wife and daughter, then one and a half years old, came along. My wife, Ruth, was pregnant with our second daughter. Yates invited us to his apartment a block and a half east of the Crossroads, and when he arrived there I bent over to pick up the stroller with my daughter, America, but Yates insisted on carrying the front end. We had eight or ten steps to climb, and the effort so taxed him that he breathed heavily. I was worried that he might drop my child, so I repositioned my hands on the stroller handle so I could support its full weight in case Dick lost his grip. He puffed so hard that I quickly worried also about his health. He smoked as heavily as he drank. At least several packs a day.

We invited Dick to join us at a restaurant we read about in a tourist guide. It was on Bunker Hill and supposedly George Washington had eaten there. When we arrived, Dick pulled out a chair for Ruth, told America how beautiful she was, asked me if I planned to see a Red Sox game before leaving town, and said he thought the tourist guide was right, that Washington had eaten in the restaurant. "I bet he didn't have green spaghetti," I joked, looking at what Dick had ordered, but I didn't think he heard me. A few minutes later, however, he said, "It's green because it's made from spinach." After dinner, when we had dropped

Dick off at his apartment, Ruth told me that he had been charming. She was right.

On my third trip to Boston, he invited me into his apartment above the Crossroads. He filled a 10-ounce glass to the top with whiskey, Jim Beam, and without asking me if I wanted it handed it to me. He filled one for himself also. We sat and talked, and after about ten minutes his glass was empty. I had taken two sips from mine. I've never liked hard liquor, and the only time I drink it is when someone hands me some in a glass without asking. He asked me if I wanted more. "I'm fine," I said, and he sat down. Another ten minutes, another empty glass in front of him, only one more sip missing from mine, and Dick stood and refilled his glass. He turned to me and said with clear annoyance, "What's wrong with your drink? Want some fucking ice?" Sometime later, maybe 30 minutes, he went into his bathroom, didn't close the door, and I heard piss hit the water in the bowl. I thought I was clever as I stood, walked to the kitchen sink, and poured most of the whiskey down the drain. I was back in my seat before he came out of the bathroom, zipping his trousers. I faked taking a sip from my glass, which now contained about two ounces. The idea was to draw his attention to how much I had consumed. Drunks, I learned long ago, often become angry when you don't drink as much as they do. They often interpret that as a criticism of their drinking. He noticed my glass, smiled or squinted or both, and said, "You need more." He went to his kitchen counter, took his bottle of Jim Beam, walked over to where I sat, and poured whiskey into my glass. I thought of saying, "I'm OK," or something but decided I could just pour more down the drain when he wasn't in the room. The bottle emptied before my glass was half full, for which I was happy, but he just went into the kitchen, took another bottle of Jim Beam from a cabinet above the sink, came back to where I sat, and poured more whiskey into my glass, which I was holding up for him. He poured more than the glass could hold. An ounce, at least, spilled onto my trousers. He didn't notice. He then filled his own glass, which was still two-thirds full, and overfilled that one, too, so some spilled onto the table. He put the cap on the bottle, walked to the kitchen, put the bottle down on the counter with a small bang, and picked up the empty bottle. He held it over a trash can, tried to step on the lever that would open the top, but missed. Stabbed twice

5. The Depths of Transition

more with his foot, missed both times, said, "Fuck, fuck, fuck," and put the empty bottle on the counter with such force I was surprised it didn't crack apart.

* * *

We talked about books and short stories, about "honesty in the use of words," a phrase from his short story "Builders," a favorite phrase of mine in one of my least favorite stories by him. We talked a little about baseball, and he talked about his regret in never having had any athletic ability. We talked about different cities and parts of the country we had visited. I once joked that the U.S. Army once paid for me to have an all-expenses-paid vacation for a full year, with housing and food and even medical care, and occasional fireworks, in Vietnam and was surprised that rather than picking up on the joke, perhaps adding to it, he offered a somber response: it didn't seem to him like it could be much of a vacation. He read some things I wrote and commented on them, at some length; clearly he read them carefully. We agreed that college teaching interfered with writing, that they, as he told me, drew from the same emotions. That did more damage even than the time teaching took away from writing. We talked about politics; we were both liberals who sometimes thought some liberals sometimes spoke with an embarrassing sense of moral superiority; we were thinking mostly of the 1960s when we said that.

But no matter what we spoke about, with seriousness or in fun, there was drinking. The later into the night, the more he drank, the more the tone of any conversation became serious. Joking was for early in the day, early evening at the latest. Dick Yates was never a mean drunk, but neither was he ever a fun-loving drunk.

* * *

In *Revolutionary Road* Frank Wheeler drinks too much. In *The Easter Parade* Emily Grimes drinks too much. In "Liars in Love" Warren Matthews drinks too much. The characters who are the most autobiographical in Yates's novels and short stories all drink too much. Especially John Wilder in *Disturbing the Peace*, a novel that is, in fact, *about* drinking too much. Wilder's drinking results in his being institutionalized, and in his going to psychiatrists and Alcoholics Anonymous meetings, and in Wilder embarrassing himself in public places. Wheeler, Grimes, and Matthews are all alcoholics, people who drink too much. Wilder is something more; he's a drunk, the kind we recognize walking down the street and want to avoid, the kind caricatured in a lot of bad films, the kind bad comedians make distasteful jokes about. There were aspects of Wheeler, Grimes, Matthews, and, most sadly, of Wilder in the Richard Yates I knew.

* * *

Often he told me stories, and often these came late at night, after his fifth or sixth drink, and I couldn't be certain whether the alcohol produced an honesty that made the story possible or a distorted memory that made it untrustworthy.

Here's one he told me about his relationship to Bobby Kennedy: In 1963 the attorney general offered William Styron a position as speechwriter, but Styron turned it down and recommended Yates instead and Yates got the job. As a result of the speeches Yates wrote for Kennedy, the attorney general got more and louder applause than he ever had before. But Kennedy was not pleased with Yates's drinking, and in November, when the attorney general's brother, the president, was murdered in Dallas and all high-ranking members of the administration were expected to offer their resignations, the new president, Lyndon Johnson, asked all cabinet members, including Bobby Kennedy, especially Bobby Kennedy, to remain in their positions. Within the Justice Department, Bobby Kennedy rejected all the resignations of his top staff, except Yates's. Yates resented that. He still resented it two decades later when he told me the story late one night, after hours of heavy drinking. He asked me, rhetorically and angrily, "The Kennedys have four hundred fucking million dollars, did you know that?"[3]

The same night he told me the story about how the script he wrote for *Lie Down in Darkness* was never made into a movie, about how director John Frankenheimer, once Natalie Wood declined the lead female role, suggested Jane Fonda replace her and play opposite her father, Henry, which would have required that the two share a passionate kiss on the screen, and how that so enraged the father that the movie project was dead. He told me this story after he told me the Kennedy story, after he had consumed another two or three drinks.

5. The Depths of Transition

* * *

Yates once asked me my age. I was at the time in my late forties, and that surprised him. "I thought I was just about the same age as your father," he said. At the time he was about 60.

I was 15 when my father died, and I cannot remember him ever having more than a single drink at a time, and even that was usually when as a family we visited someone else's home. I don't remember wine or beer in our refrigerator, whiskey or vodka or any hard alcohol in a cupboard. If there was a party at our house, my father would buy a case of beer. If that wasn't enough, so be it. If some was left over, and there seldom was, it was consumed over the next few days.

In my late teens at a party in the Poconos, where I had a summer job as a waiter, I once got drunk. Everybody else was drinking a lot of beer, so I did, too. Another time, in Vietnam, I was feeling sorry for myself, so I got drunk. And once, in my late twenties, attending a party given by an editor of the newspaper I worked for in Williamsport, Pennsylvania, I didn't turn down any of his repeated offers of martinis. Those were the only three times in my life I've been drunk.

Now I stop at two beers. There are years between the times I have hard liquor. Once, for a few weeks, I tried to drink a glass of red wine each day because I thought it might break down my cholesterol, but my cholesterol count is low. So now I have wine only when it's offered at a dinner or party at someone else's home.

Intellectually, I can understand Dick Yates's drinking. But my limited experience with that much drinking means it's impossible for me to emotionally understand why he drank, how the alcohol changed his personality, how the day-after-day-after-day act of drinking and drinking and drinking made him the man he was.

* * *

His alcoholism ruined his life. Caused two marriages to fail. Damaged most of his friendships. Probably ended his short career as a speechwriter for Bobby Kennedy. But if he was not an alcoholic he would not have been Richard Yates. An uncomfortable truth is that his drinking was needed for him to be the writer he was. He was not primarily an observer of other people. His knowledge of how humanity worked, and therefore of how to shape his characters, came from looking inward.

Drinking freed him of the inhibitions that prevent most people from doing that with honesty.

Writers need things to be honest about. If Richard Yates had been a moderate drinker or a non-drinker, I think, the things he had to be honest about would have been lesser things. His drinking, and the damage it did to his life, made him the writer he was.[4]

6

The Possibilities of Redemption: *The Easter Parade*

"Neither of the Grimes sisters would have a happy life," Yates writes to open *The Easter Parade*, and from there he goes on to chronicle the sad, often pathetic lives of Emily and Sarah Grimes. It is mostly Emily's story, although Sarah is often present physically or in thought. Emily will be called, near the end of the novel, "the original liberated woman" (p. 224).[1] She will have a brief marriage and many affairs, usually supporting herself, often living alone. She will see herself as an intellectual and will strive hard to be self-sufficient. She is doomed, however, to a life of loneliness, no more happy than her older sister, who will live what can be seen as a stereotypically unhappy life, drinking too much and married to a man who beats her. Emily and Sarah live very different lives, sharing one overwhelming trait: constant unhappiness.

While Emily is still a teenager she and her mother, Pookie, spend a lot of time just sitting around the living room being lonely. One night to avoid that loneliness, Emily goes for a walk and meets a soldier; he is Warren Maddox or Maddock, she is not sure of his name, and he takes her to Central Park, where they make love. They later have malted milks, and she is so nervous she vomits it up. She never learns what his last name actually is. Her first love making, thus, is as close to squalid as it is to romantic. Over and over the novel provides examples of a world that is not romantic and whose inhabitants suffer because they want it to be.

Just a week after that incident, Emily's father dies, and for a long time she is unable to cry, although her mother and sister, both of whom give in to romantic impulses, do. On the way to the crematorium, Emily does cry, but she realizes she is crying not for her deceased father, or even for the soldier she made love to and who since has gone off to war, but for herself, "for poor, sensitive Emily Grimes whom nobody understood" (p. 42). Emily is a woman with a large capacity for feeling sorry for herself.

Her loneliness sometimes leads to desperation. When she is 35 and the man she is living with decides to move out to return to his wife, Emily gets on her knees, embraces his legs, and begs him to stay. It is a scene she, understandably, wants to forget.

She tries at times to cover up her loneliness with a sense of dignity. Just before she turns 48, she has a fight with her boss and she says she is resigning, but the boss points out she is doing Emily a favor by firing her instead so she can collect unemployment compensation. Emily's stab at a bit of dignity, to quit rather than be fired, is thus blocked by economic necessity.

Her loneliness is tied, as so often happens in Yates's novels, to her sense of being an intellectual. While she is a student at Barnard College she is happy that other students think she is one; it is a trait she shares with Frank Wheeler in *Revolutionary Road* and one admired by William Grove in *A Good School*. She will have an affair and a brief marriage with Andrew Crawford, a graduate student in philosophy at Columbia University, despite their obvious sexual incompatibility (he has trouble getting and maintaining an erection) precisely because he *is* an intellectual who has read widely and who has many well-reasoned opinions.

Years later, while she is working on a trade journal, Emily has an affair with her boss, Jack Flanders, who has published three books of poetry, including one in the prestigious Yale Younger Poets series. But she has trouble reading his poems for pleasure; she "explicates" them, something she learned to do as an English major in college and something that is a particular affliction of "intellectuals," a group Yates continually portrays as having adopted a set of attitudes that interferes with their own happiness.

Her sense of being an intellectual is tied closely to her sense of independence, and that, too, contributes to her loneliness. One morning she wakes up in a strange room with a strange man and a hangover; she knows this is "sordid" (p. 120), and she cannot remember how she got there. Emily *is* a liberated woman, but one who does not like where her liberation has taken her. When she goes home and gets a call from that man, she tells him it is all right if he comes over. In a sense, she has accepted the sordidness of her life.

6. The Possibilities of Redemption

There is, of course, an obvious way for Emily to avoid much of the loneliness that afflicts her. At one point when a live-in lover suggests she quit a job she does not like, saying, "We don't need the money" (p. 199), she realizes he is talking as if they are married, and she likes that. If she had recognized a decade or more before the appeal that marriage held for her, she might have lived a far happier life.

But it is not the only thing that appeals to her. Near the end of the novel, when her nephew tells her his mother — Emily's sister — once called her a "free spirit" who "goes her own way" (p. 202), Emily is so overcome with emotion that she nearly cries. She sees the comment as a compliment, although her "free spirit" has assured her continual unhappiness.

Her free spirit has allowed her to engage in sex with at least eight men during the course of three decades, and seldom does that bring her emotional satisfaction. She seems to enjoy sex most with a merchant sailor who turns out to be bisexual. The worst is with Crawford, the graduate student to whom she will be briefly married. At one point he accuses her of masturbating with Sarah's husband, Tony, in mind; Tony looks just like the British actor Laurence Olivier. Crawford, just before his marriage to Emily finally does end, says he hates her body: "I hate what it put me through" (p. 76).

The lowest point in her sex life comes, however, more than two decades later, when Emily is invited by a woman friend to a party where they meet Trudy, who is said to run a "masturbation clinic" (p. 217). Trudy invites Emily and the others at the party to her "studio." In it are a large drawing of a woman masturbating with an electric vibrator and aluminum sculptures of Trudy's pupils' vaginas. This scene is a master example of Yates's subtlety. He has said that if a scene is written well enough there are things a reader does not have to be told (which, of course, is similar to Hemingway's famous iceberg principle). Nowhere does he report Emily's reaction to Trudy's bizarre studio, but clearly she must be disgusted with herself for having lived a life that might lead her into becoming one of Trudy's pupils.

Among other problems, Emily's frequent switching of sexual partners leads her to have two abortions. She does not like the father in the first pregnancy and is not certain who the father is in the second. She tries to write an article called "Abortion: A Woman's View" but does not get a good lead or acceptable article, so she files it away. The abortions and the aborted article about the abortions are passed over quickly in this novel, and they do not play the key role that April's abortion does in *Revolutionary Road*. As in that first novel, however, Yates uses the abortions as a plot device and not as a social commentary. Yates is noncommittal. He is not a writer who allows messages to interfere with his stories.

The article on abortion is not the only one Emily fails to write. After she agrees to be fired rather than resign from her job she tries to write an article about waiting for her unemployment compensation to run out and facing welfare, and when she moves to Iowa with the poet Jack Flanders she works on an article called "A New Yorker Discovers the Middle West" that praises with surprise the country between New Jersey and the Rockies. All three articles, much like her relationships with men, are never completed. At the same point that Emily cannot finish writing the article about the Midwest, Flanders fears he is losing his talent as a poet, and Emily even gets a letter from Sarah on Long Island saying she has stopped writing a book about her husband's ancestors in Montana because she cannot get there to do the research. Thus, all three — Emily, Sarah, and Jack — experience writing problems at the same time.

Jack's writing problems contribute to problems in his relationship with Emily, and when he suggests they go to Europe she happily agrees. As in *Revolutionary Road*, a trip to Europe is offered as a possible way of improving a relationship that is not working. In London Jack visits the house he had lived in after World War II with his wife, and that contributes to Emily crying because she does not want to travel with a man she does not love. When they return to Iowa, Jack asks Emily to marry him, but instead she decides to leave him. Thus, the trip that Emily Grimes and Jack Flanders make to Europe does not save their relationship, and a reader can easily speculate that if Frank and April Wheeler in *Revolutionary Road* had actually gone to Europe neither would their marriage have been saved.

Emily seems destined from an early age to be disappointed in all the men in her life, not just Flanders. When she was five and Sarah nine, they visited their father in the newspaper office where he worked, the *Sun* in New York City. They told other kids at school in Tenafly, New Jersey, where they lived with their mother, that he wrote headlines, and

6. The Possibilities of Redemption

they reported that fact with pride. After the visit, however, Emily repeats to Sarah what their father told them: "He's only a copy-desk man" (p. 7). Thus, from the beginning life is full of disappointment for the Grimes sisters. In particular, the men in their lives, their father, Sarah's husband, Emily's lovers, will never live up to the sisters' expectations.

Another childhood incident establishes another pattern that will follow them throughout their lives. While their mother is away, Sarah injures herself playing and needs seven stitches; Emily fears being left alone as a result of the accident, but Sarah holds up bravely. Likewise, Emily will years later have affairs with men she knows are not good for her because of that fear of loneliness, while Sarah will hold up bravely in a long marriage to a husband who beats her.

Part of the problem is the over-willingness of the sisters to romanticize the world. When Emily in 1942 wins a full scholarship to Barnard, she meets her father to celebrate and indicates that she thinks he is a college graduate, but he tells her he spent only one year in college. Both sisters had formed a romanticized picture of their father, a picture based on facts that never existed. It is a habit that stays with them most of their lives.

Emily's sense of romanticism never extends to the women in her life. Nevertheless, when she realizes as an adult that she feels more intelligent than her sister Emily feels as if she has betrayed her. For years Emily felt more intelligent than her mother, but that never bothered her. And it was precisely because she thought of her father as an intellectual that she was so disappointed when she found out he was "only" a copy-desk man.

Her disappointment in men, of course, extends also to lovers. Just as the Second World War ends, she meets and has a summer-long affair with Lars Ericson, a merchant seaman with an eighth-grade education who speaks English, French, Spanish, and some Italian and who quotes Milton. But he breaks off the relationship when he tells her he is bisexual and also having an affair with a man. Over and over, Emily's expectations and the men in her life do not mesh.

It is a problem that continues two decades later when she becomes infatuated with an attorney, Howard Dunninger, who is 50 and whose 28-year-old wife has left him. He moves into Emily's apartment, and she often tells him "she never enjoyed herself so much with anyone" (p.

164). But he is still in love with his wife, Linda, and often talks about her. Emily says that is "unbecoming" (p. 168) of him and not considerate of her. That relationship, like every relationship she has with a man, ends in disappointment. Sometimes she leaves; sometimes the man leaves. Always, someone leaves.

Sarah, the older sister, has only one lover, the good-looking Tony Wilson, whom she stays married to all of her adult life. During their courtship they dress up to go to the annual Easter parade on 5th Avenue in New York and their photo is taken and published in *The New York Times*. They look like "the soul of romance.... It was a picture that could be mounted and framed and treasured forever" (p. 28). The taking of that photograph provides both the novel's title and a frozen moment of happiness that will contrast sharply with the unhappiness that dominates the lives of the Grimes sisters. It is the type of image that fits so well into some movies, especially those that focus without sentimentality on a sad life (as in, for example, *Annie Hall* and other Woody Allen movies; Allen, in fact, has praised *The Easter Parade* and a character in his *Hannah and Her Sisters* approvingly mentions it).[2]

Twenty-seven years later, in 1967, Sarah dies and Emily, after the funeral, goes to Great Hedges, the run-down estate where Sarah and Tony lived, and sees a framed copy of the 1941 Easter parade photo hanging crooked. Emily straightens it. That straightening of the photo may be interpreted as symbolic, as a posthumous attempt to straighten out her sister's life, but it would be entirely Emily's symbolism, not Yates's. Yates avoids symbols as much as he does messages. The failure of Sarah's romanticized view of Tony—years earlier Sarah told Emily that she would continue to live with Tony even though he beats her: "I love the guy" (p. 151)—is emphasized when the police inconclusively investigate whether Sarah's death, at age 46, was caused by Tony.

The differences between the sisters (the only personality trait they share being their acute unhappiness) clearly derives from the differences between their divorced parents. Sarah has been so obviously shaped by her mother, Pookie, that it is the mother who selects the church her daughter will be married in. It is an Episcopal church, the same denomination selected by Mrs. Prentice in *A Special Providence*. In both novels the mothers make the selection based on the superior social position they assume goes with it rather than on any religious basis. By contrast, Emily

6. The Possibilities of Redemption

married Andrew Crawford in a civil ceremony to which the only guests invited are two friends of the groom; neither Sarah nor Pookie is present.

More than 20 years later, in 1965, Sarah calls Emily and asks to move in with her. Emily says she is not living alone and even hesitates to help Sarah find a job so she can get away from Tony. Instead Emily tells Tony on the phone to leave her sister alone. Emily realizes she says that to impress her boyfriend, Howard Dunninger, who is listening. Finally, Sarah says she had decided to stay with Tony, and Emily is relieved. The conversation reflects Emily's fear that Sarah will become a burden. Emily, much like Frank Wheeler in *Revolutionary Road*, is an intellectual who allows her sense of superiority to get in the way of her own and other people's happiness.

At one point, when Sarah is 43, she meets Emily for lunch and has three or four martinis. The two sisters have led very different lives, but both, like so many Yates characters, drink too much. After lunch Emily feels "a guilty pleasure" (p. 148) because she realizes that now that she has seen Sarah she may not have to see her for several more months. But Emily feels the breaking of her once-close relationship with her sister far more than Sarah does. That very night Sarah calls Emily to come to her hotel room, and when Emily gets there she sees that Sarah's face is bloody. This is the point at which Emily learns that Tony has been beating Sarah once or twice a month for 20 years. Sarah insists, in the melodramatic posture that she has made a part of her life, "I love the guy" (p. 151). When Tony enters the room Emily calls him "you son of a bitch" (p. 151), and she enjoys being so clearly right as she insults Tony further. But a little later she feels like an intruder. The next morning, by telephone, Emily invites Sarah to live with her, and when Sarah turns her down, saying she will stay with Tony, Emily is relieved. Emily by now clearly sees Sarah, with all her personal problems and differences in personality, as a potential burden. This scene, so ripe for melodrama because of the melodramatic personality of one of the actors, Sarah, shows the clarity and honesty of Yates's style at its best. Never does he slip into a false or confusing emotion, and every motivation is supported by subtle action and dialogue.

While Sarah clearly shows many of the same personality traits as Pookie, her mother, Emily just as clearly reflects their father's influence.

Like so many of the children in Yates's novels — William Grove in *A Good School*, for example — Emily lives with her mother but feels closer to her father. Emily will even get a job similar to her father when she takes a position on a trade journal, *Food Field Observer*, and writes headlines. At one point, when Pookie is in a hospital suffering from a cerebral hemorrhage and is near death, the two sisters visit their mother and cry not at her plight but at the long-ago death of their father. The crying suits Sarah's melodramatic nature and reflects Emily's closeness to the father.

When Sarah is temporarily placed in the same mental institution where Pookie is staying, Emily visits her sister but not her mother. The hospital has 50 buildings and Emily cannot find the building Pookie is in. Emily tells herself her mother, who by now has brain damage resulting from the hemorrhage, would not recognize her anyway. While she did make an effort to find her mother at the hospital, clearly the effort was halfhearted.

Although Emily takes more after her father, she does share her mother's mental problems. When one of Emily's boyfriends calls her "a funny girl" (p. 179) she seriously asks him if he really thinks she is. Her loneliness has led her into extreme unhappiness and it is that unhappiness that will lead her more and more, as the novel progresses, to doubting her own sanity. Unhappiness leading to doubts of sanity is typical of the type of revelation that makes so many readers uncomfortable with Yates's novels. It is just too easy for too many readers to see themselves in a Yates character they do not particularly desire to emulate.

At several points Emily tries but is unable to make herself complete telephone calls to get mental health information, and when she does make herself complete one and is told she can go to a walk-in clinic in the basement of Bellevue she does not go. Emily, perhaps like many uncomfortable readers, is extremely hesitant to make the final admission about her sanity. Instead she calls Peter, Sarah's son, now an Episcopal priest, married and with a daughter named Sarah. Peter invites Emily to visit them at the New England college where he is a chaplain, saying she can stay as long as she likes. When she gets there, Peter, now 31, tells her he has always thought of her as "the original liberated woman" (p. 224). When he says that if he and his wife have another daughter they might name her Emily, Emily cries. Then suddenly she demands to know

6. The Possibilities of Redemption

how her sister died, and Peter insists that a liver ailment killed her. But when Emily calls his father, Tony, "brutal," Peter defends him by calling him "a limited man" (p. 227). Emily insists that Tony killed Sarah "with twenty-five years of brutality and stupidity and neglect" (p. 227). She is very rude, and crude, to her nephew, saying he and his wife must play "grab ass" and must always be "talking about Jesus" (p. 228). He tells her "that's out of line" (p. 228) and she takes her suitcases and walks to the sidewalk. He comes after her and she apologizes. He invites her, at the very close of the novel, to meet his family.

The story thus ends on an odd, dual note: there is in her rudeness and crudeness clear evidence of the beginnings of a nervous breakdown, undoubtedly brought on by her intense loneliness, but there is also the clear hope of salvation by her nephew. While Emily over and over feared her sister, Sarah, would become a burden to her, her sister's son, Peter, accepts the burden that Emily imposes on him. There is hope here but also sadness, for if Emily had as openly accepted Sarah when Sarah needed her as Peter now accepts Emily, then Sarah, too, might have been saved, saved from a difficult, sometimes brutal marriage and an early death.

The novel has presented a parade of sad characters. No one is truly happy. The parade ends with the hope of salvation, with the possibility of a resurrection for Emily's sanity. Since the resurrection of Christ is marked on Easter, this has been the Easter Parade of the title.

Yates and Homosexuality

The Easter Parade is unusual, but not unprecedented, in being a novel written by a man in which the protagonist is both female and clearly autobiographical. For Yates, the writing might have caused some anguish, because as Blake Bailey, his biographer, claims, Yates "had a lifelong horror of being perceived as homosexual" (Bailey, *A Tragic Honesty*, p. 39).[3] I was unaware of any such fear by Yates when I knew him, but after reading Bailey's book years later I did rethink something Yates said to me in the mid–1980s. Talking with me about a male writer writing from a female perspective, Yates said, in a dismissive tone, "Maybe I'm a fucking queer." The tone was clearly designed to make the listener think that couldn't possibly be true, like a tall man saying people call him Shorty. But, after reading Bailey, I suspected the comment might be a mild, or not so mild, case of homophobia.

Yates told me several times he regretted that as a youngster he was not any good at sports, and while that may have nothing to do with his worries about being seen as a homosexual, it's at least possible that in his mind he made a connection.

Bailey's evidence for the fear is cumulative but circumstantial:

- In *A Good School* there's a scene where classmates attempt to masturbate an unwilling Bill Grove, the novel's protagonist. Grove is clearly based on Yates, and Bailey indicates that Yates told his daughter Monica that the incident actually happened to him, and Bailey quotes several of Yates's classmates at the Avon school in Connecticut, the model for the school in the book, as admitting that something similar happened (pp. 51–52).
- "Emily fucking Grimes is *me*," Yates told a friend, according to Bailey (p. 62).
- When the Yateses rented a cottage on an estate in Putnam County, New York, in the late 1950s, a gardener there was the actor Will Geer, who couldn't find work because he was blacklisted when he refused to testify before the House Committee on Un-American Activities. Geer, who later gained some fame in life by playing the role of the grandfather in the 1970s TV drama *The Waltons*, was the model for the character Ben Duane in *Young Hearts Crying*. Bailey writes: "Yates, who couldn't abide homosexuals, took a dim view of the folksy actor" (p. 180).
- In 1961 Yates received an unexpected telephone call from a famous writer who had read *Revolutionary Road* and much admired it. The writer, calling from California, was planning to visit New York and he wondered if Yates was willing to have dinner with him. The writer was Tennessee Williams, who was openly gay. Yates worried that Williams had something in mind other than meeting a writer whose work he admired. He thought his photograph on the cover of *Revolutionary Road* made him look "effeminate" and suspected that was the real reason behind the telephone call. Nonetheless, Yates agreed to meet Williams. He later told a friend, "We talked books and drank. I wasn't his cup of tea." To help assure that noth-

6. The Possibilities of Redemption

ing like that would happen again, he instructed Grace Schulman, who was taking a photograph of him for his second book, *Eleven Kinds of Loneliness*, to make him look "ballsy." Because of the photo on the dust jacket of his first book, he believed that many people thought he was "queer" (pp. 255–256).

- When Yates's longtime agent, Monica McCall, retired in 1980, his agent became Mitch Douglas, whom Yates disliked intensely. Part of the dislike was that Douglas, unlike McCall, was not forgiving when Yates submitted a manuscript beyond a deadline. And when Yates called to ask about a possible monetary advance, Douglas would respond with a "snitty" denial. (And, Yates told me, Douglas was a "kid" who regularly harped on Yates about his drinking.) In addition, Douglas was openly homosexual, and that, for Yates, provided an explanation for his unaccommodating behavior. Bailey writes: "Yates hated Mitch Douglas" (pp. 506–507). Yates, in talking to me about Douglas, whom he said he had "inherited" from McCall, never mentioned the homosexuality, but he made it clear he did not like the man.

Bailey's evidence is not fully convincing. Clearly he's correct in noting that Yates frequently made disparaging remarks about homosexuals, but, as he notes, Yates liked and admired Monica McCall, who was a lesbian. In fact, he named one of his daughters after her. And wanting to be seen as more manly is not something restricted to men who worry that others might think they are homosexual. America at mid-twentieth century was (as it remains) heavily sports oriented. Not being involved in (whether or not you're any good at it) sports leaves you out of much of American culture. Bailey's biography of Yates is excellent, but this point — Yates worrying that others would perceive him as a homosexual — might be a case of attaching too much weight to a minor concern. In any case, all of his writings can be read without factoring in the possibility that they are products of a latent or any other type of homosexual. The novels and stories stand independent of such interpretations.

7

Static and Memory:
A Good School

With *The Easter Parade* Yates for the first time seems to be saying that telling the truth is not the same as being pessimistic. A writer reaching this point in his progress is not much different from a cynic coming to realize that cynicism results at least as much from an attitude as it does from reality. A recognition like that would undoubtedly cause someone to adopt a new way of approaching life, at least temporarily. Up to this point, every Yates novel and short story followed a classic (if not always conventional) structure. His stories' new recognition of the possibility of redemption seemed to call for a new structure, and that comes in *A Good School*. The story's directness hides its structural innovations, yet it is in its own way as experimental as the best works of his friend William Styron. A new attitude toward life might encourage anyone to adopt a new way of telling others about it. But Yates was understandably unwilling to experiment with his style. That was the basis of his honesty, and he was not going to tamper with what was best in his writing, with what he had mastered. The other major element of storytelling, structure, was more vulnerable.

Sexual awakening, love, friendship, war, and memory are interlocking themes in this short, sensitive novel. *A Good School* is the shortest of all Yates's novels but has the most major characters and is unusual in that one of the major characters is not a human: Dorset Academy, in Connecticut, is a private secondary school for boys who cannot get into "good" schools.

The multiplicity of major characters crowded into such short space could have given the story a disjointed nature, but Yates is careful to make one scene tie into the next. Just as Hugh Britt complains about the theatrics of fellow student John Haskell, Dr. Edgar Stone, an English

7. Static and Memory

master (teacher), tells W. Alcott Knoedler, the headmaster, that he thinks Haskell is heading for a nervous breakdown. Haskell has been working too hard on the student newspaper, and his mother is divorced several times and now living with a much younger man. This interweaving from one scene to another is typical of this novel (and unusual for Yates, who usually preferred clear breaks to emphasize the essential loneliness of characters, as in "The Best of Everything" and *A Special Providence*).

Yates also uses parallels and contrasts to tie together the parts of the story. Just as Bobby Driscoll, the son in whom Robert Driscoll can take no pride, is introduced after Larry Gaines, the almost-perfect student, enters the story, so, too, is the breaking up of the Haskell/Britt friendship immediately followed by the renewed passion of Alice Drapper, wife of the chemistry master, for the French master, Jean La Prade.

Still, Yates has chosen to emphasize some of the disjointedness that is inevitable from using a large cast of characters in a short novel. Near the opening of the first chapter (following the almost nonfiction foreword), most, but not all, of the main characters are introduced, almost the same way many World War II movies opened by introducing members of the platoon. Only after the introduction of these characters does the story move into any significant action. It has the same slow, plodding start as many World War II movies, reinforcing the realization that most of this story takes place during the war.

But the element that both provides the essential unity of the story, preventing it from seeming like a mere laundry list of characters and events, and justifies the seeming disunity is the presentation of the school itself. Dorset Academy is a dominating, ever-present character that undergoes, as all well-developed characters do, a significant personality change as the story progresses. In a sense, the stories of the boys and the faculty and a few others are almost digressions, except that their personalities contribute to the personality of the school, just as the school contributes to theirs.

Where Dorset offers William Grove, the protagonist, an opportunity to mature, it offers Haskell an even greater opportunity for disaster. The pressures of his family life would have been too much for most teenagers, and the added pressures of school, particularly of being editor of the student paper, break him. Thus, Dorset Academy, as a character, is indiscriminate. It builds or destroys, not unlike nature in a man versus environment story.

The school's buildings are "Cotswold" architecture, a style found in western England and built by craftsmen who do not use plans. Thus, the very buildings of the school are pretentious: they are designed to be something that is not designed. One student, Pierre Van Loon, talks about wanting to travel to meet "real" people and he deliberately befriends a kitchen worker. He says, "Kids in private schools don't know anything about reality" (p. 95).[1] In recognizing the essential pretentiousness of the school, Van Loon seeks a pretentious remedy, similar to what decades later will become known as "slumming." Most pretentious of all is the reason Grove and some other students are at Dorset. "Dorset Academy had a wide reputation for accepting boys ... no other school would touch (pp. 5–6), and it has a deliberately created beauty, as if designed by Disney studios. Headmaster Knoedler tells Mrs. Grove, as he tries to convince her to send her son to the school, "Dorset believes in individuality" (p. 5). Knoedler, desperate to increase Dorset's enrollment above its meager 125 boys, offers to cut tuition for William Grove from $1,400 to $700. Thus, the story opens with a clear sense of pretensions: both mother and the school pretend to be something they are not (which, of course, is consistent with the opening of *Revolutionary Road*: as actors, April Wheeler and the others pretend to be people other than who they really are).

Also tying together the seemingly separate elements is an almost-unrelenting tone of sadness. Throughout the novel small touches imbue the story with a continuous sense that disappointment and sadness are inevitable. Halfway through the story (p. 87), a student, Bucky Ward, says, "To come so close to all you've ever wanted in life and then never quite — never quite attain it — I suppose that's the nature of the human condition." When student Larry Gaines is killed and his girlfriend Edith Stone grieves over his death, Yates focuses not on Edith but on her mother, Myra, who is prevented by Edgar, Edith's father, from offering comfort to their daughter. Just as Edith has a need to be comforted, so, too, does Myra have a need to offer that comfort. Neither has her need been fulfilled. Similarly, when Jack Drapper, the chemistry master, unable to find a new job, having endured his wife's sexual infidelity for a year and a half, having lived with the taunts of students, all a result of being crippled by polio, tries to kill himself, he discovers to his great shame that his handicap prevents him from doing even that. When Bobby Driscoll is humiliated by other students, his father is incapable of comforting him and, in effect, shares in his shame by deciding to hide the truth from his wife. Sadness builds upon sadness.

And amid such sadness, thoughts of suicide are inevitable. Long before he actually tries to hang himself, Jack Drapper tells Driscoll, "Sometimes I think I'd rather be dead" (p 48). And when Bucky Ward's girlfriend, Polly Clark, breaks off with him, he talks of wanting to die. Grove tells him, "Everybody wants to live," to which Bucky replies, "Wanna bet?" (p. 143).

Still, Bucky does not try to kill himself, and Drapper's humiliation at being too crippled to even kick a table from under him so he can die by hanging is immediately followed by his wife, unaware of the suicide attempt, for the first time in years making love to him. Over and over in *A Good School*, far more so than in any other work by Yates, there is a sense that despite the inevitability of sadness there is hope that things can turn out better.

Most of all that hope belongs to Grove. Despite an early sense of being out of place and alienated when he first arrives at Dorset, Grove comes to learn an important lesson during his final year at the school: "Guys were *nice* to each other" (p. 140). And at the close of the book Grove says it is only a slight exaggeration to call Dorset a "good" school, noting that it got him "through the worst of my adolescence" and that writing for the *Chronicle*, the student paper, taught him the "rudiments of my trade" (p. 178).

What Grove has learned about the rudiments of his trade — writing — are some of the same stylistic elements Yates uses in *A Good School*. At one point, on the advice of Britt, he removes from an editorial the word "beloved" to describe the school. It is a lesson similar to the one about "honesty in the use of words" that Bob Prentice learned in "Builders." Later, while Grove is helping student council president Dave Hutchins write a Thanksgiving Day speech, Grove's suggestion that they quote Shakespeare is rejected. It is a conscious rejection of being openly "literary" that is typical of Yates's own writing, although at other points in the novel characters briefly quote Kipling and Edna St. Vincent Millay. But these are things quoted by the characters and in no way reflect the author's tastes. And in the afterword Grove says that for years he wrote and rewrote drafts of letters to Britt, trying to impress him. Finally, Grove admits to being worn out trying to impress Britt and simply stops writing. *A Good School* reflects the style of a writer who has long ago accumulated enough confidence to tell a story simply and directly. It is a style as unpretentious as any in American literary history.

Grove's writing accomplishments — he wins a campus essay contest and becomes editor of the student paper — help give him the confidence he needs to have a sense of fitting in at Dorset, and that sense in turn helps make him accepted by others. He develops friendships with Britt and Bucky Ward and others, and even the English master Driscoll, who has never liked Grove, will near the end of the novel call him by his first name, Bill, largely because he is sympathetic that Grove, and many of the others, will soon go off to war.

The war oddly never makes a direct appearance in the novel, although it hovers ominously over the lives of the boys at Dorset. Pearl Harbor is attacked during Grove's first year at the school, and the French master, La Prade, joins the army OSS (Office of Strategic Services, an intelligence outfit and predecessor to the Central Intelligence Agency) as a way of adding adventure to his life and ending his affair with Alice Drapper. Larry Gaines is rejected by all the armed services for an obscure ailment he did not know he had and joins instead the Merchant Marine, but typical of how the war skirts the novel, never entering it directly, is the way Gaines dies. The freighter he is on explodes not as a result of enemy action but because of an accident. Still, it is Gaines's death that makes those at Dorset realize the significance of the war for the school. In effect, the very personality of the school changes as a result of Gaines's death, from uncaring and even hostile to grieving and confusing.

Yet Dorset fails in preparing the boys for war. During an air-raid drill, Dave Hutchins, the student council president, cries when he is taunted by fellow students as Mr. President. The students may play at war, but clearly they are more children than adults. And when Driscoll hears about-to-graduate students sing a college drinking song instead of a soldiers' song, he realizes they are really "children" (p. 173) and not ready for a world at war. The realization makes him cry.

Nevertheless, the boys do accomplish a considerable amount of growing up during their lives at Dorset, and much of that is connected

7. Static and Memory

to sexual awakening. They have strong sexual urgings and there are few girls around, and the result is a combination of frustrations and hints of homosexuality. Near the opening of the story, Grove is the victim of a prank during which several students attack him, shaving off his public hair, and one of them uses his hand to try to get Grove to ejaculate. He is unsuccessful because of Grove's "concentration" (p. 26). It is an incident that is paralleled by an attack much later on Bobby Driscoll that is discovered and stopped by Mr. Driscoll, his father. Driscoll tells his son that he did not do anything wrong but determines never to tell his mother. For Grove the attack results in a determination to become a different person, but for Bobby Driscoll there is only humiliation. The paralleling incidents and the contrasting results are typical of how Yates unifies the plot.

There are other hints of homosexual urgings in the novel. When Grove and Ward become friends, Grove thinks, "It was almost like failing in love" (p. 86). Jim Pomeroy refers to the excessive talking of his roommate Terry Flynn as being like that of a girl. And the girls at a nearby school, Miss Blair's, taunt the Dorset boys by singing a song about "fairies" (p. 146). A metaphoric clue to the origin of Dorset's confusing identification is provided when Mrs. Hooper, the wealthy woman who founded the school, confesses, "I always wanted to be a boy" (p. 163).

Under such circumstances, there is little wonder that few people have any real love for the school. When Headmaster Knoedler tells the faculty that Dorset may have to close and asks if they are willing to take a 25 percent pay cut to keep it open, they unanimously refuse. Britt at one point tells Grove, "When the war's over, you think any college in America's going to care whether you put out the paper for some dopey little school that hasn't existed for years?" (p. 145). And Grove himself asks, "What parents ... would ever have sent a son to this school if they'd had any idea it was failing ... like some sleazy little commercial venture" (p. 145).

In the afterword, more than a decade after the school does close (and is converted into a rehabilitation center for blinded veterans, giving it, finally, a usefulness in the war effort), Grove runs into fellow student Steve MacKenzie, who advises him not to look back (Tony Wilson gives the same advice to Emily Grimes in *The Easter Parade*), but Grove does look back, with a delicate mix of sadness and fondness. He thinks of his long-dead father, and once, while driving in the Midwest, he hears on the radio a recording of a tenor who reminds him of his father singing "Danny Boy."

But the rest of the recording is lost in the static of the radio. Thus the story nears its end with a strong suggestion that the recoding of events of Grove's years at Dorset may be in some way incomplete, important parts lost in the static of faulty memory. That helps to explain the disjoined nature of the narrative and helps, too, to bring into focus the nature of the story. It is something that is recalled, not something that is happening (helping also to explain why the dedication of the books is to the "memory" of Yates's father).

Grove, unlike Britt, does care about the memories that Dorset, a funny school, a good school, gave to him. The final words of the novel are "All that is in the past" (p. 178). But Yates's memory, static and all, has brought it into the present.

The Perfect Game

I met with Yates in Boston at the Crossroads bar in 1986, shortly after the first book of literary criticism that devoted significance space to him was published. The book — *The New American Novel of Manners: The Fiction of Richard Yates, Dan Wakefield, and Thomas McGuane* — by Jerome Klinkowitz, a well-known academic critic — placed the three writers mentioned in the subtitle in a category most famously occupied by Jane Austen, William Makepeace Thackeray, Evelyn Waugh, and F. Scott Fitzgerald.[2] Yates showed me a copy of the book that Klinkowitz had sent to him, and he opened the book to page 55, which he had marked with a piece of paper. He pointed to a sentence he said he thought I would like because it concerns baseball.[3] Klinkowitz was also a baseball fan, and for a while was even part owner of a minor-league baseball team (the Waterloo, Iowa, Diamonds). The quote, referring to *A Good School*, said: "If writing were baseball, this would be Richard Yates's perfect game."[4]

* * *

A Good School almost never made it into print because the only copy of the manuscript was nearly destroyed in a fire. In June 1976, Yates was

7. Static and Memory

living in Manhattan when, he told me, he fell asleep while smoking a cigarette. Bailey in *A Tragic Honesty* has a slightly different version: he says Yates put a cigarette butt in an ashtray, put the ashtray on the arm of the sofa bed in which he had been reclining, went to the bathroom, and while he was there the bedding caught on fire. Bailey's version continues: Yates often told people he then ran to other apartments in the building, knocked on doors to alert tenants, and returned to his apartment in an attempt to rescue the 100 or so manuscript pages of *A Good School*, but flames blocked his effort and he received burns on his face and hands. He ended up in the intensive-care unit of Bellevue.

Sam Lawrence, his publisher, knew Yates never made carbon copies of his manuscripts, so, when he heard about the fire, he contacted a mutual friend, Franklin Russell, who lived on Long Island, and asked if he could help. Russell, in Bailey's phrase, was "a former intelligence operator in Southeast Asia." Russell went to Yates's apartment, found the scorched manuscript, "soaked it in glycerine for a few hours, then peeled the pages apart and Xeroxed them between sheets of acetate."

The burns on Yates's face left scars and, Bailey writes, "seemed to age him.... He'd become a peculiarly feeble fifty-year-old man."[5]

Yates in the Crossroads bar told me only that there had been a fire in his apartment, that his manuscript had been damaged but was salvaged, and that he had received some burns. He was drunk at the time and not in a particularly good mood, and I had long previously learned that when he was drunk I should not press him for any information beyond what he volunteered. With the exception of falling asleep in bed, there's nothing inconsistent with the version Yates told me and the more detailed one offered by Bailey.[6]

* * *

A Good School is one in a long tradition of novels about schools, including works by Louis Auchincloss, Honore de Balzac, E. R. Braithwaite (*To Sir with Love*), Charlotte Brontë, Agatha Christie, Colette, Ivy Compton-Burnett, Robert Cormier (*The Chocolate War*), R. F. Delderfield, Lillian Hellman, John Hersey, Hermann Hesse, James Hilton (*Goodbye, Mr. Chips*), Evan Hunter, Stephen King, Rudyard Kipling, N. H. Kleinbaum (*Dead Poets Society*, a novelization of the movie), Frank McCourt (*Teacher Man*, a nonfiction book that seems to contain fictional details), Robert Parker, Muriel Spark, P. G. Wodehouse, and Tobias Wolff, to name some of the better-known writers who have written such books (and a few well-known books by lesser-known writers). But it clearly is most easily compared to what may be the best-known book in the genre, *A Separate Peace* by John Knowles.

Knowles's 1959 novel, his first, is set in a private school, Devon, in 1942, and many of the students assume that once they graduate they will go off to war. I once asked Yates if had read many school-based novels before he wrote *A Good School*, and he replied that he had read *A Separate Peace*. He did not say he had or had not read any others. He also said that he did not want to write the book Knowles had written, and clearly the differences are at least as noticeable as the similarities. One of the key characters in Knowles's book, Finney, is an excellent athlete, and when he is injured his future as an athlete is ended. When he is reinjured, he dies during an operation to reset his broken leg, probably, the doctor speculates, when bone marrow enters the bloodstream. Athletics does not play an important part in *A Good School*. Devon is based on Phillips Exeter Academy, then and now one of the most prestigious private secondary schools in the country.[7]

Yates explained that when he said he did not want to write the same book Knowles had written, he meant not only that he did not want to duplicate what was already a well-known novel but also that his experiences in a private school differed from those of Knowles. Athletics were never a big part of Yates's life, something that sometimes made him feel a bit inferior, or maybe left out, because he never experienced the camaraderie athletes often enjoy. And merely attending a school like Phillips Exeter Academy meant a student either came from a privileged background or could assume he would enter one. The attitudes of students at the Avon Old Farms School, the model for Dorset Academy, were decidedly less grandiose. And, perhaps most important, the protagonist of *A Separate Peace*, Gene Forrester, who visits the school 15 years after he graduates and has guilt feelings about the role he played in the death of his friend, Finny. Bill Grove remembers his time at Dorset with fondness, with a sense that despite the school's and his own limitations, he benefited from his time at the institution.

The two most famous alumni of the Avon Old Farms School are folksinger Pete Singer and Brian Leetch, who after a great career in the

7. Static and Memory

National Hockey League, mostly with the New York Rangers, was inducted into the Hockey Hall of Fame in Toronto. Avon's original buildings were designed by Theodate Pope Riddle, one of America's first famous woman architects and the founder of Avon. She is the model for Abigail Church Hooper, a secondary character and the founder of Dorset Academy in *A Good School.* Among the things Riddle was most famous for in her lifetime (1887 to 1946) was that she was a survivor of the sinking of the *Lusitania* in May 1915, an event that contributed to turning American public opinion against Germany during World War One and to the eventual entry of the U.S. into the war in 1917.

Knowles would later say that *A Separate Peace* was not autobiographical and that he enjoyed his time at Phillips Exeter Academy. That is one similarity that Knowles and Yates shared. In the afterword, which is close to nonfiction, Yates sums up his feelings about Dorset (Avon Old Farms) with fondness: "If my father had lived I would certainly have thanked him for paying my way through Dorset Academy.... I might even have told him — and this would have been only a slight exaggeration — that in ways still important to me it *was* a good school" (p. 178).

8

Cruelty and Optimism: *Liars in Love*

Yates's next book, *Liars in Love*, his second collection of short stories, continued his movement away from unrelieved negativity and toward at least hints of something more positive. More so than in *Eleven Kinds of Loneliness* or any of the novels, many of the characters in this collection make cruel statements. Cruelty and dishonesty are so intertwined in most of these stories that they are hard to separate. Yet the stories, despite the cruelty, mostly end with characters having something to look forward to, something to be optimistic about.

* * *

In the first story in the collection, "Oh, Joseph, I'm So Tired," two frequently used Yates themes are brought together, the non-theological discussion of religion (as also appears in *The Easter Parade*) and the explanation of the motivation of a common social type (as in "The B.A.R. Man" and "A Really Good Jazz Piano"), in this case the person who in frustration turns to anti–Semitism. Although the last names are not given here, Helen the mother and Billy the son are clearly the Groves who are central characters of *A Good School*. Through a connection Helen is permitted in 1932 to sculpt a head of President-elect Franklin Delano Roosevelt. (Alice Prentice, the mother in *A Special Providence*, of course, is also a sculptor.) She accepts it as an appropriate assignment, even though she voted for Herbert Hoover, FDR's opponent, because, she says, "I believe in the aristocracy" (p. 12).[1] She sees herself, by virtue of her artistic talent, as a member of it, despite the fact "she wasn't a very good sculptor" (p. 3). When she goes to Washington months later to personally present the sculpture to the president she is disappointed that no one from the press is present to capture the occasion. Her disappointment is heightened

8. Cruelty and Optimism

at a lunch in Washington with a friend of a friend who remarks that Bart Kampen, a recent Jewish immigrant to New York, has found some "rich, dumb, crazy woman" (p. 29) to pay him to tutor her children. The friend of a friend, Charlie Hines, does not know that that woman is Helen, and when she gets back to New York her disappointment vents itself against poor Bart. In front of the children she fires him, saying she is not dumb, not rich, and not crazy, and she adds with venom that she does not like people who say some of their best friends are Jews because "*none* of my friends are Jews" (p. 32). Earlier a friend, Sloane Cabot, had told a story to children at a Christmas party about the Virgin Mary telling her husband on their way to Bethlehem, "Oh, Joseph, I'm so tired" (p. 23). Helen has made her anti–Semitic remark out of tiredness with life in general. Her remark, unchristian as it is, can thus be seen as having an origin similar to those of Christian principles.

While Yates frequently wrote about religion, he did not consider himself an expert on the subject, so, while writing "Oh, Joseph, I'm So Tired" he called his friend writer Andre Dubus to ask him some questions. According to Dubus, Yates "asked if Mary would really have a donkey and why were they going to Bethlehem anyway." He also asked, "Well, everybody knew they were going steady, didn't they?"[2] Dubus's answers don't seem necessary to the story, but they undoubtedly gave Yates a sense that he wasn't getting anything wrong. While his primary method of research was a carefully recalled memory, he would use other methods, such as the telephone call to Dubus, for augmentation. But he didn't do much of that. For example, in all of his writings, not a single scene is set in a locale he did not live in or visit.

While many details in the story are repeated elsewhere in Yates's writing (in addition to those already mentioned, there is the fact that the father and mother are divorced, and the father sings "Danny Boy," as does the father in *A Good School)*, one is unique to this story. Helen is a Republican who voted for Herbert Hoover for president in 1932, while the father is a Democrat.

* * *

"A Natural Girl" opens with 20-year-old Susan Andrews telling her father that she does not love him anymore and nears its close with her telling the same thing years later to her husband. She defends the insensitivity of her remarks as "honest." Yates writes: "She had come to learn the value of honesty in all things: if you dealt cleanly with the world there was never any taking anything back" (p. 37). The story is set with the Vietnam War as a backdrop and at one point her husband, David, calls her "a natural girl" (p. 47), pinpointing her as representative of a group of young women in the late sixties and early seventies who saw themselves as natural, not phony, although they might spent hours each week applying subtle makeup and doing their hair to give themselves the "natural look." Susan's "honesty" twice hurts men in her life, her father and her husband. Yates is not denouncing "honesty," something that is a key to his style, but he is clearly giving an example of an honesty too easily arrived at, one based on self-serving impulses, hurting people who do not deserve to be hurt. (Similarly, Carl Traynor in *Young Hearts Crying* will distrust the use of the word "honesty" by students in his creative writing class because he has so often heard it used as an excuse for cruelty.) "A Natural Girl" provides another example of Yates's depicting a poor use of what should be a harmless word when Susan calls a dinner guest "nice" (p. 53) and David scolds her, saying "nice" is cruel, a word used to cover up an inability to find something positive to say about someone. (Again similarly, in "Liars in Love" two characters who lie make "frequent use of the word "nice.") "Natural," "honest," and "nice" should be useful words to help explain people's personalities, but they are in "A Natural Girl" used carelessly by characters and as rationalizations to excuse bits of cruelty.

This story is rounded in a way that is clearly artificial. Not only does Susan tell her father early in the story and her husband late in the story that she doesn't love them; she uses essentially the exact same wording. When her father asks her why she doesn't love him, she replies, "There *is* no why. There's no more why to not loving than there is to loving. I think most intelligent people understand that" (p. 38). Seventeen pages later she tells her husband, "There *is* no why. There's no more why to not loving than there is to loving. Isn't that something most intelligent people understand?" (pp. 55–56). If Susan were conscious of using the same phrasing, perhaps it would be a moment of self-awareness, perhaps she would recognize that she was attracted to David because he shared some personality traits with her father, or perhaps she would see that she knew only one way to react to men. Something. But that's absent,

8. Cruelty and Optimism

and the repetition of the wording is clearly contrived. It makes the story suffer from the same weakness as the novel *A Special Providence*. That is, Yates never found the right structure for the story's theme. Put another way, "A Natural Girl" is burdened with a contrived, or unnatural, structure.

* * *

In "Trying Out for the Race" one little boy cruelly asks another, Russell, "You gonna try out for the race?" (p. 88), meaning the human race, adding that "sissies" are not allowed to enter. While all characters in this story would qualify for entry into the race based on their loneliness, their essential selfishness and sometime cruelty would keep each one from crossing the finish line. Lucy Towers talks Elizabeth Baker into moving into a rented house with her in Scarsdale, New York, but Elizabeth's daughter, Nancy, and Lucy's son, Russell, do not get along. Nancy is stubborn and a crybaby and even her mother says, "Sometimes I wish that child were at the bottom of the sea" (p. 72). Elizabeth at one point goes away for more than a week with a man, who calls her and Lucy imbeciles. From New York Elizabeth calls Lucy and tells her to put Nancy on a train to come visit her. Although it is an irresponsible request, Lucy does it. Another week passes and Nancy returns by train alone. When Elizabeth finally does return, she tells Lucy she wants to break their two-year lease a year and a half early. Nancy has told Carl Shoemaker, a bigger kid at school, that Russell is a sissy, and Carl makes the remark to Russell about trying out for the human race. Lucy, in reaction to her own inability to get along with Elizabeth, scolds Nancy, saying she would not want to live with a person who says such mean things. The next day, Elizabeth and her daughter move out. Despite their loneliness, readers will find difficulty feeling sympathy for these characters. While most Yates characters have qualities that are difficult to admire — he does after all create fully developed men and women, boys and girls — the ones in this story are among the least easy to like in all his fiction. Their loneliness simply does not redeem their selfishness and cruelty. This story can easily to contrasted with almost any other one by Yates in this respect. Consider for example "Oh, Joseph, I'm So Tired," in which it is easy to sympathize with the mother despite her cruel and unnecessary anti–Semitic remark.

Likewise, no other Yates story offers so many examples of loneliness. Nearly every page of the story contains at least one comment or incident emphasizing one or more characters' loneliness. Elizabeth, 36, waits many nights for a call from Judd Leonard, 49, a PR agent in New York City, whom she loves, but he seldom calls. When Lucy calls and suggests they rent a house together, she phrases the offer by asking, "I'm awfully tired of living alone ... aren't you?" (p. 69). When Lucy tries to talk Elizabeth out of breaking their lease, Elizabeth responds by saying how different they are. Elizabeth says she is a Communist, works hard, and doesn't believe in alimony and that Lucy will probably vote for conservative Alf Landon, seldom works, and lives on alimony.

Russell is clearly based on Yates, who worried his entire life, even as an adult, that others might see him as a sissy, as unmanly. "Trying Out for the Race" offers an insight into the resulting loneliness that is absent from or less evident in Yates's other stories and novels. Much of that worry, this story says, resulted from cruelty of adults and childhood peers.

* * *

When in the book's title story, "Liars in Love," Warren Matthews's wife, Carol, and their two-year-old daughter, Cathy, leave him alone in a London flat owned by her aunt, Judith, during his Fulbright exchange year, he has an affair with Christine Phillips, a 22-year-old prostitute. Christine tells lies, among them a story about a U.S. Army major who she says is the father of her daughter and who told her to get an abortion (a subject that repeatedly appears in Yates's fiction), and when she refused and she reported him to his commanding officer the C.O. said it was her mistake. Warren thinks she is lying but does not say so. Meanwhile he tells a lie of his own, saying he would like to marry her but can't. The openness of the lies puts too much of a strain on their relationship and it shortly ends. Dishonesty here is carried to extremes. No Yates character lies as openly and with as little skill as does Christine. Her stories are designed to make her more appealing by making her more interesting but instead repulse the one man she has a real chance of being close to.

The earliest lie in their relationship propels them into a longer relationship than Matthews had originally planned. He picked up Christine

8. Cruelty and Optimism

with the intent of spending one night with her. She asks him to spend a second night without paying, and that's when they say they love each other. Warren plans to end the relationship early, but when Amy, another prostitute who, like Christine, lives with Alfred and Grace Arnold, lightly touches Warren (she puts her fingers on his thigh as a way of indicating she wants to start a conversation with him) Christine threatens her, and the two women get into a fistfight. When, on another occasion, Christine invites Warren over, she's not there when he arrives and he realizes she's beginning a process of dumping him. Days later, she calls again and again asks him to come over, but he says no and tells her not to call him again. This time, Carol's aunt, Judith, is listening in on a extension phone. Then Warren receives a letter from his wife, Carol, saying she loves him and asking him to return to New York. As he packs to return to his family, he finds a cardboard music box he had purchased as a gift for his daughter, and he throws it away because it reminds him of Christine and he wants to rid himself of memories of London.

Two autobiographical points about this story are worth noting. First, the unhappiness of much of Yates's life created a desire in him to forget much of it. Second, Warren Matthews, as he's packing to return to America, decides that "most of the books could be thrown away..." (p. 139). Yates, unlike most writers, never developed a sentimental attachment to the many books he read and his apartments were strangely devoid, for a writer, of evidence of a lifetime of reading.

The story also offers a hint of what Yates thought probably would have happened to Frank and April Wheeler in *Revolutionary Road* if, indeed, they had made their trip to Paris: "...she [Carol] and Warren hadn't been getting along well for a long time. They may both have hoped the adventure of moving to England might help set things right, but now it was hard to remember whether they'd hoped that or not" (p. 95).

* * *

In "A Compassionate Leave" Paul Colby, a 19-year-old American soldier who has arrived in Europe for the last of the fighting in World War II, seeks desperately to end his virginity but cannot. He cannot even find a prostitute in Paris at a time when the city seems to be filled with them. He requests and is granted a compassionate leave to visit his mother and 18-year-old sister, Marcia, living in London. His parents are divorced and he was raised by his father. Paul has not seen his mother and sister since he was 11. He guesses that his sister is no longer a virgin, and she guesses that he is. Marcia makes a sarcastic remark about his "virginal eyes" (p. 172), and although she quickly apologizes, he leaves her, newly determined to find a girl in London to end his virginity. A particularly recognizable emotion in this story is Paul's hatred of the city of Paris because he cannot find even a prostitute there. Like so many young men and women, he will blame his sexual frustrations on a geographic location.

A careful reading of "A Compassionate Leave" provides a useful example for examining a point Yates sometimes made to me: autobiographical is not autobiography. While a story may contain elements that are based on a writer's life, not every detail in the story should be read as emanating from that life. In "A Compassionate Leave" Colby has one sister, as Yates did, but his sister was older than Yates and Colby's is younger than him, by one year. Yates's parents were divorced and so are Colby's, but neither of Yates's parents remarried and both of Colby's did. The fact that Colby at age 19 has already read Hemingway's *The Sun Also Rises* may or may not be consistent with Yates's life. Yates read Hemingway as a young man, but in this story the novel is a plot device used to help explain Colby's attraction to Paris. The fact that Paul Colby remembering his father taking him to see the Detroit Tigers play at Briggs Stadium is consistent with Frank Wheeler's father in *Revolutionary Road* taking him to see a ball game at Yankee Stadium in New York suggests an autobiographical origin, but Yates specifically told me that he had never been to a major-league baseball game. The idea of a father taking a son to a baseball game thus seems more designed to show an incident of normality in the father/son relationship. However, the fact that Warren Matthews in "Liars in Love" remembers being on leave in London during World War II and unable to find a girl to have sex with and Paul Colby in "A Compassionate Leave" can't find even a prostitute to have sex with seems very likely to reflect what probably happened to Yates during his time in the army. The essential honesty at the heart of "A Compassionate Leave" is based on the protagonist feeling both too old to be a virgin and too incompetent to do anything about it. It's an honesty that a lesser writer would be unwilling to reveal about himself.

8. Cruelty and Optimism

* * *

"Regards at Home" is the only Yates story in which the main character — Bill Grove (who is also the main character in *A Good School* and the narrator of "Oh, Joseph, I'm So Tired") — leads a life that is envied by another important character. Grove is married to Eileen, a secretary and acting student, who is the subject of an infatuation by Dan Rosenthal, a talented artist friend. Bill and Eileen are not getting along well and Bill would in fact leave her except that she becomes pregnant. Bill loves Eileen the actress more than he loves Eileen the secretary, but Eileen gives up her acting studies because they tire her out. Dan, meanwhile, has a hard time taking his eyes off Eileen and he can make her laugh, something Bill is no longer capable of doing. But when Bill finds out he has TB the potential tragedy actually turns into a piece of good luck. The illness entitles him to enough money, since it is classified as a service-connected disability, to live in Europe while he writes the novels and stories he wants to. As he and Eileen are about to depart on the ship, Eileen gets a warm good-bye hug from Dan, and at that point Bill realizes that Dan envies him his wife, his trip to Europe, and just about everything else in his life. Bill Grove in this story has a reasonable basis for assuming he will, at least for a while, lead a happy life. Similarly, "Liars in Love" ended with Warren about to be reunited with his wife and things looking up for his personal relationships and "A Compassionate Leave" closes with Paul's clear sense of determination to end what he sees as the cause of his loneliness, his virginity. These positive (or almost positive) endings conclude stories that all appear in *Liars in Love*. Not a single one of the stories in *Eleven Kinds of Loneliness* offers the same closing potential for happiness. That is the essential thematic distinction between the two collections.

Note also that Eileen possesses notable similarities with April Wheeler in *Revolutionary Road*. Both have studied acting; Eileen is a secretary and April planned to become a secretary; Eileen is attractive to Dan, a friend of her husband, just as April is attractive to Shep Campbell, a friend and neighbor of her and her husband. Eileen might have separated from Bill, but she becomes pregnant, just as April's plan to have her and Frank go to Europe is derailed by her pregnancy. "Regards at Home" is a mini-version of *Revolutionary Road* with a far more hopeful conclusion.

There is, however, one key difference between "Regards at Home" and *Revolutionary Road*. Bill Grove has an IQ of 109 (p. 178), just as Robert Prentice has an IQ "slightly above average" (*A Special Providence*, p. 194). Frank Wheeler is clearly intended to be both intelligent and clever. Of course, when *Revolutionary Road* was being written, Yates was not yet recognized as a major writer. After its publication and positive reception by critics, he could reveal his self-doubts about his intelligence, or at least about his inability to do well in high school or on IQ tests, because he was now seen as being successful in a profession that clearly required intelligence.

* * *

Jack Fields in "Saying Goodbye to Sally" is a 36-year-old novelist who goes to Hollywood to write a film script and has an affair with Sally Baldwin, an attractive secretary of about the same age. He fancies himself a 1960s version of F. Scott Fitzgerald having an affair with Sheilah Graham, but near the end of this long story (60 pages, making it by far the longest story Yates wrote) Sally will call him a "counterfeit F. Scott Fitzgerald who comes stumbling out to movieland" (pp. 270–271). She may or may not be right. Each reader is free to draw his or her own conclusion. More interesting but far, far less appealing is the affair between two secondary characters, Jill Jarvis and Cliff Myers. Just two days after Cliff's wife dies of a heart attack, Jill invites him to dinner and he accepts. That night they make love. And when Jill wants to get rid of an old boyfriend, Woody, Cliff cruelly hands him a vase with industrial glue on it, requiring a long scrubbing with gasoline to get it off. Although many of Yates's characters have traits that are less than admirable, Myers is the only one who is downright despicable, and Jill, who will shortly marry him, is not much better. Still, this is mostly Jack and Sally's story, and they — consistent with so many other of Yates's characters — lament their lives. Sally says there are a "lot of things" she wishes for and Jack replies "So do I" (p. 234), echoing, for example, Michael Davenport's comment in *Young Hearts Crying* that he spent his whole life "yearning" for something else.

The first time I asked Yates about his time in Hollywood, he told me, "I don't want to talk about that fucking time in fucking Hollywood writing for the fucking movies." That was late one night in the Crossroads

8. Cruelty and Optimism

bar in Boston, after he had been drinking for hours. The next day, in the afternoon, before he had started his drinking for the day, he raised the subject calmly, almost apologetically, and said if I wanted to know about his time in Hollywood I should reread "Saying Goodbye to Sally." He told me everything that happened to him in Hollywood was in the story and he didn't want to talk about it because he was fired from his screenwriting job. Oddly, the protagonist, the autobiographical character, is not fired in the story, but the length of the story and Yates's comment about its completeness make detailing its plot a useful way to provide insight into an important time in the writer's life.

Jack Fields, 36, needed five years to write his first novel, which sold poorly, but he was then asked to write a screenplay for a contemporary novel he admires. So he goes to Los Angeles. On the surface it sounds like almost straight autobiography: Yates's first novel sold poorly, but he went to L.A. to write a screenplay based on William Styron's *Lie Down in Darkness*. Fields lives for a while in the expensive home of Carl Oppenheimer (who sounds very much like John Frankenheimer), the director of the film Fields is writing. An attractive starlet named Ellis lives with Oppenheimer. Fields rents a home with a view of the ocean, but it's almost as dumpy as the Greenwich Village cellar apartment he had been living in in New York. He goes to see his agent, Edgar Todd, but he's out, so he asks Todd's secretary, Sally Baldwin, about the same age as Fields, 36, to have a drink with him and she agrees. Later she takes him to her home, a Beverly Hills mansion owned by a friend, Jill, and Jill's son, Kicker Jarvis. Jill's boyfriend is Woody. Sally goes with Jack to stay at his apartment. It's at this point that Jack thinks of himself as F. Scott Fitzgerald with Sheilah Graham.

Sally tells Jack about her life. Her maiden name was Sally Munk, and she acted in some grade B movies as a teenager, went to college, married a lawyer, and divorced him nine years later. She also tells Jack about Jill: Jill Jarvis got her mansion from a divorce settlement and has had a long series of live-in boyfriends. Her son, Kicker (whose real name is Alan), got his nickname from his pre-birth kicking; his father denies he's his son, so he doesn't come to see him. Jill's current boyfriend, Woody Starr, is an "artist" who paints on black velvet. Ralph, an engineer, comes over and Jill flirts openly with him in Woody's presence.

Sally refers to Ralph as an old friend who's "a very dear person" (p.

234) and Jack wonders if Sheilah Graham ever used such an obviously phony Hollywood term with F. Scott Fitzgerald, but he decides that even if she had, Fitzgerald must still have been grateful, at that point, late in his writing life, to have her around.

Sally and Jack spend several weeks in his apartment, but then Sally says she's moving out because the place is damp and dirty and has worms. Jack's pride is hurt, but he agrees to move into her room at Jill's. Jack and Sally often drink heavily, and Jack doesn't like Sally when she drinks. Ralph tells them that the wife of his boss, Cliff Myers, whom Ralph has heavily praised as a hard worker he much admires, has died of a heart attack. She was 35. When Jack does not react with what Sally considers appropriate remorse, she calls him an "unfeeling son of a bitch" (p. 241), and he moves back to his own apartment, expecting to make up with her in a few days. Jill, meanwhile, invites Cliff Myers over for dinner two days after his wife dies, and he accepts. He's already back at work. Sally asks Jack to join them at the dinner. Cliff makes callous remarks about people offering him sympathy (example: "Funny business, this sympathy-getting bit.... I may as well enjoy it while I can, right?" [p. 247]). Jack ends up drunk on the floor of Jill's bedroom and doesn't leave until Jill and Cliff come in to make love.

Jack asks Sally to move back in with him, but she says no, that they'll just fight. A few days later, Sally calls Jack and asks him to move back in with her, and he agrees. Once there she talks mostly about how Jill kicked Woody out, is ignoring Kicker, and is having an affair with Cliff. Jack takes Sally to meet the director Carl Oppenheimer. Jack tells Sally he might stay around L.A. a little longer than the two or three weeks he needs to complete the script, but she tells him not to do her any favors.

Meanwhile, as Woody is saying good-bye to Kicker, Cliff plays a mean practical joke on him, one Jill is aware of. Cliff, whom Woody doesn't know, drives up in a truck and hands a bunch of roses in a tub to Woody, but the tub has industrial glue on it and it sticks to Woody's hands. Cliff then drives away. Kicker uses gasoline to help Woody get his hands off the tub. Jill and Cliff then go to Las Vegas to get married.

Jack finishes the script, and Oppenheimer likes it. Saying good-bye to Sally in a fancy L.A. restaurant, Jack thinks of himself again as being like Fitzgerald. For years he had been preoccupied with the author of

8. Cruelty and Optimism

The Great Gatsby but has tried to hide it. Sally jokingly refers to him as a "counterfeit F. Scott Fitzgerald who comes stumbling out to movieland" (p. 271). She also says that since they first went out they've been saying good-bye because they knew they would be together such a short time.

It is, of course, a symbolic comment. Yates knew he would be in Hollywood only a short time. A short, unhappy time.

* * *

That consistency in character dissatisfaction — coupled with the repetition of details, such as locales and ages and relationships — is what makes these stories and novels a unified work reflecting, in the tradition of all major writers, a worldview, a way of looking at life that helps explain it, that helps the reader better understand his own experiences, and that, despite what at times seems to be a sense of unrelieved depression, enriches the reader. These stories can disturb readers because they tell them things about themselves they do not want to know (that, for example, their basic dishonesty is a major cause of their loneliness), but they enlighten as well, helping readers to understand that their experiences are not unique, that others suffer the same way, that loneliness and dishonesty and dissatisfaction are universal experiences. The stories of *Eleven Kinds of Loneliness* paint the picture more bleakly than do the seven in *Liars in Love*, but both collections are convincingly realistic, and that is what is both disturbing and appealing in these writings.

9

The Artist Ages:
Young Hearts Crying

Yates's structural innovations in *A Good School* went unnoticed among critics, as did the fact that *A Special Providence* was largely a war novel. If *A Special Providence* had been seen as a highly accurate accounting of a typical wartime experience Yates might today be regularly compared to Norman Mailer or Stephen Crane or Thomas Boyd. And if the innovations of *A Good School* in its structure had been accompanied by even the slightest change in the author's stylistic approach, it might today be regularly compared to some of the works of James Joyce or William Faulkner or William Styron. Or Yates's friend Kurt Vonnegut. But so it goes.

Understandably, Yates by now was becoming increasingly aware of his role as an artist, and it was an awareness that did not always make him comfortable. But, as might be expected, it was an awareness that would work its way into a novel.

This is an area in which Yates's career differs markedly from what is, accurately or inaccurately, seen as the norm for the writer. First novels seem so often to be about being a first novelist. Or sometimes they're confessional, revealing the least appealing personality traits of the protagonist. Such books don't always work their way into print, but some writers seem to have to write them before they can go on to writing about other things. Yates did not get the confessional something out of his system until his third novel (fourth book)—*Disturbing the Peace*—and he did not get around to writing about being an artist until his sixth novel (eighth book). The difference between when Yates and other novelists write about being an artist, just as the difference between when Yates and other writers write about love or war or loneliness or any other subject they have selected is that Yates gets it right.

9. The Artist Ages

Unlike Yates's earlier works, *Young Hearts Crying* directly deals with the role of the artist, but like his other works it deals also with honesty. Many of the characters in this novel become artists, or seek to become artists, because they are dishonest, seeing artists as superior and hoping to share in that superiority. There is another tie between this and Yates's other works, and that should make it particularly appealing to those who admired those other works. Many of the characters in this novel and many of the situations in which they find themselves seem to be mirror reversals of what happened elsewhere. Lucy Blaine Davenport knows she is not an actress, unlike April Wheeler in *Revolutionary Road*, who thought she should be. Lucy has money and offers her husband, Michael, a chance to travel, think, and have time to write, the very things that April Wheeler could not give to her husband, Frank. And Michael Davenport recognizes the stability and opportunity for happiness that marriage offers, unlike Emily Grimes in *The Easter Parade*, who lived a life of constant unhappiness at least partly because she came to that realization far too late.

The structure of *Young Hearts Crying* has one strong similarity to and one strong contrast to *A Special Providence*: both have three clearly defined sections, including a middle one that could with a little rewriting stand as a separate story, but those parts interlock far more thoroughly in *Young Hearts Crying*. Part 1 is about the marriage of Michael and Lucy Davenport and how that marriage breaks up. Part 2 is about Lucy's attempts to cope with divorce and raise a daughter. Part 3 is about Michael's attempts to cope with divorce and his second marriage and the breakup of that second marriage. Each part has so many unavoidable references to the other two, however, that the reader is unlikely to get the feeling — as he might with *A Special Providence* — that the middle section not only can but should stand alone.

Michael Davenport has the severe drinking problem that will remind readers of John Wilder in *Disturbing the Peace*, and both spend time in Bellevue as a result. Each of these novels also has an important secondary character who is a writer. In *Disturbing the Peace* Chester Pratt is an "important writer," and Carl Traynor in *Young Hearts Crying* writes a novel that gets excellent reviews.

There are two notable sections that have no parallels, however, in any other work by Yates, although both are supported by themes that frequently recur elsewhere, and these two pieces lend a distinctive air to the novel. They, along with the focus on the role of the artist, prevent *Young Hearts Crying* from being a mere restatement of earlier works. The first, in which characters openly discuss the Vietnam War, is as close as Yates came to making a political statement, and the second, in which the father — Michael — rescues his daughter from some terrible, even humiliating, mistakes she has made is about as close as Yates comes to portraying a character as heroic.

In the Vietnam discussion scene, Davenport, who is teaching at a college in Kansas, and his second wife, Sarah, hold a faculty party out of a sense of obligation: they have been invited to other parties, where there are anti-war posters and upside-down flags. Michael says, "I don't think I'd mind these parties so much if the people weren't all so busy being political" (p. 280).[1] Just before his own party he gets a call from Terry Ryan, a young waiter he knew in New York, who is passing through town on his way to Vietnam. Mike invites Terry to the party, and at the party Grace Howard, wife of the English Department chairman, asks Terry, "Why do you want to kill people?" (p. 285). Terry says, "Oh, come on lady, I never killed anybody in my life" (p. 285). The next day Mike and Sarah take Terry to the airport and Yates refers to "a war that nobody would ever understand" (p. 286). The department chair later calls to say Terry was rude to Grace, and Mike apologizes with "an edge of scorn" (p. 287) and hangs up. It is a section that can stand as a separate short story (and was in fact published as one in *Esquire*) and can be read as another example of a character — Grace Howard — hurting someone else with her dishonesty, since her cruel remark to Terry clearly results from a trendy opposition to the war rather than from any moral outrage. The sense of a political statement comes in Yates's insistence that the soldier not be blamed for the war. While that statement comes close to being unique in Yates, it is supported elsewhere by a repeatedly expressed sympathy for the soldier, which is perhaps most clearly stated in "Jody Rolled the Bones," "The B.A.R. Man," and *A Special Providence*.

A little later Michael gets a call from his 19-year-old daughter by his first marriage, Laura, and she sounds as if life is terrible. In fact, for her, it is. She is using drugs, having indiscriminate sex, and living in a dumpy room in a run-down part of San Francisco. Michael immediately gets on a plane, goes to San Francisco, and takes his daughter to a decent

9. The Artist Ages

hotel. Lying in bed, he quietly recites a poem he wrote decades earlier, "Coming Clean." He is a poet and playwright, and this poem is the best piece of writing he has ever done. On the flight back to Kansas, Laura says she might be pregnant and does not who the father is and Michael says he can arrange for an abortion (which will not be necessary, since she turns out to not be pregnant). Laura has already flunked out of a prestigious New England college, and her life, as she approaches adulthood, has already reached the depths that her father's did (and that John Wilder's did in *Disturbing the Peace*) when he was much older. Michael at one point cries and says he is "proud" (p. 298) of helping Laura escape from San Francisco. But his tears are as much caused by his pride in "Coming Clean," and Laura's full recovery from the depths of depression and misery will come later largely with the sympathy and understanding of Sarah, Michael's second wife. He is, nevertheless, still justified in his pride in helping Laura. When his daughter needed him, he went, and he went immediately. There is not a single other parent in all of Yates's writing who performs a similar act.

A different type of positive emotion between father and child is expressed later when Michael is watching his infant son by his second marriage, Jimmy, play in the yard:

> He liked to watch his son toddle through sunlight and shade as earnestly as if he were discovering the world. Well, you're getting the general idea, little buddy, he wanted to say. Part of it's bright and part of it's dark, and those big things over there are trees, and there's nothing here that can ever hurt you. All you have to remember is not to go beyond the edges of it, because everything is slippery rocks and mud and brambles out there, and you might see a snake and it might scare the shit out of you [p. 320].

Laura, and Michael and Lucy and Sarah, and just about every major character in every Yates novel and short story has gone beyond the edges and tried to walk on the slippery rocks, and they have all seen their snakes and they have all had the shit scared out of them.

The mud and the brambles can be found in the world of art. There is something dirty and prickly about the way many of the artists — and nearly everyone in the novel is an artist of one type or another — practice their arts. There are poets and playwrights and painters and actors here, and nearly all of them are in one way or another pretentious. Artists — particularly the mother who is the sculptor in *A Special Providence* and

"Oh, Joseph, I'm So Tired"—appear elsewhere in Yates's writings, but only this novel is *about* art and artists. They are for the most part unappealing and they use their art to justify the pain they cause to others: they are the mud and the brambles. Paul Maitland is a painter who looks down on fellow painter Tom Nelson, deriding him as a mere illustrator, largely because Nelson is more successful. Bill Brock is writing "a working class novel" (p. 14), and he disparages Maitland's "great tragic artist horseshit" (p. 19). Ben Duane is an almost-has-been actor who was blacklisted because of an unspecified run-in with the McCarthy committee in the 1950s and is reduced to being a gardener (although he will make a comeback in a television series that sounds very much like *The Waltons*). Jack Halloran, the director of a summer theater group, has a brief affair with the divorced Lucy and then dumps her for an attractive, younger actress. Maitland wanted Nelson's success but did not get it. Ben Duane wanted an uninterrupted acting career but did not get it. Lucy wanted Jack or some other artistic man but did not get him, not on a permanent basis. At one point Michael tells Lucy, "We spent our whole lives yearning. Isn't that the God damndest thing?" (p. 126). All Yates's characters want to be somebody else; all yearn for a different life. That is what attracts them to art. Lucy at one point accuses Jack of having "a crafty little talent for inflicting senseless pain" (p. 148), which in fact seems to be the major talent of many of the artists in the novel. Lucy, better than any other character in the novel, understands the limitations of the talents of these artists. She watches young actors leaving at a train station: "...boys and girls from far and wide with their cheap hand luggage and their army duffel bags, brave entertainers who might travel for years before it occurred to them, or to most of them, that they weren't going anywhere" (p. 145). Lucy herself traveled for years before realizing she was not going anywhere artistically. She painted pictures and wrote stories and acted in a play (*A Streetcar Named Desire*). She is not very good at anything artistic. Her failures at art and the unkindness she encounters from artists justified a toast she offers on the closing page of the novel when she briefly gets together with Michael for a drink: "Fuck art" (p. 345).

There are, however, at least two artists in the book who are neither particularly cruel nor lacking in talent. Tom Nelson is successful precisely because he is not pretentious as an artist, being willing to work primarily

9. The Artist Ages

in watercolors, a medium sometimes scorned by other painters (although he is in some other ways at least mildly pretentious, such as in wearing military clothing even though he is not a veteran). And Michael Davenport has written one very good poem, "Coming Clean," and some other pretty good stuff. Carl Traynor, the novelist with whom Lucy will have an affair, may also be placed in this group, but he does make one needlessly cruel remark to Lucy to cover his hurt: when she offers him $6,000 as a gift to get over some financial difficulties, he sarcastically tells her to write "for services rendered" (p. 200) on the check.

The novel ends when Michael, leaving his final meeting with Lucy, his first wife, and uncertain if his second wife, Sarah, will ever join him in Boston, walks to his hotel alone: "Now that he was older, and now that he was home, it might not even matter how the story turned out in the end" (p. 347), which is the final line in the book. Thus, typical of Yates's later novels and short stories, *Young Hearts Crying* closes with at least a hint of acceptance, leaving open a definite possibility that Michael Davenport and Lucy will avoid much of the unhappiness that dominated their lives when they were younger. Being young had made their hearts cry, but as they matured they became more accepting of who they were. The desire to be artists made many of the characters in the novel pretentious and that contributed not only to their own unhappiness but to that of those close to them. They increase their chances for happiness when they do three things: accept work as redeeming, "fuck art," and rid themselves of pretensions.

* * *

Young Hearts Crying represents Yates's clearest statement on the possibilities of redemption. Its closing pages come as close as anything he has written to transforming a worldview into a philosophic statement. Yet the reader is unlikely to come away from the novel with the sense that he has been subjected to a message (the Vietnam War scene, of course, being an exception). The overriding tone is one of seeing the world the way it is and using the writer's craft to as clearly as possible explain to the reader what has been seen. Yates, in that sense, has imposed upon himself a double task, both parts of which continually separate him from other late twentieth-century American writers. He is never interested in either seeing the world the way he wants it to be, as the writers of emotional escapism do, or creating other worlds into which the reader can escape, as writers of adventure escapism do. And he will not allow the telling of his story to get in the way of the story — as those writers who emphasize technique do.

The Critic

Young Hearts Crying, like all of Yates's books, was admired by some critics and disliked by others. Yates, like all writers well enough known to have their books regularly reviewed, had come to accept mixed reactions to his work. But one critic's reaction to the novel angered and saddened Yates so much that it created a crisis of confidence for him. It was written by Anatole Broyard and appeared in *The New York Times Book Review* on Sunday, October 28, 1984.

To understand fully why Yates was so hurt by the review, some background to his relationship with Broyard is helpful. Yates and Broyard met when they both taught at the New School in New York in the late fifties (*A Tragic Honesty*, p. 197), and Yates admired Broyard's writing enough to overlook flaws in his personality; some people considered him mean, especially to woman (*A Tragic Honesty*, pp. 201–202). For example, Broyard, who had a reputation for bedding many women, often told a story about one woman whose "ass ... exploded like an inflatable raft" when she took off her girdle (*A Tragic Honesty*, p. 221). After Broyard married (for the second time) in the early sixties and became a full-time book reviewer for *The New York Times*, Yates seldom saw him (*A Tragic Honesty*, p. 262). Yates, however, continued to praise Broyard's writing (*A Tragic Honesty*, p. 414).

But Broyard, one of the best-known literary critics in the country — and since he wrote for the daily *New York Times* one of the most influential — was harsh in his evaluation of Yates's books. Broyard wrote a negative review of *Disturbing the Peace*,[2] saying among other things that John Wilder's continuous drunkenness is "about as interesting as having someone throw up on you."[3] The general tone of the review is captured in its first paragraph: "If I understand him, Richard Yates is saying, through the medium of his hero, John Wilder, that life in America is enough to drive a man to drink, or crazy, or both."[4] Broyard's evaluation of *The Easter Parade*,⁵ is as harsh: he denounces the "pointless incongruity" of the characters and says the characters "bow down to the imperative not of life, but of the author's sense of craftsmanship."⁶ He is at points nitpicky; when Walter Grimes tells his daughters, Emily and Sarah, that his job on a newspaper is not much to be proud of and that "I'm only a copy-desk man" (*The Easter Parade*, p. 7), Broyard questions whether any "normal father" would say that to his daughters; he asks rhetorically, "...does he say it because the author enjoys its dying fall?"⁷ Broyard in both reviews goes beyond criticizing the novels being reviewed and expands his critique to slam Yates's craft, his writing style in general, and his worldview.

Because of his friendship with Broyard, Yates — who always remained loyal to his friends and assumed his friends would remain loyal to him — was forgiving of those two reviews, choosing to see them as expressions of honest, if unnecessarily harsh, opinion. Since book reviewers and writers often end up at the same parties or share acquaintances, it's not unusual for them to become friends, and having to review a book written by someone you know is not uncommon. There are no widely accepted protocols on how to handle such assignments, but there certainly seems to be a trend for reviewers to avoid being unkind to friends.⁸ If Broyard felt he could not honestly say something positive about Yates's novels, he could have not reviewed them or could have softened his opinions with an apologetic phrase (i.e., "It hurts me to say this about the writing of a man I know and like..."). Instead, as with his unkind comments about women he slept with, he seemed to assume that the closeness of the relationship endowed him with an entitlement for mean-spiritedness.

But nothing in the reviews of *Disturbing the Peace* or *The Easter Parade* could have prepared Yates for Broyard's onslaught in his review of *Young Hearts Crying*.⁹ First, it appeared not in the daily *New York Times*, where most of Broyard's reviews were published, but in the Sunday book review section, which meant it had a larger readership and a longer shelf life in libraries.¹⁰ And, since Broyard wrote for the daily, he could have more easily avoided writing any review for the Sunday section. Second, most of the review concerned not the novel under review but Yates's full body of work and questioned the widespread praise, especially from other writers, that Yates enjoyed. Yates's characters, Broyard wrote, are not so much realistic as they "are designed to be defeated or humiliated in carefully crafted scenes."[11] He summarizes them as "literary cannon fodder."[12] As for the clean, precise style that many readers admire in Yates's writing, Broyard writes: "So far as style is concerned, there doesn't seem to be any,"[13] although he does concede that "perhaps this is by design, an emblem of Mr. Yates's realism, his refusal to embellish or distort his characters with authorial eloquence."[14] When he finally gets around to discussing *Young Hearts Crying*, he says it "fails for the most fundamental of reasons: because Michael Davenport is not an interesting or appealing man. He is so self-pitying that there is no room for our pity.... Michael is sentimental without being loving and vain without being proud."[15] Then he returns to a point that again condemns the writer's style: "As his second wife, Sarah, says, he lets his rhetoric run away with him — and it runs away with the book as well. If it were better rhetoric, that might help, but it isn't."[16] Broyard, of course, had to be very conscious of the fact that Michael Davenport is a highly autobiographical character and that condemning him as unloving, vain, and guilty of bad rhetoric was the same as accusing Yates of the same sins.

The review angered many of Yates's friends and admirers. Shortly after it was published, Yates and Dan Wakefield, drinking heavily together in the Crossroads bar in Boston, made a plan to go to New York to beat up Broyard (*A Tragic Honesty*, pp. 535–538). Only getting sober prevented them from carrying out the plan. Kurt Vonnegut wrote a letter to *The New York Times* "saying that Broyard should be fired"[17] because of the review. He told his friend Loree Rackstraw that he had called Yates about the review and Yates had told him "he hadn't been much bothered by the review."[18] But Vonnegut didn't believe his friend. "He was trying with some success not to be paranoid any more, and I warned him that he was overdoing it."[19] *The Times* published a letter from a Yates admirer in Texas, a man named Terrence Ross, who noted with deliberate irony that just as Yates was reestablishing his reputation as a major writer, Broyard's article appeared: "It is disheartening that this long overdue success has brought in the sharks."[20] Sam Lawrence, Yates's publisher, wrote to Yates in 1990, after Broyard died, that "Anatole died as he lived, with a hatchet in his hand" (*A Tragic Honesty*, p. 537).

Many of Yates's friends thought Broyard was jealous of Yates's reputation as a major writer, something Broyard had sought for himself. In

9. The Artist Ages

fact, what little bit of fame Broyard achieved (since book reviewers are known to nearly no one other than writers) came after he died, when it was revealed that he had been a black man who, in the phrase of the time, "passed for white." Some of his friends knew he was a light-skinned black man and his first wife (who was black) and his second (who was white) knew it, but many of his friends, many of his co-workers at *The Times*, and general acquaintances did not, and he never made an attempt to explain his background to people who clearly didn't understand it. Broyard died in 1990, but the full details of his background were first revealed by African-American writer Henry Louis Gates, first in an article in *The New Yorker* and later as a chapter in a book, *Thirteen Ways of Looking at a Black Man*, published in 1997. Since the facts of Broyard's race were not generally known until almost five years after Yates died, it's unlikely Yates knew his onetime friend and eventual attacker was African-American.

10

Hope for the Youngest: *Cold Spring Harbor*

There is much in *Cold Spring Harbor* that will remind readers of the full body of Yates's work. Evan Shepard, the protagonist, is at least as good looking and attractive to girls as is Tony Wilson, who marries Sarah Grimes in *The Easter Parade*. Phil, Evan's young brother-in-law, attends a private school in New England and experiences an awakening of his sexual nature, like William Grove in *A Good School*. And Gloria, Phil's mother, has the same lack of stability as all the mothers in Yates's stories. Those and other recurring themes — family strife, divorced parents, social pretensions — re-enforce the impression that Yates's collected writings form a mosaic, a larger picture made from smaller, shining pieces. Yet just as all of Yates's other novels and short stories are complete in themselves, so, too, is *Cold Spring Harbor*. It has a uniqueness resulting primarily from the North Shore Long Island town from which it gets its title. Just as Yates in *A Good School* made Dorset Academy a non-living character that shapes and is shaped by the personalities of those who attend and work there, so, too, has he made this community beyond the suburbs of New York City imbue those who live in it with longings and assumptions and opportunities for success and failure. And Evan Shepard is not Tony Wilson, Phil Drake is not William Grove, and Gloria, the mother in this novel, is not Pookie, the mother in *The Easter Parade*, or Alice Prentice, the mother in *A Special Providence*. Despite recurring themes and repeated circumstances, Yates here, as in all his writings, creates new and fresh characters, men and women, boys and girls, who despite the typical blandness of their lives become interesting. They become interesting for the same reason a man's neighbors and classmates and co-workers become interesting to him. Not because he chooses that they be, but because he gets to know them so well.

10. Hope for the Youngest

By the time Evan Shepard is 17 in 1935 he has hit a boy in the head with a brick, been arrested for disorderly conduct, and broken into a hardware store. He gets pretty Mary Donovan pregnant. They get married, and he gets a dead-end job in a factory as a machinist. He is clearly making a mess of his life and is extremely unhappy. He has fallen in love with cars, liking to repair and drive them, and that seems to be his one acceptable quality. Even his extraordinary good looks, which make him so appealing to so many girls, seem more a curse than a blessing: if he had not been so good looking he would not have been attractive to Mary and she would never have become pregnant and he might have been able to attend, as he wanted to, engineering school, although readers and other characters will quickly realize that, among his other problems, he is not very bright. There are some clear similarities between Evan and Herman Melville's Billy Budd: both suffer as a result of their good looks; but Billy is clearly a likable lad, and Evan will draw no reader's sympathy. Billy is a victim, Evan little more than a punk kid.[1]

Evan's father, Charles, a retired army captain, tells his son, "Sometimes things do get better on their own accord" (p. 13),[2] just as he had earlier thought in his frustrations over the man his son was growing into, "Maybe all you could ever do, beyond suffering, was wait and see what might be going to happen next" (p. 7). A big part of Evan's problems is that despite his strong sense of independence he is too weak to control his own life and is controlled instead by haphazardness and circumstance. Just as he never planned that Mary become pregnant or that he marry her or, for that matter, that they get divorced, as they will just a year and half after the wedding. He and his father are driving in lower Manhattan when their car breaks down and they go to a nearby apartment to ask to use the telephone to call a mechanic. It is in that apartment, in that chance meeting, that they encounter first Gloria Drake and then Gloria's children, 15-year-old Phil and his older sister, Rachel, whose expression lets Evan know she thinks he is good looking: "There might still be times in Evan Shepard's life when he was afraid he wouldn't amount to much, but he always knew what he looked like, and he knew it gave him a decided advantage with girls" (p. 24). Evan's attention makes Rachel feel pretty, as if she were in a movie.

Rachel, in fact, like so many other characters in Yates's novels and short stories, has learned too well from movies how to act and what to expect. Later, about halfway through the novel, when Gloria, Phil, and Rachel go to a movie together, Yates gives a clear sense of the appeal movies held for those who, like Rachel, like perhaps everyone, lead incomplete lives, lives short on love or hope or something:

> The movies were wonderful because they took you out of yourself, and at the same time they gave you a sense of being whole. Things of the world might serve to remind you at every turn that your life was snarled and perilously incomplete, that terror would never be far from possession of your heart, but those perceptions would nearly always vanish, if only for a little while, in the cool and nicely scented darkness of any movie house, anywhere [p. 88].

But whatever benefits movies offer are short lived; when Phil and a friend still later go to a movie mostly because there is not much else to do, "they both seemed to know it would only leave them feeling jaded and edgy afterwards, when they came out into the sun again, and it did" (p. 100). The problem is, as a secondary character about to go into the army, Aaron, will note still later (and this is a point that comes up over and over in Yates's stories, although only in *A Special Providence* does it get as much attention as it does here), "the movies don't even pretend to show the truth about the army and war, any more than they ever show the truth about love" (p. 136). Movies tell lies about life, and those who, like poor Rachel, learn to love by watching movies are doomed to live a lie. She will think Evan's extraordinary good looks are enough, but she will, despite her denials that it is happening to her, live a life of great unhappiness. Her husband will cheat on her, hit her, and insult her beyond decency (he will, among other things, deride her as being "soft as shit" [p. 179]). All of his negative qualities are there for anyone to see, and most important for Rachel to see, but she is blind to them because love, true love, in the movies overcomes all problems. Real life, of course, is different.

Rachel's mother, meanwhile, has just as much difficulty coping with real life as her daughter, but for a different reason: she is not mentally stable. She sees the world not as it is but as she wants it to be. She willingly fails to make the distinction between an army captain and a navy captain, a point that will embarrass Charles Shepard, Evan's father. He has retired as a captain in the army, a low rank for a career man, but Gloria insists on referring to him by that title because she has heard it applied with esteem to retired navy captains.[3] She wants her daughter

10. Hope for the Youngest

married in the Episcopal Church because "everybody knew it was the only aristocratic faith in America" (p. 47). And she thinks Charles, who has little money, is "representative" of the "old money" (p. 43) that she associates with Cold Spring Harbor. Near the end of the novel she will come close to a nervous breakdown when her ex-husband, Curtis, and the man she has a crush on, Charles Shepard, are together in the hospital visiting Rachel, who has just given birth: she blames Rachel and Evan's decision to move out of the house on Curtis, who has no involvement in the affair, and calls him a "coward" and "swine" (p. 162). Rachel, Curtis, Charles, and Evan will all refer to Gloria as disturbed or crazy or mentally ill. Her problems are clear to everyone but herself. When Curtis and Charles physically remove her from the hospital to protect Rachel, she goes home and locks herself in her bedroom for two weeks, coming out only when other people are not around. Not until Rachel goes to her room and asks her to come out does she, and then she pretends that nothing unusual has happened.

Gloria is not the only person who lies to herself in the novel. Grace, Charles's wife, speaks of herself as housebound because of an unspecified illness. She has had two nervous breakdowns, but her real "illness" is that she drinks too much. When a doctor suggests to Charles that Grace undergo "a course of psychotherapy" (p. 6), he responds with a Yatesian comment about the doctor's profession: "...I have no confidence in any word beginning with 'psych.' I don't think you people know what you're doing in that funny, shifty field, and I don't think you ever will"(p. 6). (Michael Davenport says something very similar in *Young Hearts Crying*.) And Harriet Talmadge, the one rich person in the town that is supposedly filled with rich people and who makes a brief appearance in the novel, will not admit to herself that she understands some things she does not want to understand, such as the fact that her daughter Jane has made as much of a mess of her life as Evan Shepard is making of his (which allows the reader to avoid the assumption that Evan's problems are classrelated):

> Harriet had long been resigned to knowing there were many things she would never understand.... She would die without hope of finding any explanation of her daughter's life. Three stunted, broken marriages, an only child left here as an infant for Harriet herself to raise, and now this bewildering parade of "friends"—what kind of life was that, dear God, for a girl who'd started out with every advantage?

> ... it was probably a blessing, in a way, that John hadn't lived to see the woman his daughter had become. He wouldn't have known what to make of her either, if only because she wasn't even pretty any more. She was too thin and sharp-faced and sarcastic as she nestled here with Warren Cox — and Warren Cox, God knew, was no prize; a commercial person, a sales person, the kind of man who said things like "X number of dollars" [pp. 94–95].

Harriet Talmadge understands too well what type of person her daughter has become, but her sense of social position will not allow her to use the words others, less refined or more honest — pick either one — would use. Many words could accurately explain the daughter, but none of them are appropriate for Mrs. Talmadge.

Yates's quick description of two very minor characters, Jane and her friend Warren, is, by the way, an excellent example of the Yates ability to select the few details that do the most work. Some critics have referred to Yates as painting with broad brushstrokes because of what they see as a scarcity of details, but that misses the point. He refuses to clutter his stories with details that do not reveal something significant about the characters. Here, in fewer than 150 words, he sums up not only two lives with a sense of completeness but also a third character's evaluation of those lives, and it is all done as convincingly as it is economically.[4]

The one person, among those given enough space to qualify as major characters, who is likely to appeal to readers is Phil, Rachel's younger brother. Rachel herself engages a reader's sympathy because she is so easy to feel sorry for, but she is not likely to be terribly appealing to most readers simply because she allows so many bad things to happen to her. A reader can almost agree, with reluctance of course, when Evan accuses her of being "soft as shit" (p. 179). Phil is 16 in the summer of 1942, the time during which most of the novel takes place, and it is an age of sexual awakening and a time to worry about having to soon go off to war. It is a confusing age, and one of the strengths of Yates's economical selection of detail is that he can focus on those seemingly minor points that clarify that confusion. When 14-year-old Gerard "Flash" Ferris, the grandson of the rich Harriet Talmadge and a fellow student at the private Irving School, tries to befriend him, Phil thinks of him as "one of the more dismal social outcasts" (p. 89) at Irving, someone to be avoided. When Phil watches a chauffeur at Mrs. Talmadge's home flirt with a maid, he realizes that "if he didn't start finding out a few things about

10. Hope for the Youngest

girls, soon, he was going to go crazy" (p. 99). (One of the many points that will prevent *Cold Spring Harbor* from degenerating into the false sentimentality of so many coming-of-age movies and novels is that at its close Phil Drake will still be a virgin.) And when Phil, who when he was younger "had failed and failed at learning how not to behave like a jerk" (p. 69), commits a shameful but minor act — he has "peeked and seen his sister locked in copulation with Evan" (p. 178) — he reacts with a combination of confusion and regret that will haunt him for a long time: "He knew it was possible for shame to be nursed and doctored like an illness ... but that didn't mean there'd be any way to keep from knowing it was there" (p. 178).

Phil differs from the other main characters in *Cold Spring Harbor* precisely because he can feel shame for his sin. When Evan slaps Rachel and decides to drive across America with his first wife, Mary, he realizes that on that drive there would be "persistent thoughts of Rachel and the baby ... but he knew they'd be obliged, eventually, to recede into the past. They would have to yield the right of way" (p. 182). The emotion that's clearly missing, and the one that would give him a sense of decency, is shame, and Rachel lies to herself about what has happened. She remains convinced that Evan will come back and is willing to accept him back when he clearly will not return and when she clearly should be unwilling to forgive him. And the last image of Gloria comes when Rachel hears her: "an old, slow, defeated person coming upstairs" (p. 182). She has not realized, will never realize, any more than Alice Prentice in *A Special Providence* or Pookie in *The Easter Parade*, that she is doomed to a life of unhappiness not because of her affinity with the old money of Cold Spring Harbor but rather because she is mentally disturbed. Rachel, in this closing scene, plans to tell her mother she is sorry for the way things turned out, convinced that will solve the immediate problems: "the Drakes had always found their own kind of renewal in tearful apologies and expressions of love" (p. 182). All four of these main characters harbor deep within themselves a great reservoir of unhappiness, and it is during the summer of 1942 that that unhappiness springs up and reveals a cold truth: only Phil has the capability of being redeemed, for only Phil has the shame that can save him, that can protect him from the type of lies that Rachel nurtures (just as in the next-to-last paragraph of the book she breast-feeds her infant son), from accepting the self-defeating pretensions that Gloria clings to, and from sliding into the self-serving punk-arrogance that dominates Evan's personality. The cold that springs from their harbor of unhappiness seems deserved by Evan Shepard, unfair but inevitable for Gloria and poor Rachel, and avoidable — and here, once again, a Yates novel is ending with a trickle of hope — for Phil. He alone in this unhappy family has the capability for feeling the shame that might save him.

Uncertain Times

I met with Richard Yates several times over three days in Boston in mid-September 1986, shortly after the publication of *Cold Spring Harbor*. He told me then something he had told me two years earlier, that his next book most probably would be about a speechwriter for Bobby Kennedy. I remember three distinct points Yates made in 1986: (1) he had not yet made a final decision that the Kennedy book would actually be his next book, although he had, in fact, already done some work on it; (2) he suspected that if he did write and publish a Kennedy book some readers, and no doubt some critics, would think he was in some way using or sensationalizing his brief ties to the Kennedys, and that didn't bother him, and (3) he wanted to make certain that he was not using or sensationalizing those ties. What others thought about the project, he said, wasn't very important, but what he thought was. But, he was convinced, he could write a book about a Kennedy speechwriter that was not exploitative or sensationalistic. He could, he told me, make certain he was writing a book designed to be a good book rather than one designed simply to attract readers. But he was aware that other writers had failed in the same attempt. He didn't mention the names of other writers, and I didn't ask.

He also told me the book would involve characters who had appeared in some of his earlier writings. Bill Grove, he said, was the most likely candidate to be the speechwriter, since in *A Good School he* had shown a desire to be a writer. But Yates wasn't certain what the plot would be, and that, more than the characters, more than the possibility somebody might see the book as exploitative, caused whatever hesitation he brought to the project.

10. Hope for the Youngest

Six years later he was dead and the novel was incomplete. There are about 400 pages of manuscript and notes for the novel, which he called *Uncertain Times*, in the Richard Yates archives at the Boston University library, but Seymour Lawrence, his publisher, who died about a year after Yates did, said at the time of Yates's death that it was not publishable. *Esquire* magazine had agreed to publish excerpts from the novel, but when Yates died those plans were dropped. I believe the manuscript is salvageable, but neither Yates's literary executor, his daughter Monica, nor any publisher has publicly expressed an interest in having it worked into publishable shape.

There are three possibilities:

1. Give the manuscript to a trusted editor and have him or her edit it as closely as possible to the form Yates intended, including the notes he made for revisions and not-yet-written parts. This is what Edmund Wilson did for F. Scott Fitzgerald's last and unfinished novel, *The Last Tycoon*. Fitzgerald died in 1940, and Wilson's edition appeared in 1941.[5]

2. Hire a trusted writer to complete the novel. This happened when the estate of Raymond Chandler hired Robert B. Parker to complete *Poodle Springs*, which was incomplete at the time of Chandler's death in 1959. The completed novel was published in 1989. The first four chapters of the published novel are exactly as Chandler wrote them; the rest is entirely by Parker.

3. Have an editor and/or a writer rework what Yates wrote into a coherent and complete novel. This happened with Ernest Hemingway's *The Garden of Eden*, which was incomplete at the time of Hemingway's death in 1961; the novel appeared in 1986. Tom Jenks, who had been an editor at *Esquire*, edited the manuscript, and his editing has been highly and widely criticized.[6]

The Chandler/Parker method probably works best when little of the manuscript is written, which is not the case with *Uncertain Times*. It's difficult to tell where Chandler was headed with *Poodle Springs*, and Parker was, in effect, given carte blanche to write what he wanted to follow Chandler's four opening chapters. Yates wrote what would probably be half or more of a novel, with notes indicating a clear sense of direction. The Fitzgerald/Wilson approach is more for scholars than readers. It's not a complete story and the last third or so of the book is wholly unsatisfying. It's not what Fitzgerald intended and Wilson makes no pretense that it is.

The Hemingway/Jenks method is, unfortunately, discredited in the minds of some readers, but that doesn't mean that the right writer or right editor couldn't do a better job with *Uncertain Times* than Jenks did with *The Garden of Eden*. What is known is that Yates wanted the book to be published. And it is publishable.

* * *

Blake Bailey's biography fills in what happened between when Yates told me he was considering working on the novel and his death six years later:

Yates had been working on the book for six years when he died (*A Tragic Honesty*, p. 3).[7] After Yates died, a friend found the manuscript in the freezer in his apartment and on the last page was written the word "END" (p. 5). A 1984 note Yates sent to Sam Lawrence says he had been "collecting notes and sketches" for several years for a novel based on the time he was a speechwriter for Bobby Kennedy, "with Bobby serving as one of the characters and even Jack having a walk-on part. Wendy Sears will be prominently featured, as will a haggard fellow who begrudges every hour spent at speechwriting because it's denying him his life's work" (p. 528). Wendy Sears was a girlfriend of Yates while he lived in Washington. The date here, of course, indicates that Yates was already making notes for several years when he told me in 1986 that he had not yet begun writing the book. That could simply mean he made a distinction between making notes for the novel and writing the novel. More likely, it meant he retained doubts at least as late of 1986 about whether he really wanted to write the novel. In 1989, Sam Lawrence, now at Houghton Mifflin, offered Yates a two-book contract that would include publication of *Uncertain Times* (p. 573). When Yates died in 1992, Lawrence told *The New York Times* that the manuscript was not in "publishable form."[8] Yates's daughter Monica, according to Bailey, said "some foolish person ... read it and said it wasn't any good," and Yates gave up on the manuscript (p. 594). Bailey does not indicate who the foolish person was. Yates's last note on the manuscript is dated August 28, 1992. He died November 7.

10. Hope for the Youngest

* * *

Bailey also provides some details about Yates's difficulty in writing the novel. The manuscript was supposed to be delivered to Lawrence in November 1987 (pp. 553–554), which was only a little more than a year after Yates indicated to me he was still uncertain that he wanted to write the book. It's possible that Yates was uncertain that he had the energy to complete the manuscript that quickly. But he had written and published six books in the 11 previous years (1975–1986). Another book by late 1987 would probably not have seemed unreasonable to him at the time. But I remember something he told me in 1970, when I was a graduate student at DePauw University in Greencastle, Indiana, and my advisor, Tom Emery, a former student of Yates at Iowa, invited him to campus. At a faculty party to which I was invited, I asked him why so much time passed between the publication of his second book (*Eleven Kinds of Loneliness*) in 1962 and his third (*A Special Providence*) in 1969. The question was a follow-up to a comment he had made in a creative writing class earlier in the day, namely that while writing too fast tended to damage writing, stretching out the time a writer took to write something did not automatically make it better. His answer was that nothing in the book had anything to do with the delay. What was outside the book, of course, was a combination of heavy drinking, other jobs (in Hollywood and Washington), and marital strife. I didn't know the details then, but I had a general sense of what he was talking about. Life gets in the way of writing.

By 1986 and 1987, the drinking was still a problem, but he didn't have the distraction of other jobs, other than occasional teaching. And his personal life was certainly no more disorderly, less so, than at any other point in his life. I believe what caused the delays in writing *Uncertain Times* had more to do with the subject than anything else. By 1987 he had had nearly two and a half decades to write a novel based on his experiences as a speechwriter for Bobby Kennedy. If he was determined to do it, he would have done it earlier.

Bailey believes one contributing factor to Yates's inability to complete the novel was that he was "intimidated" by librarians and at least once asked a friend to research something in a Boston library for him so he wouldn't have to go to the library. The intimidation was evidently based on the way librarians looked at him because of his wheezing and appearance (p. 569). In the last year of his life, Yates would sometimes ask friends their opinion of *Uncertain Times*, something he never did with earlier books, "proof of just how doubtful he'd become" (p. 590). Bailey believes Yates could not have turned *Uncertain Times* into a good book even if his health was better because he thinks Yates "couldn't quite determine the *meaning* of Grove's disaffection with public service, and was all too aware that in writing more and more about himself (that is, Grove), he was holding nobody's interest but his own" (pp. 598–599).

I almost agree. I base the "almost" on the doubts Yates expressed to me about the book in 1986. I think he was worried that a book about Bobby Kennedy, about any Kennedy, would be seen as deliberately exploitative and he didn't want to be accused of that. In trying to focus on Grove, he was in reality trying to write a book in which the reader would not focus on a Kennedy. Evaluating Yates's failure to complete *Uncertain Times* should not be separated from the negative view his protagonist, John Wilder, in *Disturbing the Peace* has for the Kennedys, as when Wilder sees some of himself in Lee Harvey Oswald:

> Kennedy had been too young, too rich, too handsome and too lucky; he had embodied elegance and wit and finesse. His murderer had spoken for weakness, for neurasthenic darkness, for struggle without hope and for self-defeating passions of ignorance, and John Wilder understood those forces too well. He almost felt he'd pulled the trigger himself [*Disturbing the Peace*, p. 196].

Disturbing the Peace was the one book Yates wrote that he very much didn't like. He didn't want to repeat the experience with *Uncertain Times*. The fact that a Kennedy plays a key role in both novels is not a coincidence. It is at the heart of why Yates couldn't complete the novel.

* * *

In the manuscript, William Grove learns that the screenplay he was writing will not be made into a movie because the two stars, Henry Fonda and Natalie Wood, have dropped out of the project. No reason is given for why they drop out. For Grove it's one more negative development in a faltering writing career: he can't complete the war novel he's writing and now the movie won't be produced. The screenplay is based, we soon learn, on a novel by Paul Cameron (who is clearly based on William Styron), and Cameron recommends Grove for a job writing

10. Hope for the Youngest

speeches for U.S. attorney general Robert Kennedy. Grove accepts the position and to his surprise likes writing speeches, but he's clearly not impressed with the Kennedys. Yet he's pleased when Bobby Kennedy tells him he wants a writer, not a journalist, for the speechwriting job and that he hopes Grove will continue working on his novel. As the new job develops we also meet Grove's girlfriend, Nora Harrington, who is a beautiful, alcoholic slob. These connected if somewhat disjointed plot developments establish the novel's chief conflicts: (1) a writer who wants to write a novel he can't write versus a writer working at a job he didn't expect to like but does; (2) an alcoholic (which we soon learn Grove is) versus a girlfriend who is even less capable of holding her liquor; and (3) the writer liking a man, Bobby Kennedy, he seemed determined to dislike.

The manuscript contains many minor details that clearly point to Grove being an autobiographical character, including the fact that he types with two fingers. Also common in the manuscript are lines Yates used in earlier novels. The most notable example of this comes in something told to Grove by Warren Pickering, a lawyer Bobby Kennedy used to deliver $53 million in food and medical aid to Cuba to free 1,200 men (Cubans) who were captured during the aborted Bay of Pigs invasion. Pickering tells how Fidel Castro asked him if there was anything he wanted to see while he was in Cuba and Pickering said, yes, Ernest Hemingway's home near Havana. So Castro took him there and boosted himself up and sat on the drain board near the sink. Pickering says to Grove, "Isn't that the God Damndest thing?" which is what Michael Davenport says to his ex-wife, Lucy, in *Young Hearts Crying*.⁹

What was probably intended as a key plot development occurs while Grove is in Bobby Kennedy's office discussing the attorney general's upcoming testimony before a congressional committee and a secretary comes in to say Grove has a call from a woman who says it's "urgent." Kennedy "winced in plain annoyance." Grove takes the call outside the office, and it's Nora, who says she needs a bag claim ticket that Grove has. He leaves the Justice Department building, meets Nora at a nearby store, and gives her the ticket, and then he yells at her for calling him out of a meeting with Kennedy. She makes it clear she doesn't care. When he returns to Kennedy's office, the attorney general asks if everything is all right with his family and Grove says yes, not explaining what the problem really was. He then spends the next hour to an hour and a half with Kennedy. Yates seemed uncertain how much he wanted to emphasize the point of Kennedy both being understanding and spending time with Yates. A potentially important sentence is crossed out. It said: "It was almost as if they were friends." If the sentence remained in the final draft of a completed novel, it no doubt would have continued development of one the three conflicts mentioned earlier: Grove starting to like a man he didn't want to like.

Nora's drinking and her consistent interference with Grove's ability to do his speechwriting job develops by the end of the parts Yates wrote into a significant plot device. Just as the manuscript ends, it becomes clear that Grove will have an affair with Holly, a secretary in Kennedy's office, with the clear implication that he will dump Nora. What's not clear, because Yates had not yet written the scene or scenes to accomplish it, is whether Grove's dumping of Nora is mostly personal, a preference for the sober Holly, or due to a belief that replacing Nora with Holly will help him succeed at a job that only a few months earlier he didn't want.

There are several references to Grove's problems in writing his World War Two novel, but perhaps the most significant comment on those efforts comes when Grove develops a useful insight into writing a better novel. He realizes that "bravery was the smallest part of what it took to be a soldier," that an effective soldier needs to be able to walk 20 or 30 miles with 60 pounds of supplies and weaponry on his back and waist, that he must learn not to lose equipment and how to dig a foxhole, to be trusted on guard duty, and to perform a seemingly endless list of other drudgery-laden skills. Nothing approaching that insight appears in *A Special Providence*, but it seems remarkably similar to the title story in Tim O'Brien's *The Things They Carried*, a story Yates and I talked about several times and which he greatly admired.

There are several versions of many scenes, and all 129 pages of one version of the manuscript of *Uncertain Times* are marked up, with words crossed out, paragraphs x'd out, marginalia, words substituted, punctuation changed, and other indications that Yates was far from satisfied with what he had so far written. (There are, conversely, few corrections of misspellings, something he and most writers tend to reserve for a final draft, again indicating he felt he was far from having completed revisions of what he had already written.)

10. Hope for the Youngest

Another copy of the manuscript contains 162 pages, several dozen of them handwritten, and seems an earlier and less complete version of the 129-page one, although it does include a scene one lacks in which Nora seduces Grove.

If all the disparate parts were combined, I estimate, they would total from 160 to 200 pages and, perhaps, 40,000 usable words. To do that, however, would require using some extended scenes that Yates clearly wanted to cut down and perhaps some scenes he wanted to abandon.

The archives contain a letter from a Hillary Liftin in the office of Seymour Lawrence, Yates's publisher, to Monica Yates, the author's second-oldest daughter, dated February 17, 1993, three months after her father died, acknowledging receipt of a manuscript of *Uncertain Times*. That manuscript is 90 pages long, 72 pages of which are identical to 72 pages found in the 129-page version, plus 18 pages of material not in the longer one, including a speech Grove wrote for John F. Kennedy, which the president did not use but which became a cover message to a civil rights bill the Kennedy administration sent to Congress.

Although there's nothing in the archives about Lawrence's reaction to the manuscript, the book has never been published.

11

The Collected Stories

The Collected Stories of Richard Yates was published in 2001. It contains all 11 stories from *Eleven Kinds of Loneliness*, all seven from *Liars in Love*, and nine previously uncollected stories. Of the nine new stories, two were previously published in *Ploughshares*, "Evening on the Cote d'Azur—1952" in 1976 and "Thieves" in 1977, and one, "The Canal," was published in *The New Yorker* in January 2001, just before *The Collected Stories* appeared. The other six were published for the first time in *The Collected Stories*.

All but the most uncritical Yates readers are likely to find each of the nine new stories inferior to all of the stories in the first collection and to most of the stories in the second. Yet each one is in some way typically Yatesian and each possesses some qualities that instill the stories with promise.

* * *

In "The Canal," Tom Brace, at a party, probably in New York City and probably in the 1950s, tells about winning a Silver Star in World War II and Lew Miller tells an undetailed story about being in battle, omitting details that would reveal him as incompetent. The story ends with Miller's wife asking him why he let Brace "eclipse you so in a conversation?" and Miller replying by asking his wife, "Will you shut up? Will you please for God's sake shut up?" (p. 379.)[1] The story is slight; that is, it doesn't probe deep into the psychology of any characters. But it is a good example of Yates's expert use of dialogue. His characters sound like real people and, yet, everything they say either reveals character or advances plot.

"The Canal" was published in *The New Yorker* nearly a decade after Yates died. It was the only one of his stories *The New Yorker* ever published, and he was saddened by the magazine's refusal to publish any of

11. The Collected Stories

his stories while he was alive. At least twice he told me that his agent frequently sent his stories to the magazine but that Roger Angell, the magazine's fiction editor, just didn't seem to like his work. He spoke of Angell with a mixture of regret and bitterness. After *The New Yorker* published "The Canal" in its January 15, 2001, issue, his daughter Sharon went into the basement of her Brooklyn home, where she kept a box containing his ashes, picked up the box, shook it, and said, "Way to go, Dad!"[2]

* * *

In "A Clinical Romance," set in a TB hospital on Long Island, probably in 1949, Tom Lynch dates a nurse, who breaks up with him and dates another patient. In the climax of the story, Lynch beats up a gay attendant.

This is another slight story that carries a significant resemblance to a much better one by the same writer. As in "The B.A.R. Man," frustration leads to an act of violence, and in both the emphasis is less on the victim of the violence (a leftist professor in "The B.A.R. Man") and more on the reason for the act. In that way, both stories are similar to "The Use of Force" by William Carlos Williams, in which a doctor forces open the mouth of a little girl in order to successfully complete his diagnosis that she suffers from diphtheria. "A Clinical Romance" was probably written prior to "The B.A.R. Man," and it's very possible that the later story was an attempt to improve upon his earlier effort.

* * *

In "Bells in the Morning" two American soldiers in Germany on Easter, 1945, hear distant church bells and speculate it means an end to the war but then decide the bells are for Easter. (Easter in 1945 fell on April 1, and Germany surrendered on May 7.)

"Bells in the Morning" is not a complete story, certainly not one with the clear Aristotelian beginning, middle, and end so typical of most of Yates's novels and other short stories. It is really a sketch, something that belongs in a larger work. Yates wrote it in the early 1950s, and his agent, Monica McCall, told him it was a "promising beginning but not saleable" (*A Tragic Honesty*, p. 124).

It does contain the preciseness and economy of detail that became typical of his stories, and one other motif he would return to. One of the characters, Murphy, when he hears the bells, says to the other, Cramer, "Don't that sound nice?" and Yates writes: "That was the word. Nice. Round and dirty" (p. 400). It's the first of three times in his writings that Yates disparages the word "nice." In "A Natural Girl" David scolds Susan for using the word to describe someone, saying it means she can't think of anything good to say about the person, and in *Young Hearts Crying* Tom Nelson tells Lucy Davenport her paintings are "nice" and she realizes that means he has nothing good to say about them. In that sense, "nice" is always a "round and dirty" word. The discussion of the word is a minor bit of metafiction that, although thrice used, is unusual for Yates. (Of course, much of "Builders" is metafictional.)

Although there's no way to know with certainty, the story is likely a remembrance of something Yates experienced when he was in the army in Europe at the end of the war.

* * *

In "Evening on the Cote d'Azur," two young American women, Betty Meyers and Marylou Smith, wives of sailors in France, go to a nightclub, the Hollywood Bar, drink, get picked up by two petty officers, and have sex. That's in 1952 (the original title when published in *Ploughshares* was "Evening on the Cote d'Azur—1952") when tens of thousands of American servicemen were stationed in France. The women feel no guilt. One of the petty officers lied about his name.

Like the other previously uncollected stories in the volume, this one contains more promise of future literary achievement than actual fulfillment. The main character for most of the 14-page story is Betty Meyers, who is bored waiting around for her husband all day, impatient with her children, and annoyed by the French, whom she considers snotty (among other proofs she has is a nasty note from the concierge of the apartment complex Betty lives in saying her children are annoying other tenants). But for the last page and a half, the point of view switches to the petty officer who called himself Tom. He tells two younger sailors that "any man who couldn't make that oughta turn in his uniform" and confesses his lie about his name: "Oh, Jesus Christ, Junior. When're you gonna grow up? Whaddya think—I told her my real name?" (p. 416).

The closing switch in point of view prevents the story's essential

11. The Collected Stories

conflict (Betty's unhappy reality in France versus her desire to return home to Bayonne, New Jersey) from being confronted. Betty has simply surrendered to a momentary loneliness. If Yates had given us one more brief scene of Betty regretting what she did, or planning to do it again, or looking for some alternative way to deal with her unhappiness — some focus on Betty's reaction to the one-night stand, not the petty officer's — the story would have been rounded out with a sense of completeness. It's an omission that does not occur in any of the 18 stories in the two volumes of short fiction published while Yates was alive.

* * *

In "Thieves" men in a veterans hospital, probably in New York City, tell stories about stealing things. The story ends with an insensitive nurse, Miss Berger, saying she's too busy to look in on a sick patient.

"Thieves," like "Out with the Old" and "No Pain Whatsoever," is set in a hospital TB ward. TB also plays an important part in "Regards at Home," and pneumonia, another serious lung disease, has a key role in *A Special Providence*. The diseases are important plot devices in each case, but unlike the role of abortion in *Revolutionary Road* and elsewhere there is no metaphoric intent.

Monica McCall, Yates's agent, praised the story when he submitted it to her but told him it was not saleable (*A Tragic Honesty*, p. 128). It is little more than a bunch of guys sitting around a TB ward and talking. Most of the talking is done by Robert Blaine, who brags about having once stolen a girl from a rich man, about once tricking a salesman in an expensive clothing store into thinking he was rich, and about other accomplishments that don't seem to much impress anyone else in the ward.

A minor but interesting point in "Thieves" is a discussion the men have about baseball. A new guy named O'Grady says, "Take a guy like Branch Rickey,[3] he knows everything there is about baseball, but that don't mean he'd of made a top ballplayer." Another patient, Jones, counters with, "Branch Rickey is *very* talented — but as a baseball *executive*. His talent is in *that* field; he's not supposed to be a player" (p. 418). Generalized, the conversation is consistent with a point Yates once made to me in the Crossroads bar in Boston: knowing how to write is not the same as being able to write, and (he seemed less certain on the second part) it might be possible to write well without knowing how to write.

* * *

In "A Private Possession" Eileen, a fourth-grade girl in a Catholic school, finds 50 cents on the school playground and her aunt Billie thinks she stole it and forces her to give it to a nun. Probably set in a suburb of New York City, maybe in the 1930s, the story has an older sister and a younger brother, Roger, like Yates and his sister, Ruth. Eileen has told Roger about finding the money, but she asks him not to tell Aunt Billie. She "wants something of her own, something Aunt Billie can't touch" (p. 429). But Roger does tell Aunt Billie, hoping it will persuade her to let each of them buy a small turtle, at 60 cents each. But Eileen lies to her aunt and claims she doesn't have 50 cents. Aunt Billie doesn't believe her and with a stern look and authoritative tone forces a confession from the little girl. But when Eileen says she found the money, Aunt Billie incorrectly believes she is lying about that, too. She takes Eileen back to the school and Aunt Billie tells Sister Katherine that Eileen stole 50 cents from another student. The nun believes the aunt and doesn't give the child an opportunity to defend herself. Later, back at Aunt Billie's home, Eileen goes out back, to a toolshed, and cries.

All four stories Yates wrote about elementary school ("Doctor Jack-o'-lantern," "Fun with a Stranger," "Trying Out for the Race," and "A Private Possession") show unhappy children. Elementary school is not a happy, nurturing experience for the youngsters in Yates's stories. By contrast, *A Good School* portrays a high school where students do mature and experience at least some incomplete happiness.

* * *

In "The Comptroller and the Wild Wind" an accountant's wife leaves him for another man. He tries to pick up a waitress but is rebuffed. It's set in New York City, probably in the late forties or early fifties. The story includes a character reading a poem by James Joyce that includes the line "I heard their young hearts crying,"[4] the last three words of which are the title of Yates's 1984 novel.

The lead character, George Pollock, is sort of a pre–Frank Wheeler of *Revolutionary Road*, with an uninteresting job (comptroller for the American Bearing Company), an attractive wife, Alice ("the wild wind" of the title), and a settled life his wife finds unappealing. If April Wheeler had left Frank instead of proposing they move to Europe, "The Comptroller and the Wild Wind" could be read as a preparatory sketch for the novel.

There are even differences that seem to have been *corrected* to make *Revolutionary Road* work better. For example, where Pollock is rejected by the waitress, Mary Hennessey, Wheeler was successful in having a brief affair with a secretary, Maureen Grube, making Wheeler less of a loser, less pathetic, than Pollock and in the process making Wheeler more of a character in which a male reader can uncomfortably recognize an image of himself. Also, we're told early in the story that when Alice was pregnant "the child died" (p. 436), presumably the result of a miscarriage, while in *Revolutionary Road* the end of the pregnancy results from a botched self-inflicted abortion that results in April's death. Relocating the miscarriage/abortion at the end, rather than the beginning, and having it self-inflicted makes the event both more powerful and more metaphoric. In the novel it represents the culmination of the two protagonists' dreams, while in the story it is mentioned only in passing, one of several sad events in the lives of the characters.

Just as "The B.A.R. Man" seems to be a successful attempt to improve upon "A Clinical Romance," "The Comptroller and the Wild Wind" seems to be an early effort to work out the details of what would become Yates's masterpiece, *Revolutionary* Road. The best writing, Yates believed, never came on a first draft; it came from rewriting and rewriting and rewriting and rewriting....

* * *

In "A Last Fling, Like" a girl talks non-stop in a diner in New York City, telling her girlfriend about her trip to Europe, a last fling before marriage. She dated many men but doesn't realize she had a boring time.

Like the other eight previously uncollected stories in the volume, this one seems like an early exercise in which Yates explored themes that would become embedded in his later, more mature writings. In this case, the heart of the story is an exploration of honesty, which, of course, is so entrenched in his other work that it can't be teased out without unraveling the whole fabric.

The story is narrated by an unnamed young woman as she talks to a girlfriend in a diner. She is so engrossed in her own story (revealing her egocentrism) that she doesn't even realize that her friend, Grace, has ordered her "another cup of coffee while I was gabbing away" (p. 459). In fact, the story is an eight-page monologue; at a normal reading speed, that means she was talking for 15 to 20 minutes without her friend being able to say anything. The reader's sympathy is with Grace when the narrator says, "So here I've been talking a blue streak and I didn't even let you get a word in edgeways" (p. 459). Certainly she doesn't engage in the careful word choice or editing or revision that is required to achieve honesty in the use of words.

She ends her monologue by telling Grace that her fiancé, Marty, "asked me did I wear my engagement ring while I was gone," and says she said, "Whaddya think I'd wear that for? Whaddya think I'm going to do, spoil the whole trip for myself? Keep myself from having fun?" That is, she ends her dishonest monologue with what seems, only on the surface, like a bit of honesty. It is in fact a bit of cruelty disguised as honesty. She closes her monologue by saying, "I says, 'Listen, brother, don't kid yourself.' I says, 'You'd do it quick enough, if you had the money'" (p. 460). Like so many other of Yates's characters, she is a continuously dishonest person who implies that her cruelty is in reality honesty.

The story "A Last Fling, Like" presages is "The Best of Everything." That "Fling" is among Yates's least satisfying pieces of fiction and "The Best of Everything" is one of his short masterpieces should not be surprising. Both are about people about to get married, and in both cases the reader realizes that neither of these couples should enter into matrimony. The difference is two major changes. In "Fling" the point of view is entirely from the bride-to-be and is thus limited, while in "The Best of Everything" the point of view switches from the bride-to-be to the groom-to-be to focusing on both. It is more sweeping and thus we feel we get a better understanding of who the characters are. Second, Martha in "The Best of Everything," while intellectually limited, is a much kinder person than the narrator in "Fling." Our sympathy for Martha entering into what will undoubtedly be an unhappy marriage seems justified; the narrator of "Fling" seems unworthy of that sympathy.

If these two stories could be hung in a museum, "A Last Fling, Like" would be the pencil sketch on paper and "The Best of Everything" would be the oil on canvas.

11. The Collected Stories

* * *

In "A Convalescent Ego" a man home from a hospital for two weeks accidentally breaks a teacup and a soap dish while his wife is out. He imagines — Walter Mitty–like — several conversations he might have with her. When she returns they argue, but then she's contrite. The time and place of the story are not indicated, but it *feels* like New York City in the early 1950s, which would make it consistent with most of the other previously uncollected stories in the volume.

The story was written before Yates published any of his better stories, and his biographer, Blake Bailey, speculates that Yates wrote "A Convalescent Ego" out of frustration. Unable to get his better stories published and aware that one of his literary heroes, F. Scott Fitzgerald, had sold what Blake Bailey calls "any number of hokey, formulaic stories [to] the *Saturday Evening Post*, and gotten rich in the process" (*A Tragic Honesty*, p. 129), a story designed to be clever and witty might have seemed to fit into the nothing-to-lose category.

The weakest part of the story is the end, where the wife ceases her nagging and says, "Oh Bill, I have been awful since you came home, haven't I? I'm so busy being tired and heroic I haven't given you a *chance* to get well.... Oh Bill, you ought to break *all* the dishes, right over my dumb head" (p. 472).

Yates once told me that he always strived for the "perfect ending," which he defined as one that is both inevitable and a surprise. His ending to "A Convalescent Ego" is not inevitable because there's nothing, absolutely nothing, in the story to justify or even hint at the change in the wife's attitude. And it's not a surprise because so many stories in what used to be called the "slicks," like *The Saturday Evening Post*, had a habit of ending the way the kindhearted reader wanted them to, not the way the development of the characters and the unfolding of the plot should require them to. It is the weakest ending of any story Yates ever wrote.

The Uncollected Stories

Collected stories are not complete stories. Four pieces of fiction by Yates that were published in magazines as short stories later appeared as parts of his novels. A story he published in a literary magazine is not included in his *Collected Stories*. Two stories he published in his high school yearbook are also excluded. Richard Russo, who wrote the introduction to the *Collected Stories*, does not explain the omissions. In addition, three stories Yates is known to have written no longer exist.

Following is a list (in alphabetical order) of all stories Richard Yates is known to have written that are not included in his *Collected Stories*. (Also included, to help avoid confusion for serious students of Yates who might come across titles not in the *Collected Stories* and not on this list, are early titles of three stories that were published under other titles and the early title of the book of stories later published as *Liars in Love*.⁵)

1. "After the Laurel Players," first published in *Esquire* in its February 1961 issue, was later published in *Revolutionary Road*. Bailey (p. 224) says that Yates was very upset with editing changes *Esquire* made to the excerpt.

2. "End of the Great Depression"—written in the mid–1950s and published in the Winter 1962 issue of *Transatlantic Review;* about a 12-year-old boy who dreams of becoming president and ending the Great Depression.

3. *Five Kinds of Dismay*—early title for the collection published as *Liars in Love*, which has seven stories.

4. "Forgive Our Foolish Ways"—Yates's first published fiction, it appeared in 1943 in *Winged Beaver*, a combination yearbook and literary magazine published at the private high school Yates attended in Connecticut, Avon Old Farms; the story is about 1,000 words long; it's about a soldier who doubts there is a God but who becomes converted into a believer after he's wounded in combat (see "Schedule," also on this list).

5. "Forms of Entertainment"—story written in the early 1970s that Gordon Lish, one of the editors at *Esquire*, wanted to publish, but he was overruled by higher editors; the manuscript does not survive.

6. "Foursome"—a story written in the early fifties; no manuscript survives.

7. "The Game of Ambush"—early title of "A Glutton for Punishment."

8. "A Good and Gallant Woman"—published in September 11, 1965, issue of *The Saturday Evening Post*; published later as "Prologue"

11. The Collected Stories

of *A Special Providence* (a second excerpt was also published in *The Saturday Evening Post* two weeks later, September 25 (see "To Be a Hero" later).

9. "Lament for a Tenor"—published in *Cosmopolitan* in February 1954. Jack Warren, 16, is in an unnamed prep school when he is informed by the headmaster that his father has died. The headmaster tells Jack he should go to his morning classes because the train that will take him into the city doesn't leave until that afternoon. Jack, responding to a question from the headmaster, says his masters (i.e., teachers) shouldn't be told what has happened. Jack's parents were divorced, and Jack saw his father only three or four times a year He remembers his father as "a pretty boring guy, but he tries "to reconstruct a father he could mourn." But what he remembers most is his parents arguing, although he also remembers that they were polite to each other after their divorce. And he also recalls looking at a picture on the wall in his father's office in Manhattan of a picnic for his company's salesmen, and he assumes that his father probably struck out four times in a softball game. (In this clearly autobiographical story, Yates is revealing that his own acknowledged lack of athletic ability was inherited.) Jack has, however, another assumption: his father, who once studied singing formally, must have thought of himself as "an operatic tenor lost among salesmen." He does remember his father, Mike, once singing at the insistence of his brother, Jack's uncle George, something operatic in Italian. Jack's father, his memory tells him, sang with "pride and love." But just as he finally has latched on to a fond memory of his father (during lunch at the prep school), Fred Larkin, the school's best athlete and something of a bully, makes fun of Jack for looking sad. He calls Larkin an S.O.B., but everyone in the school cafeteria laughs at Jack. Later, on the train home, he cries: "Jack knew he wasn't crying for his father at all, but for himself—a boy bereaved." (This line is very close to one that appears in *The Easter Parade*, after Emily Grimes attends a memorial service for her father: she was crying "for poor, sensitive Emily Grimes whom nobody understood, and who understood nothing"—p. 42.) "Lament for a Tenor" ends with Jack whispering on the train, "I'm sorry, dad. I guess that's the best I can do." In tone this story is very similar to the afterword of *A Good School*, in which an adult Bill Grove fondly remembers his long-deceased father. Yates, according to Blake Bailey, thought this story was very sentimental,

and that is probably the reason he did not include it in either of his two collections, although it does not explain why the editors of *The Collected Stories of Richard Yates*, published a decade after the author died, also omitted it. Yates's mother, Bailey says, did not like the story but defended her son's right as an artist to write it (*A Tragic Honesty*, p. 154). It's not clear why his mother wouldn't have liked it, since there's nothing unkind said about either the mother or father. Another reason Yates may not have liked it is that it was published in *Cosmopolitan*, which he thought lacked prestige, but he happily accepted the $850 the magazine paid him for the story (*A Tragic Honesty*, p. 153). In the early 1950s, many families were living on less than that each month. While the ending does seem sentimental, there are clearly elements in the story Yates must have liked, evidenced by his near repetition of the line about Jack Warren feeling sorry for himself to Emily Grimes in *The Easter Parade* and the concluding warmth suggested by the endings to both "Lament for a Tenor" and *A Good School*, written more than two decades apart.

10. "Nuptials"—early title of "The Best of Everything."

11. "The Ordeal of Vincent Sabella"—early title of "Doctor Jack-o'-lantern."

12. "The Right Thing," first published in *Esquire* in 1984, is an excerpt from *Young Hearts Crying*.

13. "Schedule"—published in the 1944 edition of *Winged Beaver* (see "Forgive Our Foolish Ways"); about a boy who, at his father's insistence, drops out of high school to deliver ice and later is derided by his wife for wanting to complete his high school education and who still later attacks a co-worker for calling him ignorant.

14. "Shepherd's Pie on Payday"—story written in early fifties; the manuscript no longer exists.

15. "To Be a Hero"—excerpt from *A Special Providence*, first ran in *The Saturday Evening Post* on September 25, 1965 (see "A Good and Gallant Woman" earlier).

12

Rethinking Richard Yates

Richard Yates always rethought what he had written. Good writers always do. A first draft is never the best draft. His manuscripts in the archives at Boston University show revisions on nearly every page. Many stories and parts of novels have multiple typed versions that often are inconsistent. Rethinking the choice of words, the order of scenes, the inclusion of this, the exclusion of that, having doubts, turning those doubts into revisions, that's how Richard Yates worked.

Yates also rethought what he considered good in his own writing. In notes he made for revisions of *Revolutionary Road*, he said he wanted to capture "elements of the mood of my best stories" such as "Jody Rolled the Bones," "Lament for a Tenor," "Evening on the Cote d'Azur," and "I'll Be All in Clover" (which was an early title for "The Best of Everything"). But three decades later he told me he wished he had never published "Jody Rolled the Bones" because he thought the protagonist was a stereotype, and his opinion of both "Lament for a Tenor" and "Evening on the Cote d'Azur" was not high enough for him to include either in the two collections of his short stories that were published while he was alive, *Eleven Kinds of Loneliness* and *Liars in Love*. Of the four stories he listed, he would retain a high opinion for the rest of his life only of "The Best of Everything."

Sometimes his change of opinion about his own writing seemed unclear even to him. In a letter dated May 7, 1971, to DeWitt Henry he said of *A Special Providence* that he disliked the "damn book" and that he regretted with bitterness the years it took him to write it. That was consistent with what he told me in 1970 when I was a graduate student at DePauw University in Greencastle, Indiana, and he came to campus to give a reading. At a faculty party to which I was invited, he said, in response to my question, that there was nothing in the book that explained why it took so long to complete. He was at the time clearly unhappy with the final product. But when I spoke with him several times in the mid–1980s about *A Special Providence* and expressed my admiration for the war parts, he indicated that what he regretted was the way he conceived the novel. He saw it in its original conception not so much as a war novel but rather as a story about how a son breaks free of a mother's attempts to shape him into someone he doesn't want to be. And he seemed then to be very much in agreement with my judgment that if he had conceived the story differently, conceived it as a war story, he would have written a different and better book. And he left me with the clear impression that his regrets about the book, a decade and a half after its publication, centered around a belief that he had missed an opportunity to write, as so many of his contemporaries had (writers such as Norman Mailer, Joseph Heller, Thomas Heggen, and James Jones) *his* war novel. This became more and more clear as he questioned me about my own experiences in Vietnam and about the two Vietnam War novels I had published. Blake Bailey's *A Tragic Honesty* notes that when younger Yates often downplayed, even belittled, his army service in Europe near the end of World War Two, but that over the years he developed, as so many war veterans do, a quiet pride in that service. He said he liked my statement, made one night in the Crossroads bar in Boston, that I had been opposed to the Vietnam War, thought it was wrong for the U.S. to send as many troops as it did to that conflict, but that I never regretted that I went and that the more distance there was between my service in the war and the present, the easier I found it to feel positive about having been there. He said he thought the same emotion applied to him and his military service during the Second World War.

Richard Yates clearly changed his views over the years about his own writing. A rethinking of what is good in the writings of Yates, and why it is good, is appropriate for a new evaluation of his work.

* * *

An obvious place to rethink Richard Yates has already been indicated. The military training scenes and the war scenes in *A Special Providence* should be ranked among Richard Yates's best writing. Their focus on a young soldier's doubts about his ability to simply be competent captures a near-universal emotion largely absent from other great war literature, from Homer to Tolstoy to Stephen Crane to Hemingway.

12. Rethinking Richard Yates

Some of it is found in Tim O'Brien's National Book Award–winning Vietnam War novel, *Going After Cacciato*, but it is nowhere to be found in what has come to serve as the standard canon of American Second World War novels (which includes *The Naked and the Dead*, *Mr. Roberts*, *Catch-22*, and *From Here to Eternity*). *A Special Providence*'s basic training and war scenes deserve a place in that canon both because they explore near-virgin territory and because the writing, in its crispness and directness, is so honest.

Another clear place to rethink Yates's work is with *Revolutionary Road*. It should be recognized as a great novel not because it condemns a transitory phenomenon, American suburbia of the 1950s, but because it examines with honesty and depth a universal human trait, the tendency of all humans to be pretentious and self-deluding. To emphasize either suburbia or marriage (as Alfred Kazin did[1]) is to misunderstand what the novel is really about. As Yates said in notes to himself outlining revisions he wanted to make in an early draft of the novel,[2] blaming the suburbs for the unhappiness of people who live in them is a "minor point." Blaming "America" or "our time," he also said in the same notes, would be misleading. Any of these three — suburbia, America, or the times — has only the limited responsibility of failing to provide something "true and big enough to believe in." Who or what, then, is to blame? "Human weakness," he writes. We are unwilling to be honest about our limitations, and we allow ourselves to be encouraged to be unrealistically optimistic. Movies and, by extension, television, popular music, and all of American popular culture have a particular responsibility because they make money off of people's willingness to delude themselves. Exploitation of a human weakness for monetary gain is not a morally defensible activity.

A less obvious place, perhaps, to rethink Yates should be in his attempts to be innovative. Many critics, even those who generally admired his novels and stories, felt he too often returned to the same themes and that his style and stories were highly repetitive. Perhaps because he wrote with such clarity, what was truly innovative in his writing is sometimes overlooked. Consider three examples: (1) For a writer so indentified with creating autobiographical characters and who simultaneously worried that in his personal life he was not viewed as manly, he displayed considerable daring in writing *The Easter Parade* with a woman as protagonist. Emily Grimes was indeed autobiographical, and

Yates never denied that fact. (2) In *A Good School* he unified varying short plots and an array of characters by tying them all to Dorset Academy, which he developed as a character in itself. (3) In *Disturbing the Peace* he gave us a character who seems to deserve his self-loathing. None of this is unprecedented, but all of it is unusual, and Yates deserves credit for these mostly successful attempts to expand his range of points of view and structures.

Richard Yates belongs in the canon. And rethinking what is good in his writing, and why, as indicated earlier, could result in placing him there. I say that with a realization that Yates and I once agreed that the very idea of a literary canon was wrongheaded. And also I understand that there are many canons and that they are not rigid and that some works of literature once in a canon are no longer there and some very deserving works are in no one's canon. So, to be more specific, I think some works written by Richard Yates should be read by anyone who wants to consider himself well-read, especially anyone who wants to be self-considered well-read in American literature of the second half of the twentieth-century. And some of his writings should be required reading in high schools and colleges. To be even more specific, and with the hope of starting a few friendly arguments in college English departments, I think *Revolutionary Road* should be ranked with *The Great Gatsby*, *The Sun Also Rises*, and a handful of other novels as a contender for the title of Great twentieth-century American Novel. And it should be considered better than *Moby-Dick* (too sprawling, to use Yates's criticism), *The Scarlet Letter*, and a dozen or so other books that lack its unity, stylistic grace, and intellectual honesty. *The Easter Parade*, the basic training and war scenes in *A Special Providence,* the first ten stories in *Eleven Kinds of Loneliness* (especially "The Best of Everything"), *A Good School,* and "Oh, Joseph, I'm So Tired" cannot remain unread by anyone wanting to seriously study the best in American literature.

Appendix 1:
Lie Down in Darkness

In the early 1960s Yates was asked by director John Frankenheimer to write a screenplay based on William Styron's first novel, *Lie Down in Darkness*. It was a promising if somewhat odd combination of superb talents. Yates had just published *Revolutionary Road* and *Eleven Kinds of Loneliness,* establishing him as one of the most important fiction writers in America. Frankenheimer had recently directed such unusual but appealing films as *Bird Man of Alcatraz* and *The Manchurian Candidate,* and Styron, since the publication of *Lie Down in Darkness* in 1951 was widely esteemed as one of America's finest novelists. The combination was odd, however, because of basic differences each of the three men brought to his art form. Styron's style was innovative and complex, in the tradition of a fellow Southerner, William Faulkner, while Yates's was stark and direct, far more in the tradition of Ernest Hemingway. That combination might work: Faulkner, after all, had co-written the script for the movie based on Hemingway's *To Have and Have Not*. The problem with the comparison to *To Have and Have Not* is that *To Have and Have Not* was a bad movie. Complicating the matter was Frankenheimer, who already had a well-earned reputation for the off beat. That is probably what attracted him to *Lie Down in Darkness* in the first place, but what is off beat about Styron's novel is not the same types of things that easily translate to the screen, for both artistic and commercial reasons.

It is a complex story that demands a long script, and one of its central themes concerns a near-incestuous relationship between a father and daughter. When stars Natalie Wood and Henry Fonda withdrew from the project, it could not attract the needed studio support. But the script, published more than two decades after it was written, reads almost like a novel, so complete did Yates make the descriptions of sets and actions.

Appendix 1

Yates has in effect translated Styron's complex style into his own direct delivery and, remarkably, done no damage to the original intent. As George Bluestone notes in his revealing introduction to the published script:

> As a good craftsman, Yates freely drops characters, ... changes locales ... rearranges sequences, all in the interest of finding visual equivalents for Styron's fatal struggle between faith and death. Sometimes a sharp deviation from a striking detail in the novel improves the nuances of a scene [p. 14[1]].

The script is not pure Yates. The symbolism of death and faith and illicit sex that dominates the Styron novel comes through clearly. Everything from a hearse breaking down to a hymn played by bells inside a church tower rings out with a sense of *significance*. Even if the reader (or viewer) is not always certain what the meaning is intended to be, he can always have certainty that there is a meaning. Such symbolism is rare in Yates's own stories. Still, there is much in the script that *is* consistent with Yates's own stories: Milton, a lawyer, tells Dolly, "I wasn't cut out for the law. I wish I'd been a poet" (p. 110). Like all of Yates's own major characters, he yearns to be someone else. Also typical of Yates's stories are the divorces (Dolly and Pookie), troubled marriages (Helen and Milton, Peyton and Harry), heavy drinking, and constant tensions neatly summed up in key lines (such as Helen to her daughter Peyton: "You've got your *own* husband now. Leave mine alone" [p. 177]), lines that in a lesser writer could easily slip into melodrama.

Three of Yates's own novels, *Revolutionary Road*, *The Easter Parade*, and *Disturbing the Peace*, were also sold to Hollywood and like Yates's script for *Lie Down in Darkness* did not find their way to the screen while he was still alive. *Revolutionary Road*, which was made into a film a decade and a half after Yates died, in its form as a novel is really more cinematic than *Lie Down in Darkness*, and that is not surprising since Yates credits his earliest knowledge of stories to those he encountered in movie theaters rather than those he read. He comes as much out of a film tradition as does Styron out of a literary one (even though they were born only one year apart). Little wonder, then, that Yates has so expertly taken a highly literary novel — the kind that does not normally translate well to film — and made of it what could be a remarkable screen experience. But, unless it is finally produced, no one will know for sure.

Appendix 2:
Alternative Yates

Richard Yates, like most writers, often considered alternatives to what was eventually published. Most of these involved the type of editing common to any manuscript, a word crossed out and replaced, a sentence added, a paragraph deleted, and similar changes made as the manuscript progresses from first to final draft, and sometimes beyond that.[1]

An example of this type of editing is visible on the proofs (that is, copy already set by the publisher) of *A Good School*. Publishers typically discourage changes this late in the production process because it often holds up press runs and disrupts schedules, therefore costing money. A typical way to discourage the writer from such late and costly alterations is to charge him for each change made on page proofs. Yates, however, despite never having much money, continued to make changes on proofs. On the proofs of *A Good School*, some sentences are crossed out, some added, and individual words are changed, deleted, and added. That is, on the proofs Yates is not just correcting (publishers don't charge for corrections) but continuing to write his novel. There are dozens of changes. For example, on the first line of page 131 of the proofs, he adds a sentence in pencil: "He looked as though he regretted saying 'thanks,' but it was too late." In the published book, the added line appears on page 131 on the seventh and eight lines.

Similarly, fragments of his handwritten manuscript of *Cold Spring Harbor* contain notes written by Yates in pencil, mostly in block lettering, some in cursive, on yellow and white legal pad sheets. The writing is single spaced and mostly legible (more specifically, most of it can be read without difficulty). As with the proofs of *A Good School*, some stuff is crossed out, some added, some changed. There is no readily apparent distinction between the nature of the alterations made in the proofs of one book and the manuscript of the other. Yates does, however, seem to have been neater with the proofs. They contain none of the coffee (presumably) stains that discolor several pages of the manuscript.[2]

Probably the most significant change visible on the manuscript of *Cold Spring Harbor* is a note on page 150 telling himself to work one or two songs into the chapter. The note is dated December 3, 1984, and indicates the songs should be on page 155 of the manuscript. Page 155, however, is not included in that manuscript. A later draft, part handwritten and part typed, does have some lyrics. The intended place to add the lyrics corresponds to Chapter 9 in the published book, which does in fact contain lyrics from "Don't Get Around Much Anymore" by Duke Ellington and Bob Russell and from "He Wears a Pair of Silver Wings" by Eric Maschwitz and Michael Carr.

At least four of the short stories in *Eleven Kinds of Loneliness* came close to having titles other than the ones that were used when they appeared in print:

- "Doctor Jack-O'-lantern" was first called "The Ordeal of Vincent Sabella," after the story's protagonist.
- "The Best of Everything" was the third serious choice for a title for what is probably Yates's best-known short story. The first two were "Nuptials" and "I'll Be All in Clover."
- "A Glutton for Punishment" was originally called "The Game of Ambush."
- "A Wrestler with Sharks" was originally called "Sobel." Leon Sobel is one of the principal characters in the story.

And the title of his second collection of short stories, *Liars in Love*, was originally going to be *Five Kinds of Dismay*, which would have clearly made his fans think of his first collection, *Eleven Kinds of Loneliness*. The collection eventually was published with seven stories.

More significant is the fact that his best-known novel, *Revolutionary Road*, was originally called *The Getaway*. And the two protagonists, Frank and April Wheeler, were originally Frank and April Garvey. And, in addition to the epigraph to the novel that did appear ("Alas! When passion is both meek and wild!" from John Keats), Yates evidently considered, according to a handwritten note he made on a separate sheet included with an early draft of the novel, a second or alternative epigraph: "We are a disappointed generation.... The ache of unfulfilled experience throbs within us. Our eyes hurt. Vicarious pleasures buzz in our heads. Isn't there something more, something more?" The quote is from an essay by Herbert Gold, "The Age of Happy Problems." The essay appears in a collection of the same title published by Gold in 1962.[3]

Another alteration, in a different format, is indicated in a letter dated July 24, 1972, sent from Wichita, Kansas, where Yates was teaching at Wichita State University, to DeWitt Henry, founder and editor of *Ploughshares* magazine in Boston. Henry had conducted a long interview with Yates and sent him the typed transcript, and Yates had rewritten virtually the entire thing. The letter was an explanation (and defense) of the changes. He said he didn't like the post-realism school of fiction in general, that he didn't like Robert Coover personally, and that he didn't respect the writing of such realists as Saul Bellow or J. P. Donleavy. He specifically exempted Kurt Vonnegut from any criticism that might apply to post-realists (a group Vonnegut is sometimes included in; Yates didn't think Vonnegut should be included in that group). The question-and-answer type of interview that was eventually published in *Ploughshares* is normally considered a joint work by the interviewer and interviewee, but Yates so thoroughly altered the transcript that he made it almost entirely his own work. It appeared in the magazine in December of 1972.

There's one further type of alternation worth noting because it reveals much about Yates's personality when he was still an unknown writer. It involves his first publication, "Jody Rolled the Bones" in *The Atlantic Monthly*. In the draft of a letter he wrote in 1952 to Emily P. Flint, managing editor of the magazine, he expresses strong disagreement with changes she has made in his story. He discovered the changes when he received the galleys (that is, the story was already set in print). And, in wording reflecting both anger and petulance, he changed many of them back to the way he originally had them. For example, she changed "hotshot" to "hot shot," and "hod damn" to "God damn," and "what the hella" to "what the hell," and "keep your nose clean" to "keep your noses clean." Flint wrote back, in a letter dated December 13, 1952, noting that Yates's letter was clearly written in "heat" and pointing out that

Appendix 2

changes on galleys cost money because they disrupt schedules. But she agreed to most of the alterations he wanted. In a letter dated December 27, 1952, Yates was both polite and contrite and he apologized for the "heat" of the earlier letter. He said he would accept the changes that remained.

Appendix 3:
"The World on Fire"

Late in his life, just three years before he died, Yates was still trying to make money in the movies despite his intense dislike for the institution. He wrote a treatment (i.e., a detailed synopsis, which reads much like a short story) for a movie based loosely on his own experiences writing PR copy for Remington Rand in the early 1950s. He called it "The World on Fire," the title coming from what one character tells another, namely that just because he got a promotion he's not going to set the world on fire.[1]

The story is set in the early fifties and opens in Wichita, Kansas (where Yates once taught at Wichita State University in the early seventies). Harold Clark makes the first ever sale of a Univac, the world's first commercially viable computer, and that earns him a promotion to the New York office. His wife, Elaine, is a "secret intellectual" who reads literary books. His bosses in New York include Al Sears and Ed Grundy, neither of whom has much imagination. Harold and Elaine live in Riverdale, a suburb of New York City, and Elaine takes a literature course at the New School for Social Research, where Yates also taught, in the late fifties and early sixties. The course is taught by Thurston Picard, who is accustomed to seducing his female students. Picard seems to be based on Anatole Broyard, who also taught at the New School and with whom Yates became friends; the friendship ended bitterly in the 1980s when Broyard, by then a book reviewer for *The New York Times*, wrote a review of *Young Hearts Crying* that not only was negative about the book but alos attacked Yates's writing in general. Picard seduces Elaine, something Harold evidently never finds out about. However, his secretary, Mary Pomeroy, has a crush on him, and he has no difficulty in seducing her (very much like Frank Wheeler in *Revolutionary Road* had no difficulty in seducing a willing Maureen Grube), something Elaine never seems to discover. Meanwhile, Jack Ardsley, a Remington Rand PR man, is trying to woo Mary.

Harold talks Remington Rand into using Univac to try to predict the outcome of the 1952 presidential election ahead of everyone else. In Yates's version, Univac performs badly, giving the wrong outcome and giving it very slowly. That, however, is inconsistent with what actually happened. Univac, in reality, accurately predicted a landslide victory for Eisenhower over Adlai Stevenson after only 1 percent of the vote was counted. Probably Yates's memory was simply wrong, since he did little research for his fiction, although it's possible he was writing a form of alternative history. Mary expresses concern that Harold will be depressed, and he snaps at her petulantly, which prompts her to leave with Jack Ardsley. The next day, Al Sears is furious, believing Remington Rand has been made to look foolish, and he orders Ed Grundy to fire Harold. Also the next day, Thurston in the classroom comments on Univac's failure and crudely compares Elaine to Emma Bovary, in *Madame Bovary*, whom Flaubert at one point compared to a dying carp on the floor thrashing about for love. The story ends with Harold and Elaine driving back to Wichita, apparently happy with each other, even though, or maybe because, they didn't set the world on fire.

One possible interpretation of the treatment, which is essentially a plot synopsis, is that Yates once again was attacking something in the American middle class, but that seems too pat. The treatment should be put in the context of when it was written — a handwritten date on the manuscript says February 9, 1989. By that time Yates had abandoned the sense of inevitable unhappiness that permeated his earliest work. By that date, much of his writing displayed at least a hint of optimism. The fact that Harold and Elaine each seem never to have learned of the affair the other had (or a director might have had them become forgiving of each other's transgression), combined with the closing scene in which they are returning to Wichita without any sign of remorse, suggests that Yates saw the treatment as being consistent with Hollywood's typical happy endings and his own emerging willingness to accept the world for what it is, with our own individual inabilities to set the world on fire being in no way a sign of failure.

Yates's agent was unable to interest a studio in the treatment.

Chapter Notes

Introduction

1. Blake Bailey, *A Tragic Honesty: The Life and Work of Richard Yates* (New York: Picador, 2003), p. 242. Pages 240–241 of Bailey's biography of Yates, in fact, provide what he calls "a nice summary of the Yatesian aesthetic." Yates told Grace Schulman, a young woman he befriended in the early 1960s and who wanted to be a writer, that she should read Jane Austen and Gina Berriault. He said *Billy Budd* was better than *Moby-Dick*, *Ulysses* better than *Finnegans Wake*, and praised Ford Maddox Ford's *A Good Soldier* and Joseph Conrad's *Heart of Darkness*. Yates's aesthetic judgment was also revealed to James Crumley on the first day Crumley attended a novel-writing course taught by Yates at the Iowa Writers' Workshop: "...he thought *All the Kings Men* [by Robert Penn Warren] was a fake novel and at the end of the seminar tossed his copy into the wastebasket" (James Crumley, "The Last Gentleman," *Boston Review*, April/May 2001). And in response to a query from *The New York Times Book Review* in 1977 Yates said J. D. Salinger was the living writer he most admired. (Once he told me that in response to a similar question he had said in the 1980s that he expected John Updike to be the next American to win the Nobel Prize in Literature, a prediction that of course did not come true.)

2. At least one critic, William H. Pritchard, takes a slightly different view of the comparison between Yates and Updike. In *Updike: America's Man of Letters* (South Royalton, Vermont: Steerforth Press, 2000), he compares Yates's *Revolutionary Road*, published in 1961, with Updike's *Rabbit, Run*, published in 1960 (both are set in the 1950s). Pritchard sees Yates's middle-class characters as being at least a little richer than Updike's and, more significantly, notes that Yates's story is set in a suburb and Updike's in a "hometown."

3. Andrea Barrett, winner of the 1996 National Book Award for her collection of short stories, *Ship Fever*, once told me about the contrasting reactions she and an editor, whom she did not name, had about a comparison I had made between her and Yates. In a review of her 1991 novel, *The Middle Kingdom*, I had written that Barrett is often "compared to Gail Godwin and Anne Tyler, but I think a more apt comparison would be Richard Yates [because] unhappiness in the fictional worlds of Yates and Barrett is inevitable, and the source of that unhappiness is loneliness." A few months later, while I was interviewing her for an article, she told me she "loved" the comparison, but "my editor hates it." She said her editor said, "'Oh, you're so much more life affirming than Richard Yates,' which, actually, I don't think I am.... I love Richard Yates, so I was very flattered by that. I just think he's a terrific writer." (Interview was May 14, 1991, at Barrett's then-home in Rochester, New York.)

4. Woody Allen, *Hannah and Her Sisters* (New York: Vintage Books, 1987), p. 17.

5. Tim O'Brien once told me, "I know Yates doesn't like a couple of his books, a lot; one in particular, I think it's *A Special Providence*." He added, "Which I like a lot." Yates no doubt would have been pleased with O'Brien's evaluation of his World War Two novel, especially since O'Brien has a reputation of having written the best fiction to come out of the Vietnam War. (The quotes come from my interview with O'Brien on April 21, 1989,

at his then-home in Boxford, Massachusetts.) O'Brien, actually, was wrong on one point. The one novel of his that Yates most disliked was *Disturbing the Peace*.

6. Rust Hills, editor's note accompanying "The Right Thing," an excerpt from *Young Hearts Crying*, *Esquire*, August 1984.

7. While Yates was alive, few articles, other than book reviews, were published about him. Seven years after he died, Stewart O'Nan, in the *Boston Review*, lamented the fact that Yates's books were out of print and that he was so little known. Shortly after that, however, Yates's fame achieved a status it never enjoyed while he was alive. This was brought about by a series of publications, including the first Yates story ever to appear in *The New Yorker* (2001); Yates's *Collected Stories* (2001); Bailey's biography, *A Tragic Honesty* (2003); a remembrance of Yates by his friend and former student, James Crumley, in the *Boston Review* (2003); a special section devoted to Yates in the *Harvard Review* that included an introduction by the *Review*'s editor, Michael Shinagel, some letters Yates had written to a young woman in the early sixties (Barbara Singleton Beury), and tributes by Bailey and Kurt Vonnegut; articles I wrote about Yates for the *North American Review* (2001), *The Writer's Chronicle* (2007), *Firsts: The Book Collector's Magazine* (2008), and *Authors Guild Bulletin* (2009); and production of the movie version of *Revolutionary Road* (2008).

Chapter 1

1. Richard Yates, *Young Hearts Crying* (New York: Delacorte/Seymour Law-rence, 1984), p. 342.

2. Richard Yates, *Revolutionary Road* (Boston: Atlantic/Little, Brown, 1961), p. 223.

3. Richard Yates, *The Easter Parade* (New York: Delacorte/Seymour Law-rence, 1976), p. 3.

4. Richard Yates, *A Good School* (New York: Delacorte/Seymour Law-rence, 1978), p. 87.

5. Yates, *Young Hearts Crying*, p. 126.

6. Richard Yates, *Eleven Kinds of Loneliness* (New York: Delacorte/Seymour Lawrence, 1962), p. 192.

7. Richard Yates, *Liars in Love* (New York: Delacorte/Seymour Lawrence, 1981), p. 32.

8. Richard Yates, *Cold Spring Harbor* (New York: Delacorte/Seymour Law-rence, 1986), p. 136.

9. David Castronovo and Steven Goldleaf have a similar but much shorter list in their 1996 book, *Richard Yates* (New York: Twayne), which is part of Twayne's United States Authors Series. Their list is limited to the six stories that appear in *Liars in Love*, Yates's second collection of stories. See p. 99 of their book.

10. A book containing the winning entries, *Stories for the Sixties*, was published in 1963 and contains winning stories in a contest sponsored jointly by *Esquire* magazine and Bantam Books. Rust Hills, fiction editor of *Esquire* and a big Yates fan, offered him what Yates called "a considerable amount of dough" to select the winners from an estimated 5,000 entries. Yates came to regret accepting the assignment because, unlike most writers in similar situations, he actually read all the entries in their entirety. He confessed in the introduction he wrote for the volume that all that reading caused him to suffer from "literary snow-blindness." Among the winners, only Judith Rossner (who would later write *Looking for Mr. Goodbar*) would become well known, although George Cuomo, Helen Hudson, and Silvia Tennenbaum would also have some success. (See Yates's introduction to *Stories for the Sixties*, and Blake Bailey, *A Tragic Honesty: The Life and Work of Richard Yates* [New York: Picador, 2003], pp. 258, 266, 275; and Castronovo and Goldleaf, *Richard Yates*, p. 34.

11. Details of the home that both Richard Yates and John Cheever lived in as boys can be found in the biographies Blake Bailey wrote about the two writers, *A Tragic Honesty*, pp. 30–33, and *Cheever: A Life* (New York: Alfred A. Knopf, 2009), chapter 14.

12. Blake Bailey says in a footnote in *Cheever: A Life* (p. 371) that the Beechwood Players at Scarborough-on-Hudson were the model for the Laurel Players in *Revolutionary Road*, but more likely Yates was aware that such amateur acting companies exist all over the country.

Chapter 2

1. Parenthetical numbers in this chapter, unless otherwise indicated, refer to pages in the 1961 edition of *Revolutionary Road* published by Atlantic/Little, Brown (Boston). Page numbers for various trade paperback editions since then are identical. Page numbering for the mass market edition issued when the movie based on the novel was released is not the same.
2. Richard Yates, "Some Very Good Masters," *New York Times Book Review*, April 19, 1981, p. 1. In this essay Yates says that when he was 20 years old "I embarked on a long binge of Ernest Hemingway that entailed embarrassingly frequent attempts to talk and act like characters in the early Hemingway books." He goes on to note that he was heavily influenced by F. Scott Fitzgerald's *The Great Gatsby* and Gustave Flaubert's *Madame Bovary*.
3. The comment appears as a blurb on the top of the front cover of the first edition of *Revolutionary Road*. The publisher had send out advance copies of the book to famous critics and writers, and Kazin was as well known as any literary critic in the country at the time, and Yates did not know about it until he was informed it would appear on the book. Yates told me he was grateful for the quote, although he knew there's no proof that blurbs help sell books. He also told me he disagreed with Kazin's interpretation of his novel.
4. "Little Boxes" was written by Malvina Reynolds in 1962 and recorded by dozens of artists, including Pete Seeger.
5. There are of course many editions of Aristotle's *Poetics* (also sometimes called in translation by other titles, such as *On the Art of Poetry*). The discussion of a beginning, middle, and end appears in what is usually called chapter 7, although not all translations divide the work into chapters.
6. *Seinfeld* also once did an episode where the character George learns that his father once had a homosexual relationship with John Cheever. Blake Bailey notes in *Cheever: A Life* (New York: Alfred A. Knopf, 2009) that Larry David, who wrote both the Yates and Cheever episodes, said he used Cheever's name only because he was a well-known homosexual writer. David told Bailey the fact that George in the episode had a girlfriend named Susan, the same name as Cheever's daughter, was "just one of those things" (p. 672).
7. Paul Haggis, *Million Dollar Baby*, http://www.awesomefilm.com/script/million_dollar_baby, pdf, pp. 57–58.
8. Sean Gregory, "Pump Up the (Alcohol) Volume," *Time*, May 24, 2010, p. 50.
9. Conversation with Nancy Kress, April 2010, at her then-home in Irondequoit, New York.
10. All references to comments made by Sam Mendes and others about the production of the movie come from the 2009 DVD of the film. The DVD contains, in addition to the full movie, a version with running commentary by Mendes and screenwriter Justin Haythe, and other extras with commentaries by Leonardo DiCaprio, Kate Winslet, and others.

Chapter 3

1. Parenthetical numbers in this chapter, unless otherwise indicated, refer to pages in the 1962 edition of *Eleven Kinds of Loneliness* published by Delacorte/Seymour Lawrence (New York). Page numbers for various trade paperback editions since then are identical.
2. Gina Berriault built a writing career that was very similar to that of Richard Yates, who, in fact, played a small but significant role in her success. The similarities are that both

were highly praised by fellow writers, both had just enough success to keep writing and publishing, and neither made much of a living as a writer. Both published short stories in *Short Story I* in 1958, and Yates liked hers so much that he wrote her a fan letter, which became the beginning of a lifelong friendship, conducted almost entirely at a distance. They did not meet until 1969 and only a few times after that (Blake Bailey, *A Tragic Honesty: The Life and Work of Richard Yates* [New York: Picador, 2003], pp. 190–191). She was one of the few female writers he regularly recommended to others, along with Jane Austen, George Eliot, and Alice Munro (Bailey, *A Tragic Honesty*, p. 241, pp. 482–483), and he said she was unfairly neglected by critics and the public (Bailey, *A Tragic Honesty*, p. 415). He even named his youngest daughter, Gina, after her (Bailey, *A Tragic Honesty*, p. 413). But his most telling praise of her came in one of his few published pieces of non-fiction, "The Achievement of Gina Berriault," which appeared in *Ploughshares* in 1979. The article says Berriault writes "remarkably sensitive and powerful fiction. Her style is lucid, lyrical and very much her own, and she seems to have any number of strategies for breaking your heart." He adds: "Gina Berriault knows that ill-educated or inarticulate people are as sensitive as anyone else. She renders their speech with a fine and subtle ear for the shy or strident inaccuracies, for the bewilderment of missed points and for the dim, sad rhythms of clichés; but when she takes us into the silence of their minds, their thoughts and feelings come out in prose as graceful, as venturesome and precise as she can make it. That's a rare ability and reflects a rare degree of insight. It may be one of the most valuable skills a writer can learn." He closes the essay with "she is telling us what the great writers of the past have always wanted us to understand: that ignorance and terror are never far from possession of our hearts...." (All quotes from the article are taken from the version that appeared in *The Tea Ceremony: The Uncollected Writings of Gina Berriault* [Washington, D.C.: Shoemaker & Hoard, 2003].) I've quoted extensively from the essay because, in many ways, Yates could have applied everything he said about Gina Berriault to his own writing. In fact, DeWitt Henry, a friend and fan of Yates and now retired as the longtime editor of *Ploughshares*, where the essay first appeared, used excerpts from it to explain why Yates's fiction was so good (see DeWitt Henry, "Points of Craft from Richard Yates" at www.richardyates.org).

3. The anecdote is contained in *George Being George: George Plimpton's Life As Told, Admired, Deplored, and Envied by 200 Friends, Relatives, Lovers, Acquaintances, Rivals — and a Few Unappreciative Observers*, edited by Nelson W. Aldrich, Jr. (New York: Random House, 2008), pp. 159–160.

4. The quote is contained in *Andre Dubus: A Study of the Short Fiction*, by Thomas E. Kennedy, Twayne's Studies in Short Fiction Series No. 1 (Boston: Twayne, 1988), pp. 113–114.

Chapter 4

1. Parenthetical numbers in this chapter, unless otherwise indicated, refer to pages in the 1969 edition of *A Special Providence* published by Alfred A. Knopf (New York). Page numbers for various trade paperback editions since then are identical.

2. The 13 references in *A Special Providence* to movies, all of which suggest they are fraudulent, appear on pp. 14, 55, 60, 89, 97, 103, 104, 262, 280, 301, 317, and twice on 320. Similar and particularly notable references appear in *Disturbing the Peace* and *Cold Spring Harbor* and in such short stories as "Saying Goodbye to Sally." *Disturbing the Peace* is largely about making a movie and "Saying Goodbye to Sally" is about a man hired to write a movie script.

3. Yates doesn't mention the title of the poem, but it is "Ode to a Nightingale," which John Keats (1795–1821) wrote in 1819, and the lines (from the seventh stanza) are:

> *Perhaps the selfsame song that found a path Through the sad heart of Ruth, when, sick for home, She stood in tears amid the alien corn....*

Chapter Notes

Keats, in fact, appears several times in Yates's writing. The epigraph of *Revolutionary Road* is from one of Keats's lesser-known poems, "Isabella" (the full title, not often used, is "Isabella, or the Pot of Basil"). The epigraph—"Alas! When passion is both meek and wild!"—clearly applies to Frank and April Wheeler. In "Isabella" the young woman of the title loves Lorenzo, but her brothers think he isn't rich enough, so they murder him. Isabella buries her head in a pot with a basil plant and cares for it. She eventually dies while pining for him. The story is taken from a tale found in the *Decameron* by Boccaccio. The poem was written in 1820 and the line Yates quotes is the final one in the sixth stanza.

Yates credits Keats with being one of the writers who most influenced him. In "Some Very Good Masters" (*New York Times Book Review*, April 19, 1981, p. 3), he wrote: "...my discovery of John Keats ... made most other English lyric poets seem insubstantial ... certain of Keats's poems ... [leave] you with a stunning illumination of the world."

4. The historical basis for considering Episcopalians aristocratic is twofold. The American Episcopalian church is an offshoot of the Church of England, to which all British monarchs must belong, and 12 of the 43 men who have been president of the U.S. have belonged to the church. This includes George W. Bush, who made a switch just the opposite of Alice Prentice's: he was raised an Episcopalian and as an adult became a Methodist. The other American presidents who belonged to the Episcopalian church are George Washington, James Madison, James Monroe, William Henry Harrison, John Tyler, Zachary Taylor, Franklin Pierce, Chester A. Arthur, Franklin D. Roosevelt, Gerald Ford, and George H. W. Bush. Yates does not mention this historical background in any of his writings, but in conversations with me he clearly indicated his awareness of it. He assumed most readers would also be aware of it and that it did not need explanation.

5. Stewart O'Nan, "The Lost World of Richard Yates: How the Great Writer of the Age of Anxiety Disappeared from Print," *Boston Review*, Nov. 5, 1999. O'Nan also says the writing in *A Special Providence* is as good as what's found in *Revolutionary Road* and that both Bob and April Prentice are "deep and credible characters."

Chapter 5

1. Parenthetical numbers in this chapter, unless otherwise indicated, refer to pages in the 1975 edition of *Disturbing the Peace* published by Delacorte/Seymour Lawrence (New York). Page numbers for various trade paperback editions since then are identical.

2. Stewart O'Nan, for example, calls *Disturbing the Peace* "Richard Yates's only bad book" and thinks it almost ended Yates's career. He writes that the novel "confirmed for some that Yates was finished, that, like Fitzgerald and so many others, he'd squandered his talent, drank it away." See O'Nan's "The Lost World of Richard Yates: How the Great Writer of the Age of Anxiety Disappeared from Print," *Boston Review*, Nov. 5, 1999.

3. Regardless of the accuracy of the story an inebriated Richard Yates told me, there is no doubt that he did not like the Kennedys. For example, Arthur Schlesinger, Jr., the historian, who wrote speeches for John F. Kennedy as both candidate and president, writes in his biography of Bobby Kennedy (*Robert Kennedy and His Times*, Volume II [Boston: Houghton Mifflin, 1978]): "Richard Yates, the novelist, who worked at Justice in 1963, did not like [Bobby] Kennedy" (p. 851).

4. Yates, of course, was not the only American writer who drank heavily. The two activities, drinking and writing, are so linked in the public mind that there has been a great deal of speculation about why so many American writers drink. (The public perception of an inevitable connection between writers and drinking is not nearly so pronounced in other countries.) One common view is that writers drink because it is expected of them, it's part of the way they tell the world they are writers. Another often-expressed theory is that intoxication provides inspiration. A third and more convincing explanation was offered by Donald W. Goodwin, M.D., in his 1988 book, *Alcohol and the Writer* (Kansas City: Andrews &

McMeel, 1988). His view can be summed up in a quote from his book: "Creative writing requires a rich fantasy life; loners have rich fantasy lives — the ultimate loner is the schizophrenic who lives in a prison of fantasy. Alcohol promotes fantasy." That view suggests that at least some writers could not write well if they did not drink.

In any case, the list of American writers who were alcoholics is long. A fun-to-read book that sadly glorifies writers' alcoholism is *Hemingway & Bailey's Bartending Guide to Great American Writers* (Chapel Hill, North Carolina: Algonquin Books of Chapel Hill, 2006). (The Hemingway of the title is Edward Hemingway, grandson of Ernest Hemingway. Edward illustrated the book; Mark Bailey wrote it.) The book provides amusing anecdotes about 43 American writers who suffered from severe drinking problems. Each author is also quoted as paying tribute to alcohol (example: Raymond Chandler once said, "I think a man ought to get drunk at least twice a year just on principle" [p. 22]). There's an alcohol-related excerpt from each writer's work and a recipe for a favorite drink for each writer. The list of writers covered by Hemingway and Bailey is long and impressive in the quality of writing they produced. More so than in Goodwin's book, the length of the list and the quality of the writers confirm there is a connection, at least in the United States, between writing and alcoholism. On the list are James Agee, Conrad Aiken, Sherwood Anderson, James Baldwin, Djuna Barnes, Robert Benchley, John Berryman, Charles Bukowski, Truman Capote, Raymond Carver, Raymond Chandler, John Cheever, James Gould Cozzens, Hart Crane, William Faulkner, F. Scott Fitzgerald, Dashiell Hammett, Lillian Hellman, Ernest Hemingway, Chester Himes, James Jones, Jack Kerouac, Ring Lardner, Sinclair Lewis, Jack London, Robert Lowell, Carson McCullers, H. L. Mencken, Edna St. Vincent Millay, John O'Hara, Eugene O'Neill, Dorothy Parker, Edgar Allan Poe, Dawn Powell, Anne Sexton, Jean Stafford, John Steinbeck, Hunter S. Thompson, Jim Thompson, James Thurber, Tennessee Williams, Edmund Wilson, and Thomas Wolfe.

On the list are five winners of the Nobel Prize in Literature and 15 winners of Pulitzer Prizes.

Chapter 6

1. Parenthetical numbers in this chapter refer to pages in the 1976 edition of *The Easter Parade* published by Delacorte Press/Seymour Lawrence (New York). Page numbers for various trade paperback editions since then are identical.
2. Woody Allen, *Hannah and Her Sisters* (New York: Vintage Books, 1987), p. 17.
3. Parenthetical numbers in this section for Bailey quotations refer to Blake Bailey's *A Tragic Honesty: The Life and Work of Richard Yates* (New York: Picador, 2003).

Chapter 7

1. Parenthetical numbers in this chapter refer to pages in the 1978 edition of *A Good School* published by Delacorte/Seymour Lawrence (New York). Page numbers for various trade paperback editions since then are identical.
2. Wakefield and Yates had a personal relationship for a few years that centered around Wakefield visiting Yates at Boston's Crossroads bar, the same place I most often visited with Yates. Yates, in the mid–1980s, indicated to me that the friendship was no longer close, although he didn't go into detail. Wakefield, however, indicated in a 2008 article he wrote for *The Boston Globe* ("A Writer Revived," Dec. 28) and in talking to Blake Bailey, Yates's biographer, that he and Yates remained close for the ten years Yates lived in Boston.
3. In *A Tragic Honesty* (New York: Picador, 2003), Blake Bailey says writer Andre Dubus would visit Yates at the Crossroads in the late seventies and "sometimes ... would coax his friend to Fenway for a Red Sox game, but Yates was immune to such ancillary enthusiasms and mostly they stayed at the Crossroads" (p. 472). Yates specifically told me he had never

been to either Fenway Park or any other professional baseball stadium. One among the very few references to baseball in his writings appears in "A Clinical Romance," when we are told patients in a Long Island tuberculosis hospital listen to radios "drone": "It's a high, high fly ball out to left field. Woodling's under it — a — and — takes it, to retire the side" (see *The Collected Stories of Richard Yates*, introduction by Richard Russo [New York: Henry Holt, 2001], p. 391). The use of the word "drone" reflects Yates's attitude toward a sport that in 1949 (the likely date of the story's action) could still be called America's pastime, which could be seen as surprising for a writer who was so good at reflecting the minutiae of American middle-class society. What I remember most about Yates and baseball, however, is that several times he questioned me about playing on my college baseball team and on a semi-pro team and each time he expressed considerable regret that as a youngster or young man he had displayed so little talent for athletics. Not a single character in a Yates novel or short story who is in the least autobiographical is either athletic or interested in sports.

4. Jerome Klinkowitz, *The New American Novel of Manners: The Fiction of Richard Yates, Dan Wakefield, and Thomas McGuane* (Athens: University of Georgia Press, 1986), p. 55.

5. See Bailey, *A Tragic Honesty*, pp. 455–457, 463.

6. The story of the fire in Yates's apartment is a reminder of two other stories from literary history, each from more than a century earlier. English historian Thomas Carlyle in 1834 had just completed writing the first volume of his three-volume history of the French Revolution and sent or brought (there are several versions of the story) his only copy of the manuscript to his friend, philosopher John Stuart Mill, who in fact was the writer who had signed a contract to write the book. Mill was too busy to write it and asked Carlyle to fulfill the contract instead, which is why Carlyle wanted Mill to see the manuscript. However, Mill's maid, believing the pile of papers was trash, threw it into the fireplace. Carlyle then rewrote the manuscript in its entirety. It's often said he rewrote it from memory, and sometimes the story insists he rewrote it word for word. That seems unlikely, given the frailty of human memory, but since he had already done the research and had labored on the project for more than a year, and also had some notes, writing a second draft that was close in tone, intent and content to the first draft would no doubt be possible. Would Yates have been able to do the same with *A Good School* if the manuscript could not have been salvaged? Probably, since he had an excellent memory for his own work and his research was largely dependent on recalling his own childhood.

The other story concerns American poet Henry Wadsworth Longfellow, who on July 9, 1861, was napping in his Cambridge, Massachusetts, home when he heard his wife, Fanny, screaming. He rushed into the room where she was and saw her in flames. Her dress had caught on fire, perhaps from dripping sealing wax as she was closing an envelope containing locks of her children's hair, or perhaps from a knocked-over candle, or perhaps from a dropped, self-igniting match (Longfellow thought it was the sealing wax, although a candle was later found on the floor, and decades later Longfellow's daughter Annie said it was a match). He at first tried to extinguish the flames with a small rug, but that didn't work, so he used his own body. That did put out the flames, but it was too late. Fanny died the next morning. Longfellow was badly burned over much of his body, especially his face. He was so badly burned that he was unable to attend his wife's funeral. After that, shaving was very painful for him, so he grew a beard. Biographers note that Longfellow was constantly depressed after that and sometimes used laudanum (a mixture of water and opium, a common narcotic in the nineteenth century). He worried about his sanity and begged his friends to assure that he never be sent to an insane asylum. The parallels with Yates are clear but not complete. No one died in the Yates fire; he already had a beard before the fire, although he believed the fire damaged his appearance; he already consumed large quantities of his drug of choice, alcohol, before the fire; he worried about his sanity before the fire; and he did spend time in an asylum (that is, in Bellevue).

7. Among the school's more famous alumni are James Agee, George Bancroft, Peter Benchley, John Irving, Pierre du Pont, Dwight Macdonald, Franklin Pierce, Drew Pearson,

Chapter Notes

George Plimpton, several Rockefellers, Arthur Schlesinger, Jr., Gore Vidal, Daniel Webster, and, of course, Knowles.

Chapter 8

1. Parenthetical numbers in this chapter, unless otherwise indicated, refer to pages in the 1981 edition of *Liars in Love* published by Delacorte/Seymour Law-rence (New York). Page numbers for various trade paperback editions since then are identical.
2. The anecdote is cited in "Good-bye to Richard Yates," published in *Meditations from a Movable Chair: Essays*, a collection of essays by Andre Dubus (New York: Alfred A. Knopf, 1998).

Chapter 9

1. Parenthetical numbers in this chapter refer to pages in the 1984 edition of *Young Hearts Crying* published by Delacorte/Seymour Lawrence (New York). Page numbers for various trade paperback editions since then are identical.
2. See Anatole Broyard, "No Label on the Bottle," *New York Times*, Sept. 9, 1975, p. 37.
3. Broyard, "No Label on the Bottle," p. 37.
4. Broyard, "No Label on the Bottle," p. 37.
5. See Anatole Broyard, "Craft Versus Character," *New York Times*, Sept. 7, 1976, p. 29.
6. Broyard, "Craft Versus Character," p. 29.
7. Broyard, "Craft Versus Character," p. 29.
8. These observations are based partly on my reading of various journalistic codes of ethics, partly on conversations with several editors and book reviewers I've known, and partly on my experiences as the book reviewer for *The Salt Lake Tribune*, the largest-circulation daily news-paper in Utah, from 1997 to 2007, and for *Private Eye Weekly* (now *Salt Lake City Weekly*), the largest-circulation weekly paper in the state, for a year and a half prior to switching to *The Tribune*.
9. See Anatole Broyard, "Two-Fisted Self-Pity," review of *Young Hearts Crying, New York Times Book Review*, Oct. 28, 1984, p. 3.
10. The daily *New York Times* did, in fact, run a review of *Young Hearts Crying*. It was published on Monday, October 15, 1984, about two weeks before Broyard's review appeared, and was written by Christopher Lehmann-Haupt, who found much not to like in the protagonists, Michael and Lucy Davenport (example: "I got so terribly tired of the weakness of Michael Davenport") but found room to praise Yates's full body of work ("impressive") and the novel's accomplishments (example: "beguilingly vivid" characters) and concludes with an appropriate mixture of both his praise and criticism: "... what is most infuriating of all is that because of Mr. Yates's skill at bringing these people to life, you go right on reading and raging at them").
11. Broyard, "Two-Fisted Self-Pity," p. 3.
12. Broyard, "Two-Fisted Self-Pity," p. 3.
13. Broyard, "Two-Fisted Self-Pity," p. 3.
14. Broyard, "Two-Fisted Self-Pity," p. 3.
15. Broyard, "Two-Fisted Self-Pity," p. 3.
16. Broyard, "Two-Fisted Self-Pity," p. 3.
17. Loree Rackstraw, *Love as Always, Kurt: Vonnegut As I Knew Him* (Cambridge, Massachusetts: Da Capo Press, 2009), p. 112.
18. Rackstraw, *Love as Always, Kurt*, p. 112.
19. Rackstraw, *Love as Always, Kurt*, p. 112.
20. Terrence Ross, "Success and the Sharks," letter to the editor, *New York Times*, Jan. 6, 1985.

Chapter Notes

Chapter 10

1. Yates told me he considered Billy Budd a good example of a well-developed character, although he did not expand on the point; the comment came during one of several times he told me that *Moby-Dick* was not a very good novel because it was "sprawling." Blake Bailey, likewise, reports that Yates preferred *Billy Budd* to *Moby-Dick*, and he, too, quotes Yates as saying *Moby-Dick* "sprawled" (*A Tragic Honesty: The Life and Work of Richard Yates* [New York: Picador, 2003], p. 242).
2. Parenthetical numbers in this chapter refer to pages in the 1986 edition of *Cold Spring Harbor* published by Delacorte/Seymour Lawrence (New York). Page numbers for various trade paperback editions since then are identical.
3. In the U.S. military, a navy captain is equal to an army colonel and an army captain is equal to a navy lieutenant.
4. Yates, of course, was an admirer of Hemingway, and in his selection of details follows the "iceberg principle" Hemingway advocated. Only 10 percent of an iceberg is visible above the waterline, but the observer knows the other 90 percent is there. Similarly, a writer who selects details carefully need only present a small percentage of the total available and the reader will know the rest are there.
5. In 1993 Scribner's published a somewhat different version of Fitzgerald's unfinished novel under the title *The Love of the Last Tycoon: A Western*.
6. See "Where's Papa?" by Barbara Probst Solomon, *The New Republic,* March 9, 1987, in which Solomon persuasively argues that *The Garden of Eden*, as published the previous year is not the novel Hemingway intended.
7. Parenthetical page numbers in this section, unless otherwise noted, refer to Blake Bailey's *A Tragic Honesty*.
8. Eric Pace, "Richard Yates, Novelist, 66, Dies; Chronicler of Disappointed Lives," obituary, *New York Times*, Nov. 9, 1992, p. B-9.
9. While the quote is the same, it should be noted, as it is used in the *Uncertain Times* manuscript, the speaker is expressing surprise either that Fidel Castro is acting in what some might see as an undignified manner or that he, the most powerful man in Cuba, is acting like an ordinary guy. As used in *Young Hearts Crying* (New York: Delacorte/Seymour Lawrence, 1984, on p. 126), Michael Davenport is making an observation about the human condition that helps explain why people are unhappy. The use in *Young Hearts Crying*, in that sense, clearly has more depth than the use in *Uncertain Times*.

Chapter 11

1. Parenthetical numbers in this chapter, unless otherwise indicated, refer to pages in the 2001 edition of *The Collected Stories of Richard Yates* published by Henry Holt (New York) with an introduction by Richard Russo.
2. Blake Bailey, *A Tragic Honesty: The Life and Work of Richard Yates* (New York: Picador, 2003), p. 611.
3. Branch Rickey (1881–1965) played in the major leagues for three years and managed for 10, but he is best known as a front office executive with the St. Louis Cardinals (where he created the modern "farm" system in which minor-league players are employees of a major-league club), and the Brooklyn Dodgers, where he signed the first African-American, Jackie Robinson, to play major-league ball in the twentieth century. Rickey is a member of baseball's Hall of Fame in Cooperstown, New York. He is the only baseball figure whom I heard Richard Yates praise (for signing Robinson).
4. The poem by James Joyce is "Watching the Needleboats at San Sabba." "Comptroller and the Wild Wind" quotes the entire eight-line poem, as does the epigraph to the novel *Young Hearts Crying*.

5. For additional choices Yates made as he revised his work, see appendix 2, "Alternative Yates," which contains not only alternative titles but some additional options Yates at some point rejected, such as the names of the protagonists in *Revolutionary Road*.

Chapter 12

1. See note 3 in chapter 2.
2. The notes are in the Richard Yates archives at Boston University.

Appendix 1

1. Parenthetical numbers in this chapter refer to pages in the 1985 edition of *Lie Down in Darkness: A Screenplay* published by Ploughshares (Cambridge, Massachusetts).

Appendix 2

1. All factual information in this section comes from materials in the Richard Yates archives at the Boston University library.
2. Yates told me that when he thought he had a completed manuscript he would type it up as neatly as he could, maybe make a few changes in pencil, and then send it to a professional typist. The copy typed by the professional was the one sent to an editor or publisher.
3. "The Age of Happy Problems," in *The Age of Happy Problems* by Herbert Gold (New York: The Dial Press, 1962), pp. 12–13 (because the Gold book was published after Yates's novel, Yates's source for the quote must have been the essay as it originally appeared in *The Atlantic Monthly*, in March 1957).

Appendix 3

1. The manuscript of the treatment, which has not been published, is located at the Richard Yates archives at Boston University.

Bibliography

Books by Yates

Revolutionary Road. Boston: Atlantic/Little, Brown, 1961.
Eleven Kinds of Loneliness. New York: Delacorte/Seymour Lawrence, 1962.
Stories for the Sixties, edited by Yates. New York: Bantam, 1963.
A Special Providence. New York: Alfred A. Knopf, 1969.
Disturbing the Peace. New York: Delacorte/Seymour Lawrence, 1975.
The Easter Parade. New York: Delacorte/Seymour Lawrence, 1976.
A Good School. New York: Delacorte/Seymour Lawrence, 1978.
Liars in Love. New York: Delacorte/Seymour Lawrence, 1981.
Young Hearts Crying. New York: Delacorte/Seymour Lawrence, 1984.
Lie Down in Darkness: A Screenplay. Cambridge, Massachusetts: Ploughshares, 1985. Screenplay by Yates based on William Styron's novel.
Cold Spring Harbor. New York: Delacorte/Seymour Lawrence, 1986.
The Collected Stories of Richard Yates. Introduction by Richard Russo. New York: Henry Holt. 2001. This book, published nine years after Yates died, contains all of the stories in *Eleven Kinds of Loneliness* and *Liars in Love*, plus nine other stories.

Poetry by Yates

"QWERTYUIOP 1/2." *Esquire*, October 1966. This is the only poem ever published by Yates. The title comes from the top row of letters on a typewriter keyboard. Yates once told me he did not consider himself a good poet and that becoming a good poet would mean he would have to learn a new profession. He once said the same thing about writing non-fiction.

Articles by Yates

"The Achievement of Gina Berriault." Literary criticism in *Ploughshares*, v. 5, no. 3 (1979). Yates offers high praise to a contemporary writer who has much in common with him in style and content: "...she seems to have any number of strategies for breaking your heart." This essay was republished as an afterword in *The Tea Ceremony: The Uncollected Writings of Gina Berriault* (Washington, D.C.: Shoemaker & Hoard, 2003).
"Some Very Good Masters." Personal essay in *The New York Times Book Review*, April 19, 1981, pp. 1, 21. Yates discusses early influences on his writing, including movies, Hemingway, Fitzgerald, and Flaubert.

Bibliography

"R.V. Cassill's Clem Anderson." *Ploughshares*, v. 14, nos. 2-3 (1988). Praise for a novel written by a friend: "...the best novel I know on the subject of writing."

In an untitled article in *The New York Times Book Review* on Dec. 4, 1977, in response to a question "Who is the living writer you most admire?" Yates answered J. D. Salinger. He said: "I have never read a novel of adolescence as penetrating, as funny and as sad as 'The Catcher in the Rye.' And at least five of his 'Nine Stories' are astonishing, most notably the tragic 'Uncle Wiggly in Connecticut.'"

Letters by Yates

"Excerpts from the Correspondence of Richard Yates and Barbara Singleton Beury, September 1960–November 1961." Letters to a young woman, in *Harvard Review*, no. 25 (Fall 2003), pp. 64–77.

Interview with Yates

Henry, DeWitt, and Geoffrey Clark. "An Interview with Richard Yates." *Ploughshares*, v. 1, no. 3 (December 1972), pp. 65–78.

Works About Yates

BOOKS

Bailey, Blake. *A Tragic Honesty: The Life and Work of Richard Yates*. New York: Picador, 2003. A thorough, highly readable, reliable biography. Janet Maslin, a book reviewer for the daily *New York Times*, admired this book so much that she recommended that her husband encourage Bailey to write a biography of his father, John Cheever. Bailey agreed and the book, *Cheever: A Life*, was published in 2009.

Castronovo, David, and Steven Goldleaf. *Richard Yates*. Twayne's United States Authors Series. New York: Twayne, 1996.

Klinkowitz, Jerome. *The New American Novel of Manners: The Fiction of Richard Yates, Dan Wakefield, and Thomas McGuane*. Athens: University of Georgia Press, 1986. Argues that Yates, Wakefield, and McGuane have reinvented what was once thought to be a dying literary form, the novel of manners, which is based on an author's ability to select details that reflect values of the characters. The one-third of this book devoted to Yates is a highly favorable commentary.

ARTICLES

Appelo, Tim. "Auteur chose: Five Voices from New England." *Boston Phoenix*, Oct. 7, 1986, pp. 20, 24–25. Classifies Yates as a New England writer because his style has "linguistic thrift, a brisk chill."

Bailey, Blake. "Poor Dick: Looking for the Real Richard Yates." *Harvard Review*, no. 25 (Fall 2003), pp. 53–63. An appreciation of the writer and his writing by his biographer.

Broyard, Anatole. "Two-Fisted Self-Pity." Review of *Young Hearts Crying*. *New York Times Book Review*, Oct. 28, 1984, p. 3. This extraordinarily harsh review actually discusses Yates's full body of work. It also was the cause of the final break in what had once been a close friendship.

Bibliography

Chappell, Fred. "Fred Chappell on Richard Yates's *Revolutionary Road*." In *Rediscoveries*, edited by David Madden, pp. 245–255. New York: Crown, 1971.

Cox, Elizabeth. "Meet Richard Yates." *Pif Magazine*, May 2, 2001 (at http://www.pif magazine.com/2000/10/meet-richard-yates/). A young writer recalls, in this online magazine article, the help she received with her first novel from Yates, whom she met at a writers conference.

Crumley, James. "The Last Gentleman: A Friend and Student Remembers Richard Yates." *Boston Review*, April/May 2001. Crumley writes of the friendship he formed with Yates when he was a graduate student at the Iowa Writers' Workshop and Yates taught there.

Cuomo, George. "Richard Yates: The Art of Craft." *Denver Quarterly*, v. 19, no. 4 (Spring 1985), pp. 127–132. Focuses on Yates's ability to select details that build credible characters.

Dubus, Andre. "A Salute to Mr. Yates." In *Broken Vessels:Essays*. Boston: David R. Godine, 1991, pp. 93–96. This essay, which originally appeared in *Black Warrior Review*, describes a small, unattractive apartment Yates lived in on Beacon Street in Boston for several years. The essay closes with Yates saying he doesn't want money: "I just want readers." The book opens with a thank-you to Yates and nine other writers who held a reading to raise funds for Dubus after "I was struck by a car and lost a leg." (The other writers he thanks are Ann Beattie, E. L. Doctorow, Gail Godwin, John Irving, Stephen King, Tim O'Brien, Jayne Anne Phillips, John Updike, and Kurt Vonnegut.)

_____. "Good-bye to Richard Yates." In *Meditations from a Movable Chair: Essays*. New York: Alfred A. Knopf, New York, 1998, pp. 83–84. This very brief essay was first read at a memorable service in Boston for Yates.

Henry, DeWitt. Untitled review of *Disturbing the Peace*. *Ploughshares*, v. 3, no. 1 (1977). Uses one Yates novel to explore his "difficult moral artistry."

_____. "Points of Craft from Richard Yates" (at www.richardyates.org). Talk delivered at the 2008 conference of the Association of Writers & Writing Programs.

Lehmann-Haupt, Christopher. Review of *Young Hearts Crying*. *New York Times*, Oct. 15, 1984.

Naparsteck, Martin. "Richard Yates at the Crossroads." *The San Francisco Review of Books*, v. X, no. 1 (Summer 1985), pp. 13–14, 22.

_____. "The Company of Writers." *Weber Studies*, v. 15, no. 2 (Spring/Summer 1998).

_____. "Drinking with Dick Yates." *North American Review*, v. 286, nos. 3–4 (May–August 2001).

_____. "Righting a Reputation." Review of Blake Bailey's *A Tragic Honesty: The Life and Work of Richard Yates*. *Salt Lake Tribune*, Sept. 27, 2003.

_____. "The God Damndest Thing: Learning from Richard Yates." *The Writer's Chronicle*, v. 39, no. 6 (May/Summer 2007).

_____. "Collecting Richard Yates." *Firsts: The Book Collector's Magazine*, v. 18, no. 1 (January 2008).

_____. "Dick Yates Goes to the Movies." *Authors Guild Bulletin*, Winter 2009.

O'Nan, Stewart. "The Lost World of Richard Yates: How the Great Writer of the Age of Anxiety Disappeared from Print." *Boston Review*, Nov. 5, 1999. Laments the fact that in 1999 all of Yates's books are out of print and hopes someone will write a biography of him and make a movie of one of his novels. This article was the first in a series of publications that contributed to a revival of Yates's literary reputation.

Pace, Eric. "Richard Yates, Novelist, 66, Dies; Chronicler of Disappointed Lives." Obituary. *New York Times*, Nov. 9, 1992, p. B-9. The second line of the headline—"Chronicler of Disappointed Lives"—has become one of the most common ways to sum up Yates's writing.

Penner, Jonathan. "The Novelists: Richard Yates." *The New Republic*, Nov. 4, 1978, pp. 42–45. The economy and honesty of the writer's style are seen as the basis for his literary achievement.

Ross, Terrence. "Success and the Sharks." Letter to the editor, *New York Times*, Jan. 6, 1985.

Shinagel, Michael. "Richard Yates: An Introduction." *Harvard Review*, no. 25 (Fall 2003), pp. 50–61. Introduction to a special section on Yates.

Solotaroff, Theodore. "The Wages of Maturity." In *The Red Hot Vacuum and Other Pieces on Writing of the Sixties*, pp. 44–49. New York: Atheneum, 1970. Argues that *Revolutionary Road* offers "so much of the truth about suburbia" that it must be considered a major work.

Vonnegut, Kurt. "Remarks at the Richard Yates Memorial Service." *Harvard Review*, no. 25 (Fall 2003), pp. 78–79. An appreciation of a friendship.

Wakefield, Dan. "A Writer Revived." *Boston Globe*, Dec. 28, 2008. Wakefield recalls his friendship with Yates, including the times they drank together at Boston's Crossroads bar.

Other Books and Articles Cited in Text

Aldrich, Nelson W., Jr., editor. *George, Being George: George Plimpton's Life As Told, Admired, Deplored, and Envied by 200 Friends, Relatives, Lovers, Acquaintances, Rivals—and a Few Unappreciative Observers*. New York: Random House, 2008.

Allen, Woody. *Hannah and Her Sisters*. New York: Vintage Books, 1987.

Bailey, Blake. *Cheever: A Life*. New York: Alfred A. Knopf, 2009.

Berriault, Gina. *The Tea Ceremony: The Uncollected Writings of Gina Berriault*. Washington, D.C.: Shoemaker & Hoard, 2003.

Chandler, Raymond, and Robert B. Parker. *Poodle Springs*. New York: G. P. Putnam's Sons, 1989.

Fitzgerald, F. Scott. *The Great Gatsby*. New York: Charles Scribner's Sons, 1925.

_____. *The Last Tycoon*. Edited by Edmund Wilson. New York: Charles Scribner's Sons, 1941.

Flaubert, Gustave. *Madame Bovary*. Paris: Michel Lévy Frères, 1857.

Gates, Henry Louis. *Thirteen Ways of Looking at a Black Man*. New York: Random House, 1997.

Gold, Herbert. *The Age of Happy Problems*. New York: The Dial Press, 1962.

Goodwin, Donald W., M.D. *Alcohol and the Writer*. Kansas City: Andrews & McMeel, 1988.

Heller, Joseph. *Catch-22*. New York: Simon and Schuster, 1961.

Hemingway, Edward, and Mark Bailey. *Hemingway & Bailey's Bartending Guide to Great American Writers*. Chapel Hill, North Carolina: Algonquin Books of Chapel Hill, 2006.

Bibliography

Ernest Hemingway. *A Farewell to Arms.* New York: Charles Scribner's Sons, 1929.
———. *The Garden of Eden.* Edited by Tom Jenks. New York: Charles Scribner's Sons, 1986.
Jones, James. *From Here to Eternity.* New York: Charles Scribner's Sons, 1951.
Kennedy, Thomas E. *Andre Dubus: A Study of the Short Fiction.* Twayne's Studies in Short Fiction Series No. 1. Boston: Twayne, 1988. At six different points in this book, Kennedy quotes Dubus talking about the influence Yates had on his writing.
Kovic, Ron. *Born on the Fourth of July.* New York: McGraw-Hill, 1976.
Mailer, Norman. *The Naked and the Dead.* New York: Rinehart and Company, 1948.
Melville, Herman. *Moby-Dick, or, The Whale.* New York: Richard Bentley, 1861.
Naparsteck, Martin. "Living in the Present. Third Novel by Rochester Writer Is Set in China." Rochester (N.Y.) *Democrat and Chronicle*, March 24, 1991, p. 8D. This review of Andrea Barrett's novel *The Middle Kingdom* compares Barrett to Yates.
O'Brien, Tim. "The Things They Carried." In *The Things They Carried*, pp. 1–25. Boston: Houghton Mifflin/Seymour Lawrence, 1990.
Pritchard, William H. *Updike: America's Man of Letters.* Royalton, Vermont: Steerforth Press, 2000.
Rackstraw, Loree. *Love as Always, Kurt: Vonnegut As I Knew Him.* Cambridge, Massachusetts: Da Capo Press, 2009. In discussing her brief affair and long friendship with Vonnegut, Rackstraw makes numerous references to Vonnegut's friendship with Richard Yates.
Schlesinger, Arthur, Jr. *Robert Kennedy and His Times*, Volume II. Boston: Houghton Mifflin, 1978.
Solomon, Barbara Probst. "Where's Papa?" *The New Republic*, March 9, 1987. Solomon argues that *The Garden of Eden* as published is not the novel Hemingway intended.
Styron, William. *Lie Down in Darkness.* Indianapolis: Bobbs-Merrill, 1959.
Toole, F. X. *Rope Burns: Stories from the Corner.* New York: HarperCollins, 2000.
Vonnegut, Kurt. *Slaughterhouse Five.* New York: Seymour Lawrence/Delacorte, 1969.
Williams, Tennessee. *A Streetcar Named Desire.* New York: New Directions, 1947.

Films Cited in the Text

Bridge at Remagen, The. Directed by John Guillermin, produced by David L. Wolver, screenplay by Richard Yates and William Roberts, starring George Segal, Robert Vaughn, Ben Gazzara, Bradford Dillman, E. G. Marshall. 1969. Although he received screen credit for writing the script of this World War Two drama, Yates disowned it, refusing to even list it on his résumé. He felt that very little of the final movie had anything to do with the script he wrote.
Hannah and Her Sisters. Written and directed by Woody Allen, produced by Robert Greenhut, starring Woody Allen, Mia Farrow, Michael Caine, Barbara Hershey, Dianna Wiest, Lloyd Nolan, Max Von Sydow, Carrie Fisher. 1986. Yates's novel *The Easter Parade* is mentioned in this movie, although Yates himself is not.
Lonesome Jim. Directed by Steve Buscemi, produced by Plum Pictures, screenplay by James C. Strouse, starring Casey Affleck, Liv Tyler. 2005. Yates is favorably mentioned by a character in the movie.
Million Dollar Baby. Directed by Clint Eastwood, produced by Clint Eastwood, Albert

Bibliography

S. Ruddy, Tom Rosenberg, Gary Lucchesi, screenplay by Paul Haggis, starring Clint Eastwood, Hilary Swank, Morgan Freeman. Some Yates fans mistakenly believe that the Clint Eastwood character says at one point in this movie that he is reading a book by Richard Yates. However, the character is reading a book by William Butler Yeats.

Revolutionary Road. Directed by Sam Mendes, produced by John N. Hart, Scott Rudin, Sam Mendes, Bobby Cohen, screenplay by Justin Haythe, starring Leonardo DiCaprio, Kate Winslet, Michael Shannon, Kathy Bates. 2008. Based on Yates's first novel.

Index

abortion 17–18, 20, 30, 32, 33, 37, 38, 49, 71, 97–98, 120, 131, 155, 157
"After the Laurel Players" 160
Alabama 8, 16, 28
Allen, Woody 8 44, 100
Aristotle 11, 19, 38, 153
Avon Old Farms School 16, 25, 114, 115, 160

Bailey, Blake 41, 44, 74, 75, 103, 104, 105, 113, 146, 147, 148, 159, 160, 161, 162,
"The B.A.R. Man" 25, 57–59, 80, 116, 130, 153, 157
Barrett, Andrea 175
baseball 5, 76–77, 91, 112, 122, 155, 161 181
Beattie, Ann 12
"Bells in the Morning" 153
Berriault, Gina 56, 175, 177–178
"The Best of Everything" 11, 14, 19, 20, 25, 52,–53, 74, 107, 158, 162, 163, 166, 170
Bluestone, George 168
Boston University 11, 16, 28, 88, 145, 157, 163
Bridge at Remagen 7, 16, 26, 41
Broyard, Anatole 3, 134–137, 173, 182
Bryan, C.B.D. 77–78
Bryant, Sheila (Yates's first wife) 26, 27
"Builders" 6, 14, 19, 20, 21, 25, 60–61, 64, 90, 109, 154
Burroughs, William 13, 62

"The Canal" 9, 152–153
Carlyle, Thomas 181
Catch-22 63, 165
Cheever, John 6, 29, 176, 177 180, 186
Ciardi, John 12
"A Clinical Romance" 60, 153, 157, 181
Cold Spring Harbor 3, 4, 7, 15, 17, 18, 19, 23, 25, 28, 42, 55, 83, 138–144, 169, 170, 178

The Collected Stories of Richard Yates 3, 28, 152–159, 162
Columbia University 26, 32, 96
"A Compassionate Leave" 25, 121–122, 123
"The Comptroller and the Wild Wind" 156, 157, 183
"A Convalescent Ego" 60, 159
Cosmopolitan 64, 161, 162
Crossroads bar 11, 12, 14, 39, 86–94, 112, 113, 124, 136, 155, 164, 180
Crumley, James 175, 176

Disturbing the Peace 2, 3, 14, 15, 16, 17, 18, 21, 25, 28, 43, 80–86, 91, 128, 168, 176, 178, 179
"Doctor Jack-o'-Lantern" 25, 51–52, 170
Douglas, Mitch 105
Dubus, Andre 61, 117, 180, 187

The Easter Parade 2, 4, 8, 15, 17, 18, 19, 21, 24, 28, 43, 44, 65, 69, 71, 73, 83, 84, 91, 95–103, 106, 111, 116, 129, 135, 138, 143, 161, 162, 165, 168
"The Eighty Yard Run" 10
Eisenhower, Dwight 50, 174
Eleven Kinds of Loneliness (album) 61
Eleven Kinds of Loneliness (book) 3, 6, 28, 39, 51–61, 104, 105, 116, 123, 127, 147, 152, 163, 166, 167, 170
Emery, Thomas 157
"End of the Great Depression" 160
Episcopal Church 9, 19, 21, 73, 100, 102, 141, 179; *see also* religion
"Evening on the Cote d'Azur" 152, 154, 163

Faulkner, William 128, 167, 180
Fitzgerald, F. Scott 43, 112, 124–127, 145–146, 159, 177, 179, 180, 183
Five Kinds of Dismay 160, 170
Flaubert, Gustave 19, 174, 177

191

Index

Fonda, Henry 16, 40, 41, 92, 148, 167
Fonda, Jane 40, 41, 92
"Forgive Our Foolish Ways" 160, 162
"Forms of Entertainment" 160
"Foursome" 160
Frankenheimer, John 10, 16, 26, 40, 41, 92, 124, 167–168
From Here to Eternity 63, 165
fuckup (Yates's use of word) 69–71, 74
"Fun with a Stranger" 25, 51, 57, 156

"The Game of Ambush" 160, 170
Gass, William 13
Gates, Henry Louis 137
"The Girls in Their Summer Dresses" 10
"A Glutton for Punishment" 25, 55, 160, 170
A Good School 2, 4, 9 15, 20, 21, 23, 24, 25, 28, 31, 51, 59, 64, 65, 69, 83, 85, 96, 102, 104, 106–112, 113, 114, 115, 116, 117, 123, 128, 138, 144, 156, 161, 162, 166, 169, 181
Greer, Will 105

Hannah and Her Sisters 8, 44, 100
Heggen, Thomas 77, 164
Heller, Joseph 63, 77, 164
Hemingway, Ernest 19, 31, 70, 74, 77, 85, 97, 122, 145, 146, 149, 164, 166, 167, 177, 180, 183
Henry, DeWitt 163, 171, 178
Hicks, Grantville 12
homosexuality 2, 103–105, 111, 153, 177
honesty (as element of Yates's style) 6, 9, 12, 21, 22, 23, 54, 60, 61, 91, 92, 94, 101, 106, 109, 118, 122, 129, 157, 158, 165, 166

Iowa Writer's Workshop 8, 10, 16, 27, 44, 147, 175

"Jody Rolled the Bones" 3, 9, 16, 25, 26, 53, 57, 130, 163, 171
Jones, James 63, 164, 170
Joyce, James 128, 156, 183

Kazin, Alfred 12, 35, 164, 177
Keats, John 73, 170, 178–179
Kennedy, John 16, 80, 81, 82, 92, 151, 179
Kennedy, Robert 10, 11, 15, 16, 27, 28, 58, 80, 81, 92, 93, 144–149, 179
Klinkowitz, Jerome 112
Knowles, John 2, 114, 115
Kovic, Ron 77–78

Krantz, Judith 12
Kress, Nancy 46

"Lament for a Tenor" 25, 64, 161–162, 163
"A Last Fling, Like" 157–158
Lawrence, Seymour (Sam) 113, 136, 145, 146–147, 151
Liars in Love (book) 4, 28, 43, 51, 65, 66, 116–127, 152, 160, 163, 170
"Liars in Love" (story) 25, 91, 118, 122, 123
Lie Down in Darkness (novel) 2, 16, 28, 40, 125, 167–168
Lie Down in Darkness (screenplay) 2, 3, 10, 16, 28, 40–41, 92, 125, 167–168
Lonesome Jim 44
Longfellow, Henry Wadsworth 181

Mailer, Norman 13, 63, 71, 77, 128, 164
McCall, Monica 105, 153, 155
Michener, James 13
Million Dollar Baby 44
Moby Dick 6, 166, 175, 183
The Moviegoer 26

The Naked and the Dead 63, 71, 165
National Book Award 26, 165, 175
"A Natural Girl" 25, 117–119, 154
New School for Social Research 16, 26, 134, 173
The New York Times 3, 6, 7, 65, 77, 100, 134, 135, 136, 146, 173, 175, 182, 186, 187
New Yorker 9, 56, 137, 152–153, 176
nice (Yates's use of word) 20, 118, 154
"No Pain Whatsoever" 25, 54–55, 60, 155

Oates, Joyce Carol 21
O'Brien, Tim 78, 150, 165, 175
"Oh, Joseph, I'm So Tired" 21, 22, 24, 25, 28, 51, 65, 73, 116–117, 119, 123, 132, 166
Olivier, Laurence 7, 43, 97
O'Nan, Stewart 74, 169, 176, 179
"Ordeal of Vincent Sabella" 162, 170
"Out with the Old" 25, 54, 59–60, 155

Parker, Dorothy 12, 180
Percy, Walker 26
Phillips Exeter Academy 114–115
Ploughshares 152, 154, 171
Pritchard, William H. 175
"A Private Possession" 156

Index

psychiatry, psychology 17, 18, 19, 27, 32, 80, 82, 83, 84, 91, 152

Rackstraw, Loree 136
"A Really Good Jazz Piano" 25, 58,-59, 116
"Regards at Home" 24, 25, 55, 66, 123–124, 155
religion 9, 19, 73 84, 100, 116, 117; *see also* Episcopal Church
Revolutionary Road (movie) 2, 8, 39, 43, 45–50
Revolutionary Road (novel) 2, 3, 6, 8, 10, 15, 17, 20, 21, 25, 26, 28, 30–39, 45–50, 55, 69, 71, 74, 84, 91, 96, 98, 101, 104, 108, 121, 122, 123, 124, 129, 155, 156, 157, 160, 163, 165, 166, 167, 168, 170, 173, 175, 177, 179
Richler, Mordecai 12
Riddle, Theodate Pope 115
"The Right Thing" 162, 176
Russo, Richard 160

Salinger, J.D. 175, 185
Saturday Evening Post 159, 160–161, 162
"Saying Goodbye to Sally" 25, 43, 124–125, 178
"Schedule" 160, 162
Schlesinger, Arthur, Jr. 179, 181–182
Seinfeld 10, 44, 177
Shaw, Irwin 10
"Shepherd's Pie on Payday" 162
A Special Providence 2, 3, 5, 9, 14, 15, 23, 25, 28, 41, 42, 59, 60, 62–79, 83, 85, 100, 107, 116, 119, 124, 128, 129, 130, 131, 138, 140, 143, 147, 150, 155, 161, 162, 163, 164, 166, 175, 179
Speer, Martha (Yates's second wife) 27
Stone, Robert 12
Stories for the Sixties 176
A Streetcar Named Desire 84, 132
Styron, William 2, 3, 6, 8, 12, 16, 28, 40, 92, 106, 125, 128, 148, 167–168

"Thieves" 60, 152, 155
Tikaram, Tanita 61
Time 6, 12, 46
"To Be a Hero" 161, 162
A Tragic Honesty see Bailey, Blake

"Trying Out for the Race" 25, 119–120, 156
tuberculosis 26, 54, 59, 123, 153, 155, 181

Uncertain Times 3, 28, 55, 144–151, 183
University of Alabama at Tuscaloosa 16, 28
University of Southern California 16, 28
Updike, John 6, 175

Veterans Administration 26, 28, 54, 55, 59, 60
Vietnam War 75–78, 91, 93, 118, 130, 133, 164–165
Vonnegut, Kurt 6, 12, 77, 87, 128, 136, 171

Wakefield, Dan 112, 136, 180–181
The Waltons 48, 104, 132
Warren, Robert Penn 175
Wichita State University 16, 28, 171, 173
Williams, Tennessee 6, 12, 104–105
Williams, William Carlos 153
Winged Beaver 160, 162
Wolff, Tobias 12, 114
Wood, Natalie 16, 40–41, 92, 148, 167
The World on Fire 3, 173–174
"A Wrestler with Sharks" 25, 56, 170

Yates, Gina (Yates's daughter) 27, 178
Yates, Monica (Yates's daughter) 27, 44, 104, 145, 146, 151
Yates, Richard: alcoholism 2, 11, 14, 26, 27, 28, 39, 86–94, 105, 125, 136, 147; apartment fire 112–113, 181; athletic abilities 91, 104, 105, 161, 181; bipolarity 2, 27; books owned 121; military service 9, 16, 25–26, 74–77, 122, 154, 164; patience 39, 88; smoking 23, 113; teaching 10, 16, 26, 27, 28, 44, 88, 134, 147, 171, 173; writing 28, 59–60, 60–61, 169–172
Yates, Ruth (Yates's sister) 7, 25, 43, 156
Yates, Sharon (Yates's daughter) 9, 27, 153
Young Hearts Crying 3, 4, 5, 15, 17, 21, 25, 28, 45, 48, 63, 65, 83, 84, 87, 104, 118, 124, 128–134, 135, 136, 141, 149, 154, 156, 162, 173, 192

www.ingramcontent.com/pod-product-compliance
Lightning Source LLC
Chambersburg PA
CBHW032101300426
44116CB00007B/837